BUYING A HOUSE IN

NEW

ZEALAND

Alison Ripley

Distributed in the USA by
The Globe Pequot Press, Guilford, Connecticut

Published by Vacation Work, 9 Park End Street, Oxford
www.vacationwork.co.uk

BUYING A HOUSE IN NEW ZEALAND
by Alison Ripley

First edition 2006

ISBN 13: 978-1-85458-350-5
ISBN 10: 1-85458-350-6

Publicity: Charles Cutting

Cover design by mccdesign ltd

Typeset by Guy Hobbs

Illustrations by Mick Siddens

Cover photograph: typical New Zealand house, Coromandel Peninsula

Printed and bound in Italy by Legoprint SpA, Trento

CONTENTS

PART I
LIVING IN NEW ZEALAND

PART II
LOCATION, LOCATION

WHERE TO FIND YOUR IDEAL HOME

NORTH ISLAND

SOUTH ISLAND

PART III
THE PURCHASING PROCESS

FINANCE

FINDING PROPERTIES FOR SALE

PART IV
WHAT HAPPENS NEXT

SERVICES

FOREWORD

On my first trip to Waiheke Island, I remember asking the bus driver which side of the bus had the best scenery and he fell about laughing. And he was right, of course. It didn't matter whether I sat on the left or the right – the shimmering waters of the Hauraki Gulf were visible from every direction. And from my vantage point it looked for all the world as though I was on a sub-tropical version of a Greek island. But man (or woman) can't survive on scenery alone and those of us, privileged enough to call New Zealand home do so not just because it's a beautiful country but a very liveable one too.

Some of you may have relatives or friends who moved out to New Zealand and made a new life for themselves. And from their information, as well as your own observations from reading about the country, going to New Zealand films or watching the occasional documentary, you will no doubt have formed some opinion on what New Zealand might be like.

But I can guarantee that whatever your perceptions about the country, when you experience first-hand the real 21st century New Zealand, it will be so different from the one in your imagination. No matter who you talk to or where you go, you will find many different New Zealands in one country. Crave the urban life but with a South Pacific flavour? – then give Auckland a go. Prefer mountains and skiing over messing about on boats? – then Christchurch might suit. Or if cities aren't your thing there's plenty on offer for families in the regional centres.

You can mix with the locals without worrying about whether you'll be understood. You can drink great local wine and feast on fantastically fresh produce without having to put up with the seemingly endless bureaucracy of an EU country. And there will be enough of a common culture – whether you come from Australia, Ireland, South Africa, the United Kingdom, Canada or the United States, that it won't take too long for you to feel like New Zealand is 'home'.

Whether it's a holiday house or a complete change of lifestyle that you're after – I do hope that you get to see the real New Zealand along the way. Will you find what you're searching for in New Zealand? Only you can answer that. But I hope you enjoy looking.

Alison Ripley, Auckland
February 2006

ACKNOWLEDGEMENTS

There were many people who assisted in the writing and research of this book and I am indebted to the following: Former colleagues and clients of Woburn International, whose relocation experiences helped me shape some of the ideas for this book.

Thanks to July Rea for her insights into New Zealand culture, Ian McAleese for information on apartments in Mount Maunganui, Ashley Smith for generously giving up his time to show me around parts of the Bay of Plenty I would otherwise never have known about, Vicky Bowmer for encouragement and advice, the Taylor family for their experiences, Sean Cubitt for his culinary expertise and Zebedee Cubitt for following doggedly in pursuit of yet another photograph. Thanks are due to Sarah Carradine for reading the first section and helping to launch the book to a good start. Thanks also to Rebecca Russell and Andy Williamson.

Finally a special thanks to the contributors for their generosity in sharing their case histories: Helen Davies, Laura Totis and Sandro Lionello, Mike Cole.

Thank you to Charles James for all his support and everyone at Vacation Work who helped in the production of this book.

Photo of art deco houses, Napier, courtesy of The Art Deco Trust Napier and photo of 'Willowbrook' B & B near Arrowtown courtesy of Roy Llewellyn.

Part I

LIVING IN NEW ZEALAND

LIVING IN NEW ZEALAND

RESIDENCE & ENTRY

LIVING IN NEW ZEALAND

CHAPTER SUMMARY

- There is no need to learn a new language to live the Kiwi lifestyle.
- The standard of living is still good enough to persuade high-fliers from London and New York that it is worth taking a cut in salary to move there.
- **History.** The 1840 Treaty of Waitangi is regarded as New Zealand's founding document.
- **Mythology.** Maori mythology is as evocative and powerful as the stories of Ancient Greece.
- **Getting There.** Competition between the airlines that fly the route allows travellers a greater choice of stop-overs than ever before.
- **Geography.** Packed within this one small country is a diversity of landscapes that is generally only found in entire continents.
  - Nobody is more than a couple of hours drive from the beach.
- **Politics.** The 'first past the post' voting system was abandoned in the mid 1990s in favour of a version of proportional representation called MMP.
- **Crime.** It is a safe destination where violent crime inflicted on strangers is rare.
- **Food and Drink.** The first person to make wine in New Zealand was a Scot.
- **Communications.** Broadband speed is much slower in New Zealand than in the UK.
  - There is one telephone area code for all of the South Island.
- **Media.** Only on satellite television can you watch sports or

films without advertisements.
○ **Education.** Schools are of a good standard with a number offering either Cambridge A Levels or the International Baccalaureate.
○ **Health.** New Zealand operates a no-fault accident compensation scheme covering visitors and citizens alike.

INTRODUCTION – FRIENDS IN COMMON?

The last landfall before Antarctica, New Zealand is the ultimate destination to 'get away from it all'. While this geographical isolation might deter some, for those of you reading this book, New Zealand's perceived remoteness only adds to the allure. After that marathon plane journey, you might never want to leave. New Zealand offers a way of life with access to the great outdoors that is unsurpassed and with a population of just 4.1 million you are sure to find an isolated beach somewhere.

For anyone coming from Britain, Australia or the USA one of the attractions of moving to New Zealand is that you don't have to learn a new language to live the Kiwi lifestyle. And although you are bound to miss family and friends back home, staying in touch with loved ones has never been cheaper or easier now that phone calls can be made over the internet.

Even though the strong ties between Britain and New Zealand have started to unravel in recent years, the two nations still have much in common and British visitors report that there is much still about New Zealand that is reassuringly familiar. Competing internationally in many of the same sports allows for events such as the 2005 British and Irish Lions rugby tour. And as many Lions fans found out – New Zealanders are generally easy going – except during a rugby tournament. Rugby is not just a sport -it's a national obsession with the mood of the nation reflected by how well or how badly the All Blacks are playing. But despite the healthy degree of rivalry amongst the supporters and the teams during the tour, off the pitch, the thousands of fans who had travelled half way around the world to watch their team play were given a very hospitable welcome.

But New Zealand has maintained important ties with other countries too, including the USA and its closest neighbour, Australia. The film industry is but one of the important cultural links that have helped forge better relations between New Zealand and the USA. And in recent times the nations have engaged in quiet diplomacy to heal the political rift between the two countries, since New Zealand took its non-nuclear stance. Politics aside, individual visitors from the USA have always been well received.

But despite the occasional silly public digs that the media on both sides of the Tasman Sea like to indulge in; it is Australia that continues to be New Zealand's closest trading partner, favourite holiday destination as well as sporting rival. And although a handful of New Zealanders like to heckle from the sidelines when their bigger and more powerful neighbour flexes its muscles, the rest of the country knows that even good friends squabble occasionally. When it really counts, the ties that bind these two nations are just too strong.

The lure of Australia, Britain or the USA has proved too much to resist for the thousands of young (and some not so young) New Zealanders who go to seek opportunities abroad that are denied them in a country of only a few million people. In the early 20th century many of the brightest and best had no option but to leave. Katherine Mansfield went in search of a literary peer group and Earnest Rutherford left for Britain as he was unable to find a suitable academic post. There he founded the discipline of nuclear physics.

However film director and local hero Peter Jackson bucked this trend and stayed put. He is admired just as much by New Zealanders for persuading Hollywood come to him as he is for his extraordinary feat of making the blockbuster Lord of the Rings trilogy and King Kong back-to-back. Being able to make highly successful work on home turf, without the need to export intellectual capital to the US, Britain or Australia has instilled a new vigour in the creative industries. The once dreary capital of Wellington, or Wellywood as some wags call it, is now a vibrant place to live and work.

As much as there are similarities between Britain and New Zealand, there are a number of important differences. As historian Michael King describes it, many came to New Zealand looking to create 'a better Britain.' And although New Zealand may have been a 'better Britain' in the boom years of the 1960s, it was a fairly boring one, with everything except the beach closed on Sundays. The lingering perception of the country as Britain's dairy farm, (now under the stewardship of a few hobbits) still exists. Some migrants are surprised at what a Pacific feel the city of Auckland has, a combination of cultures of which the British heritage is just one part.

New Zealand once had one of the highest standards of living in the developed world. Although that changed when Britain joined the Common

Market, and the standard of living might not be as high as it once was, there are immeasurable qualities about New Zealand life that remain. Nobody is more than a couple of hours drive from a beach. Children attend schools that have green space and playing fields. Universities have pleasant campuses. There is no heavy industry. The urban poor do not have to live in endless blocks of depressing high-rise housing estates. The most modest house will generally have some outdoor space.

The wages might be better in neighbouring Australia but the downside is that there are much greater divisions between rich and poor and social problems on a scale not yet seen in New Zealand. And despite the continued rumblings over the Treaty of Waitangi, New Zealand is much further along the path of reconciliation with its indigenous people, not only apologising for the wrongs of the past but also continuing to pay compensation for seized land.

That stunning South Island scenery as seen in the Lord of the Rings trilogy is there for everyone to visit and enjoy. Although there are still remote rural areas where doors are left unlocked, the majority of New Zealanders, who still have to work for a living lead an urban or suburban lifestyle, far removed from that rural idyll.

However, cities in New Zealand are on nothing like the scale of those in the UK, the USA or even Australia. Even if you live in Auckland, the largest city, with 1.3 million people, you can still be out in a wilderness or on the sparkling waters of the Hauraki Gulf within half an hour of leaving town. That same evening you could go to a concert of classical music, or the theatre, attend a cultural performance by a Pacific Island group, dine out at a top restaurant or eat your fish and chips at a local beach.

Whether you want to spend a few months of the year escaping the northern hemisphere winter or are planning to make New Zealand your permanent home, there are many more options available to house hunters than there would be back home. You can buy a plot of land and commission an architect to build your dream home, or one as close to the dream as the budget permits. Or how about a house and land package? If it is a question of best house, worst street, then the house can be trucked to somewhere better. You can renovate a church, build an earth house, or buy a good old Kiwi holiday house or bach (pronounced batch).

The most expensive place to buy a house according to Quotable Value in April 2005, was Auckland's eastern suburbs, where the average sale price was NZ$589,801 (£233,980, US$402,540) although the Queenstown Lakes area is poised to overtake that.

Stop press: Although the Real Estate Institute's figures have yet to be supported by any QV data, a press report in January 2006 stated that the Central Otago Lakes now has higher median house prices than Auckland.

The biggest price increase shown in property in the past twenty years has not surprisingly been waterfront or cliff-top. Expect to pay around NZ$2,000,000 plus for a four bedroom cliff-top house on Auckland's North Shore with uninterrupted views of the Hauraki Gulf. But there are still plenty of places with an excellent quality of life where house prices are much lower. In September 2005, median house prices were NZ$262,250 in Nelson/Marlborough, the sunniest place in the country, NZ$256,150 in Northland and NZ $250,000 in Hawke's Bay.

Houses or plots of land in rural areas, especially in pockets of the North Island may not be as much of a bargain as you thought. Rural in New Zealand means remote and the concept of villages every few miles does not really exist. The nearest supermarket or general practitioner could be 30km away by a narrow winding road. Many overseas buyers attracted to the Far North because of its sub-tropical climate do not realise that once you get away from the affluent areas of the Bay of Islands and Kerikeri the infrastructure is poor and there are pockets of rural poverty. An unoccupied house in an isolated area is as vulnerable to theft in New Zealand as it is in any other country unless you have a regular property management system in place. Alarms are of limited use if it is a forty five minute drive for the alarm monitoring company to get there.

- Places like Nelson, Napier, Kerikeri and Whangarei offer a mix between a great outdoor lifestyle and accessible facilities that attracts city dwellers from Auckland as well as expatriates.
- The area around Warkworth, just North of Auckland is another area worth considering as it is less than hour's drive to the biggest city yet has a sense of community, great beaches and a number of wineries.
- For anyone who for work reasons has to be close to a big city, Christchurch is a good alternative to Auckland.
  - The schools are excellent and family homes can be as much as 20% cheaper than they would be in Auckland or Wellington.
  - The climate is dry and although colder in winter, it has long hot summers.
  - The Mount Hutt ski field can be reached easily after work on a Fri-

day night and has the longest season of any ski resort in the country.

o And of all the cities in New Zealand, Christchurch still retains a distinctly British feel.

THE CREATION MYTH – MAUI LANDS A FISH

The creation myth of Maori mythology is but one of many wonderful stories in a culture that celebrates this most ancient form of oral storytelling.

When *Ranginui* (the Sky father) and *Papatuanuku* (the Earth mother) joined together, their union created some powerful offspring: *Tu Matauenga*, the God of War, *Tawhirimatea* the God of winds and storms, *Tangaroa*, the god of the oceans, *Rongo ma Tane* (the God of cultivated food and men, *Haumia Tiketike* god of wild food, and *Tane Mahuta*, the God of the Forests.

Rangi and Papa were so tightly joined that no light was visible between sky and earth. But Rangi and Papa's children, were no different to any others. They wanted their own way. Tired of living in perpetual darkness, they demanded that there be light. In order to have light their only option was to somehow separate their parents. Tawhirimatea stood up to his brothers and opposed the plan. He was so angry that he flew up into the sky and threw down great bolts of thunder and lightning.

The other siblings tried but failed to prise Earth from Sky. And then it was Tane Mahuta's turn. The giant kauri tree placed his shoulders against his mother, the Earth and his feet against his father, the Sky, and with all his might he finally forced his parents apart. At last the world was awash with light but Ranginui cried tears enough to fill the oceans. And even now the grief of their parting manifests itself as rain and mist.

But Tane's work was not over. Creatures and gods were not enough to inhabit the world. A woman had to be created. Made from the red earth found at Kurakawa, *Hinetitama*, the Dawn Maiden went on to form a union with Tane. And from this union came the human race. But when Hinetitama found that her husband and father were one and the same, she escaped to the spirit world. Because of her the dawn rises in the east and sets in the west. Not far behind her is Tane, and like all of mankind, must follow her for eternity down her chosen path.

Maui Goes Fishing and Comes Back with the North Island. The exploits of the half-human demi-god, Maui are known in myths right across the Pacific, from Hawaii, to the Solomon Islands and across to New Zealand. Even before Maui went fishing he did man a favour, slowing the sun down so the days were longer and the nights were shorter.

Out fishing with his brothers, Maui slung his enchanted fish-hook (made from the jawbone of a female ancestor) over the side. The water started to froth and foam as Maui chanted. His brothers could scarcely believe what Maui had fished up. This was not the usual catch that could be baked in a pie.

Te Ika a Maui (the fish of Maui) was a great tract of land. Maui asked his brothers to look after his find while he went and made an offering to the gods but they disobeyed him and started to scale this fish and hack pieces off it. The gods became angry at this insult. They had not been even been offered their promised fish.

The fish of Maui started to move and writhe about, and that is why much of the land of Aotearoa is mountainous and uncultivated. Had the brothers done as Maui told them the land would have been smooth and flat.

The dry land fished up by Maui, Te Ika a Maui, which had lain beneath the sea, became the North Island of Aotearoa. And when you look at a map you can see that fish-like shape. The mouth of the fish is Wellington Harbour, the East Coast and Taranaki are its two fins, Lake Taupo is the heart and Northland is its tail. And the hook (Te matau a Maui – Maui's Fishhook) is the cape at Heretaunga (Cape Kidnappers).

According to some tribes the South Island is the canoe Te Waka o Maui from which Maui went fishing. To steady himself, Maui placed his foot on the Kaikoura Peninsula and Stewart Island was the anchor stone that kept the canoe steady while he hauled up his enormous catch.

A Voyage of Mythic Proportions. Like the creation myth, the story of how New Zealand was first settled was written in the early 20th century not by Maori but by Europeans. The story was so powerful it was soon embraced by both cultures. It went like this: In 950 AD the great Polynesian navigator, *Kupe* came to a land filled with only birds, which he named Aotearoa 'the land of the long white cloud'. On his return to Hawaiki, the ancestral home of all Polynesians, he gave instructions on how to retrace his voyage.

Where Hawaiki is exactly, no one knows. The Society Islands (which includes Tahiti) or the Cook Islands are the two main contenders.

Kupe's voyage was retraced in 1350AD when a 'Great Fleet' of seven canoes arrived simultaneously to settle, staying together, establishing a tribal structure that formed the basis of the seven main tribal groups found today. Generations of school children were told this tale but the real story of how New Zealand came to be settled may never be known. Flying across the Pacific in a modern jet, and looking down upon that vast ocean, it is hard to imagine what kind of extraordinary courage, strength and navigational skills it took to set out on such a voyage.

HISTORY

The First Settlers

Scientific evidence suggests that New Zealand was first settled within a 100 years of the 'Great Fleet' myth, around the thirteenth century AD. An initial population of between 100 to 200 was needed for the numbers to grow to the 100,000 reached by the 18th century, and although *Aotearoa* has since been adopted as the Maori name for New Zealand, it was not known as this when the first Europeans arrived.

The social structure of Maori society was established long before the white man set foot on this land. It was an agricultural society where food crops, (all of which had to be brought by canoe on those early voyages) of *taro*, yams and *kumara* (sweet potato) were cultivated. Maori lived in villages centred around a *marae* (meeting house) and strict protocols had been established about encounters between social groups meeting for the first time.

Moriori and Maori. A tribe settled on the Chatham Islands who called themselves *Moriori*. Now regarded as just a different term for the word Maori, the story went that this group were settlers from West Polynesia who had arrived before Maori. These peaceful people, it was alleged, had got there first and were therefore the rightful indigenous inhabitants of New Zealand and Maori were the colonisers who behaved as badly to the Moriori as the white man did to Maori. Although the Moriori were unsuccessful at defending themselves and did suffer at the hands of other Maori tribes, they were one and the same people. The theory that they arrived before Maori was disproved as early as the 1920s, but even as late as the 1980s, the story was promoted for political gain as a way of justifying the seizure of Maori land, without having to pay financial compensation.

The First Europeans

In the 17th century, an era of remarkable scientific and technological advancement, visitors from one of the world's richest trading nations ventured further south than any earlier expedition had done. Abel Tasman had strayed that far south, in his search for *terra australis incognito*, the elusive southern continent. While that discovery would, no doubt have made Tasman a favoured son of Holland, the main purpose of his voyage was far more pragmatic. On behalf of the Dutch East India Company he was seeking further opportunities for trade in precious metals, minerals and spices. Tasman managed to miss the enormous continent of Australia on his voyage and brushed past a much smaller landmass which was named Van Diemen's Land – Tasmania as we know it today.

Catching sight of the South Island he anchored in a bay that must have looked idyllic. But when a group of Maori in a canoe challenged the occupants of a rowing boat, the lack of any understanding of Polynesian protocol led to the deaths of four of Tasman's crewmen. When another canoe got too close to Tasman's ships, one of the Dutch vessels fired upon it, killing one of its occupants. This deadly encounter marked the first killing of a Maori by a European. To the First People the force of the firepower unleashed by these visitors must have been terrifying. Tasman had not so much as set foot on the land before he had to flee, before any further damage could be done. He named the new land 'Staten Land' later to be renamed Nieuw Zeeland. That idyllic spot was named Murderer's Bay although now locals prefer the name Golden Bay. The visitors may have been from one of the world's richest and sophisticated trading nations but their failure to comprehend the local social customs meant that Tasman was unable to claim the territory for Holland. For the First People this meant that they were left undisturbed from outsiders for another 125 years.

In 1769 Captain Cook was in the Pacific completing his observations of the transit of Venus across the sun, a very rare event. Under the command of the Royal Navy he was instructed to sail south, either to find the elusive terra australis incognito or, failing that, to continue on to 'the land discover'd by Tasman.' Cook was far better prepared than Tasman as he had on board the *Endeavour* a translator from Tahiti who could not only act as interpreter but more importantly understood custom and protocol. Cook aimed to ensure cordial relations with any native peoples he encountered.

Despite his best intentions, misunderstandings were inevitable, particularly among frightened crew who fired on and killed indigenous people when they mistook bravado for aggression. But Cook was able to observe social customs and although initial social contact appeared hostile, he observed that much of it was for show. Careful to avoid any confrontation, he was able to barter goods in exchange for fresh food for his crew.

On that first voyage Cook spent six months circumnavigating both islands. His charts were so accurate that he was able to determine that terra australis incognito, the mythical southern continent that Tasman had tried in vain to find, had never existed. Where Tasman had observed one landmass, Cook found that there were two main islands of New Zealand.

He noted that this land had a plentiful supply of timber and flax and that there were seals and whales offshore that could be commercially harvested. Cook made two further voyages in 1773 and 1774 and again in 1777, before he was killed in a disastrous skirmish in Hawaii. Closely followed by Cook were two French expeditions one of which ended in calamity for crew and locals alike. A breach of protocol resulted in most of the remaining French sailors being killed then eaten. Firepower from what crew that was left caused the deaths of up to 300 Maori.

By the 1790s the barbaric practice of transportation to the penal colonies in what is now Australian territory brought many ships off New Zealand's coast. These ships needed to take shelter from storms and sailors needed somewhere to rest. But as many New Zealanders will tell you, the prosperity of the early settlers was not built on the convict trade. Nor are they the descendents of those that survived the misery of transportation. Europeans had already learned from the deaths on the Dutch, British and French voyages that Maori would not hesitate to fight back if anyone tried to subdue them. They would no doubt have fiercely contested any such attempt to use their land in such a way. Norfolk Island was selected as a penal colony instead.

Although sealers and whalers were the first to harvest the natural resources off New Zealand's shores, it was not until the 1820s that the land was exploited. An abundant stock of tall, straight, top quality native hardwoods was needed to build more ships, necessary to expand Britain's naval fleet. With the assistance of Cook's artists', who had so meticulously recorded the flora of New Zealand, shipbuilders knew exactly where such a plentiful supply existed.

By the 1820s the first major European settlement was in the Bay of Islands. Considered a rough and lawless place, the missionaries had no difficulty imposing their Christian values on the indigenous population; it was the sealers and whalers who were the problem. As well as drunkenness and loose morals these visitors brought something far worse. With no immunity to any European diseases Maori were unable to withstand the onslaught on their health and many died.

Despite Cook's painstaking efforts in charting and circumnavigating the coastline on his three voyages, New Zealand had never formally been recognised as a British possession. Britain was having enough trouble with its two major colonies of America and Canada, so there was little enthusiasm for adding this small South Pacific outpost to its empire. A compromise was made over governance and it was decided that the nearest neighbour, New South Wales should extend its laws to include New Zealand. It was a fine theory but was very difficult to administer from so far away and was as a consequence largely ineffective.

By the early 1830s a group of northern Maori chiefs concerned at the lawlessness of the colonists, decided to approach the British government for formal protection. Maori were concerned at the growing number of European settlers who were trying to buy land in one-sided deals that were highly unfavourable to the indigenous people. Regulation was needed to protect Maori interests. *Ngai Tahu* of the South Island in particular were concerned about their established and lucrative trade with New South Wales.

As well as the need to impose law and order on the British in the Bay Of Islands, Maori were concerned about French imperial ambitions in the region. A French Catholic mission in the Hokianga had already been set up and this brought French ships and traders to the area. As the French retaliation for the killing of Marion de Fresne earlier had been so brutal, Maori had no desire to enter into negotiations with such a regime and out of the two, Britain seemed to be the better choice.

The Treaty of Waitangi

The British government responded in half-hearted fashion by sending the inexperienced and under-qualified James Busby as British Resident. Busby's low standing was underscored by the modest cottage at Waitangi that he was expected to live in, since preserved for the nation as the site where the historic treaty was signed. Appointed as a civilian administrator, he had no real powers of governance.

Busby's assertion that Maori were unable to manage their own affairs meant that the 1840 Treaty of Waitangi, regarded as New Zealand's founding document was instigated by the British Government. The Maori translation of the Treaty, signed by 500 of the 539 Maori chiefs was at odds with the English version. The Treaty that Maori signed stated that the British Crown would preserve law and order between Maori and the Europeans, would protect Maori trade and ensure that Maori controlled land and other resources that they wished to keep. The English version gave full sovereignty to the British Crown.

Maori were asked to concede sovereignty but the word in Maori was translated as governorship. It is unlikely that Maori would have signed away their right to sovereignty had they understood what exactly it was. In the Maori text the Crown guaranteed to the *tangata whenua* (people of the land) the right to possess their properties as long as they wished to keep them. In perhaps the worst mis-translation of all, the English version expressed this as individual property rights, something that did not exist in a culture based on collective ownership.

The English version stated that the Crown had exclusive right to buy Maori land, something that has caused considerable disagreement as Maori were unable to sell any land to a third party, even if the Crown rejected it. That Maori were now under the jurisdiction of British law and what citizenship meant in practice was another significant part of the Treaty that was not understood. In international law it is the indigenous text that should have been agreed to but as it was clearly the Crown's version that was, these major discrepancies have ensured that there continues to be on-going debate around the Treaty.

The New Zealand Wars

Almost as soon as the Treaty was signed there were allegations of breaches. *Hone Heke*, who was a supporter of the Treaty, believing that it would bring more opportunities for trade was so frustrated by these transgressions that he chopped down the flagstaff at Russell in protest. Frustrations with British incursion into territory deemed to be under the authority of Maori erupted into what is now known as the New Zealand Wars in 1845 which lasted until 1872. According to the historian James Belich, these were not mere skirmishes but involved 18,000 or so armed troops against 60,000 Maori, including women and children. That Maori were able to hold out against colonial expansion was remarkable, given the uneven odds. Belich's view is that the New Zealand Wars marked a turning point in the country's race relations.

In the late 1950s conservative Maori groups chose to work within the system to champion Maori rights. But these groups were accused by younger activists of being part of the establishment and did not necessarily represent urban Maori. In the 1970s a younger group of activists demanded to have their voices heard. Through a series of well-publicised marches and demonstrations they became noticeably more politicised.

Land Marches and Treaty Settlements

In 1975 30,000 protestors marched to Parliament under the slogan, 'Not One More Acre of Maori Land.' Government and other New Zealanders had to address issues around the Treaty that had been forgotten in the ensuing years. One of the most high profile demonstrations occurred at Takaparawha or Bastion Point in Auckland.

The Waitangi Tribunal was established but a government bill sought to restrict the amount that could be paid in reparations in total as a billion dollars. Through the Office of Treaty Settlements some of the first claims began. The settlements were neither perfect nor fair but the participating tribes saw settlement as a way to move forward and a chance to re-build their assets.

To illustrate the limits of settlement, the Waikato settlement of 170 million dollars was a fraction of the estimated 21 billion dollar estimated loss to the tribe. And to many Maori the settlements ignores the issue of sovereignty altogether.

To those coming to New Zealand now it can seem that the issues with the Treaty are about looking to the past rather than to the future. Although the Treaty is far from perfect it is still New Zealand's founding document, and some New Zealanders regard it the way Americans see their Constitution.

One contemporary issue that has highlighted the grievances of the past is the ownership and access to the seabed and foreshore. In 2003 a court decision stated that Maori could claim customary title over this coastal land but the government contradicted that saying that the Crown owned the land. Protests over this move forced a compromise and the government sought to defuse the situation by putting the land in question into the public domain for all New Zealanders.

European Settlement

At Te Papa, New Zealand's national museum a former exhibition traces the origins of European settlement. Between 1840 and 1850 over 22,000 immigrants arrived from England through the New Zealand Company. Part of a social experiment instigated by Edward Gibbon Wakefield, the concept was to ensure that many of the settlers were middle-class so that they would have a 'civilising' effect on the country. But like so many attempts at social engineering, this one failed as uncontrolled immigration came from the rest of the British Isles including Scotland and Northern Ireland. And despite conflicts with the indigenous people, life for the settlers prospered, thanks to wool, gold and timber.

In 1893, New Zealand gave women the vote, the first country in the world to do so. New Zealand suffered as much as any country did during the Depression in 1929, with food queues and riots. In World War 1 out of a population of one million people, New Zealand sent 100,000 of its able bodied men to fight for Britain in a war 12,000 miles away. And in World War II the dominion again sent its young able-bodied men in the same numbers to fight in Europe, the Middle East and in South East Asia.

An Enviable Lifestyle

For a country still suffering from rationing, the attraction of New Zealand was a strong one and from the late 1940s until the mid 1970s over 75,000 Britons moved there with the assistance of the government. These 'ten pound poms' who came over on an assisted passage were brought in to make up numbers in the rapidly expanding work force. The marketing campaign promised them a life they could only dream about in urban industrial Britain – fresh air, a detached house, good weather and a beach lifestyle.

In the 1950s and 1960s New Zealand prospered and had one of the highest standards of living in the world. Britain's joining of the Common Market was inevitable but New Zealand did not have any long-term strategy in place and was unprepared when it did happen. Although other markets had been found for exports the morale of the nation was gloomy.

End of the Boom Years

In 1975 the National Government was led by the blustering Robert 'Piggy' Muldoon who perfected the art of the 'sound-bite' media comment, long before the term had been invented. When asked if he was worried about the country's brightest and best moving to Australia, Muldoon in typical fashion, managed to put a sarcastic spin on it, claiming that 'New Zealanders who leave for Australia raise the IQ of both countries'. Muldoon was quick to blame the outgoing Labour government for the country's woes but National's spending habits under Muldoon put Labour's in the shade. As unemployment rose and New Zealand's famed standard of living began to drop, thousands left to seek a better life overseas.

The 1970s saw the formation of a number of bike gangs in South Auckland. At the same time Polynesian immigrants arrived in large numbers causing tensions not only with Maori groups, concerned that the immigrants would have access to housing and social welfare at their expense, but with white society as well. Muldoon responded by instructing police to conduct spot identity checks to ensure none were in the country illegally. Those that were found to be so were deported with little or no right to appeal.

During the Muldoon era African nations boycotted the Montreal Olympics because New Zealand had sent an All Black team to South Africa during the boycott. In 1981 the New Zealand Rugby Union chose to ignore public opinion by planning a Springbok tour of the country. It caused serious civil unrest with marches and demonstrations and even caused divisions within families between those that believed that the tour should go ahead and those that passionately opposed it.

Muldoon's reign although full of grandiose schemes such as his 'Think Big' economic strategy, was largely ineffectual. By 1984 the country was tired of Muldoon and his over-spending and returned a Labour government to power, headed by David Lange. But once voted in, Labour abandoned its traditional left-of-centre policies to solve the country's considerable economic problems. Under the stewardship of Finance Minister Roger Douglas the government embarked on a range of free market economic reforms that went further than even those of Margaret Thatcher's government.

Standing Tall

In 1985 all nuclear-armed and nuclear-propelled vessels were banned from New Zealand waters. New Zealand's allies in the ANZUS treaty, Australia and the USA did not much like this move. That same year the Greenpeace vessel *Rainbow Warrior* which was at the forefront of protesting about nuclear testing in the Pacific, was sunk by French intelligence agents while docked in Auckland harbour. One crew member was killed in the explosion. This cowardly act hardened New Zealand's resolve to maintain a firm anti-nuclear policy, and the country was much admired by many in the developed world, particularly amongst smaller nations, as a role-model and one that dared to stand up to its much bigger and more powerful allies.

In 1987 those New Zealand investors who had embraced free market reforms found out the hard way that there was a downside to their speculation. The economic crash hit New Zealand hard and a period of economic recession ensued. There was one event during the era of all that belt-tightening that gave the whole country the morale boost it needed:- In 1995 Team New Zealand won that most prestigious yachting title, the America's Cup.

By the end of the 1990s recession was over and New Zealand had much to look forward to. In 2000 it was the first country to see the sun rise on the new millennium and later that year Team New Zealand successfully defended its America's Cup title only to lose it in 2004 after a disappointing race series. But the mood of the nation was buoyed by the total domination of the 2004 Academy Awards by Peter Jackson and his crew. If only Gollum could have got his hands on 'the precious' – the biggest haul of gold statuettes that New Zealand has ever seen. A triumphant Return of the King indeed.

THE POLITICS OF POWERSHARING

New Zealand's system of government is a parliamentary democracy with Queen Elizabeth II as the Head of State. The Governor-General is appointed as her representative. There is only one legislative chamber, the House of Representatives. The Prime Minister and Members of Parliament are elected by New Zealanders. The two main political parties are the centre-right National and Labour on the centre-left. Up until 1996 elections were won or lost using the 'first past the post system' but when New Zealand's version of proportional representation (Mixed Member Proportional – referred to as MMP), was introduced, the situation became somewhat more complex.

With MMP voters have two votes, one to elect their MP and the other to choose a party. Proportional representation is a much fairer system but problems arise when the majority party has to form a coalition with a minor party that may be at odds with them on certain key issues. It was the National government in the mid 1990s that introduced MMP and they were in coalition with the right-wing New Zealand First. But the two parties fell out over key policy and the situation became so bad that the coalition was dissolved and National struggled to govern alone.

In 1999 a Labour-led coalition headed up by Helen Clark ousted National. In 2002 Labour was returned to power for a second term. National had lost its way in the worst election defeat in 70 years. Labour has found aspects of MMP to be equally as challenging as National. Either the relationships have soured over the three-year term or their preferred coalition partner has not passed the crucial 5% vote threshold. The paradox of MMP is that power sharing can only work where the parties share a common ideology. But even natural allies like Labour and the left-leaning Greens had a major falling-out out over the issue of genetic modification.

Life for the minor parties is perilous as every three years not only does the individual risk losing their seat in parliament but if the party doesn't manage to retain 5% of the vote the entire party risk's political oblivion. In a small country like New Zealand, career politicians have a habit of re-inventing themselves and returning to power either in local government or as representatives of a minor party.

The September 2005 Labour-led election victory was won under such a narrow margin that for some weeks while the special votes were still being counted, it was unclear which party had actually won. This election was much more of a contest as Don Brash's National Party had started to rise significantly in the polls. The budget delivered in 2005 by Labour was seen as parsimonious, given that Labour had significant surpluses.

The 'jam tomorrow' attitude of the Minister of Finance, Michael Cullen, whose smug public persona did not go down well with an electorate that believed that the economy was in good shape because of their contribution and that it was pay-back time, especially as the opposition were making noises about tax cuts if they were elected.

Labour responded swiftly to the real threat that they might lose the election and suddenly found there was enough money to woo not just the students but the mums, dads and grandparents as well.

When the election results were confirmed in October 2005, the final count delivered the mandate to Labour but only just. In the new parliament out of a total of 121 seats, Labour won 50, National 48, NZ First 7, Greens 6, Maori 4, United Future 3 and Act 2. Labour won 41.10% of the Party votes and National 39.10%.

It took many weeks for Labour to talk with its potential coalition partners to work out just how the party was going to govern the country. Labour has previously been accused of cosying up to the Green Party who are seen as able on environmental matters but soft on economic issues. With nearly as many National MPs in Parliament as there are Labour, Labour abandoned the Greens and the newly formed Maori Party in favour of Peter Dunne's United Future Party and the controversial Winston Peters – with or without his party, New Zealand First.

National may have lost the election because of one controversial speech made by its leader Don Brash, which addressed issues of race based funding. Although the content of his speech pleased some sectors of the community, it alienated the important Maori and Pacific Island vote. Instead of seeking to build bridges with Maori, Brash's political naivety was reinforced, when he hastily removed his only Maori minister from the portfolio of Opposition Spokesperson on Maori Affairs, the highly regarded Georgina Te Heuheu, when she dared to raise objections from the Maori community regarding Brash's stand.

GEOGRAPHICAL INFORMATION

Physical Features

The size of the United Kingdom, Italy or the US state of Colorado but spread across two main islands the total land mass of New Zealand is 104,454 sq miles (270,534 sq km). A body of water as wide as the English Channel, the Cook Strait separates the two islands. There are numerous offshore islands, the largest of which is Stewart Island, at the southern tip of the South Island. Lake Taupo in the central North Island is the largest lake at 235 sq miles (607 sq km) and is the source of the longest river, the Waikato, which runs for 264 miles (425 km). Packed within this one small country is a diversity of landscape that is generally only found in entire continents, with lakes, mountains, volcanoes, sub-tropical beaches and rainforest.

Geological Features

New Zealand is a geological upstart as its present shape was formed barely 10,000 years ago. But rocks found dating back 500 million years that originated in Australia and Antarctica suggest that New Zealand was once part of that super-continent, Gondwanaland. After the land broke away a combination of continental drift, volcanic and seismic activity formed more land and the country over the centuries gradually began to take shape.

Volcanoes and Earthquakes. The restless activity of two tectonic plates ensures that it is a land that never sleeps. As the Indo-Australian plate pushes against the Pacific plate, where the two overlap, it can get a little shaky. Out of the 400 or so earthquakes recorded every year, few of them are strong enough to be felt, although earthquakes have caused damage and fatalities in the past. A quake measuring 7.9 hit the city of Napier in the Hawke's Bay in 1931. Out of the rubble of the 1931 Napier earthquake a new city was created in the Art Deco style. From the Bay of Plenty a fault line runs diagonally through New Plymouth and down through Wellington. Across Cook Strait the fault line passes through Marlborough, Nelson and then on a diagonal to join the Alpine fault on the west coast of the South Island.

In May 1968 a recently emigrated British family living near Nelson recall shattered glassware and their newly surfaced tennis court developing a large crack running down its length. Measuring 7.1 on the Richter scale the epicentre was over 100km away at Inangahua Junction, on the South Island's west coast, But tectonic plates crashing against each other cause more than earthquakes. This geological disturbance has been responsible for some of the country's most spectacular scenery, including the Southern Alps. This icy spine runs along most of the length of South Island. stretching from peak to peak for nearly 300 miles (500km). Aoraki Mount Cook (the cloud piercer) is the tallest at 12,316 feet (3754m) high.

In the central North Island the atmosphere can get a little heated. In the volcanic heartland is the Taupo Volcanic Zone, part of the Pacific Ring of Fire that links the mountains around Lake Taupo (an enormous crater lake) beyond the coast of the Bay of Plenty to White Island. The plumes of steam can be seen from the coast and the country's most active volcano can be visited on a day trip. While the volcanic cones that dot Auckland, especially the sleeping giant Rangitoto out in the Hauraki Gulf, have lain dormant for the past 500 years, in the centre of the North Island in the recent past, things have been rather less benign.

Close to Rotorua, partial excavations have unearthed a village on the shores of Lake Tarawera where, in the 19th century a catastrophic eruption not only buried a village but destroyed the famous Pink and White Terraces. And as recently as 1995 and 1996, Mount Ruapehu erupted, forcing the closure of the ski fields for a number of seasons.

But all this geological and geo-thermal activity has meant that visitors and locals alike have plenty of opportunity for recreational escapes. After skiing down a mountainside you can relax in a hot pool or if you'd rather pack two activities into one, at Hot Water Beach on the Coromandel Peninsula you can lie on a beach and soak in a hot pool at the same time.

CLIMATE

Surrounded by the Pacific Ocean to the north and east and the Tasman Sea to the west, all that water gives New Zealand a maritime climate where temperatures at sea level never get too hot or too cold. But as more than 75% of the country is over 200 metres high, variations in temperature, amount of rainfall and wind vary significantly. In all there are nine climate zones, ranging from sub-tropical in the north to cool and temperate in the far south to alpine conditions in the Southern Alps. These microclimates occur because of proximity to the west or east coasts, their situation near mountains, whether sheltered from winds such as Nelson and Marlborough or exposed in coastal areas buffeted by gales, like Wellington. Mean annual temperatures in the north are as high as 16 degrees Celsius and as low as 10 degrees Celsius in the south.

The seasons in the Southern Hemisphere are an exact reversal of those in the northern, with winter from June to August, spring from September to November, summer from December to February and the autumn months March, April and May.

Seasonal variations are more marked in the South Island while in the sub-tropical north, temperatures are more evenly spread throughout the year.

Weather systems forming in the Tasman Sea and the Southern Alps protect the east coast of the South Island from the full force of the prevailing westerlies. The west coast of the South Island experiences some of the wettest weather while the east coast remains the driest due to the protective barrier created by the mountain ranges.

In the north and the central North Island winter is the season for the highest rainfall whereas in the southern areas winters are generally drier.

Most of New Zealand has more than 2000 hours of sunshine a year, the sunniest place being Nelson at the top of the South Island. But the sun brings with it a very high and potentially damaging UV level to those with fair skin, especially in summer, autumn and spring. It is particularly high in mountainous areas.

AVERAGE TEMPERATURES, (FAHRENHEIT/CELSIUS) AND RAINFALL (MM)

Bay of Islands	Summer	Autumn	Winter	Spring
Max	77 /25	70/21	62/17	77/19
Min	57/14	53/12	46/8	52/11
Rainfall	101	134	158	113
Auckland				
Max	75/24	68/20	59/16	65/18
Min	58/15	55/13	48/9	50/10/
Rainfall	83	92	133	95
Napier				
Max	74/23	65/18	57/14	66/19
Min	57/14	50/10	43/6	48/9
Rainfall	66	82	95	58
Wellington				
Max	68/20	63/17	54/12	59/15
Min	55/13	52/11	53/6	47/9
Rainfall	85	103	127	90
Nelson				
Max	73/23	65/18	55/13	63/17
Min	55/13	52/11	43/6	48/9
Rainfall	65	82	88	82
Christchurch				
Max	72/22	65/18	54 /12	64/16
Min	54/12	46/8	37/3	45/7
Rainfall	49	57	58	45
Queenstown				
Max	72/22	61/16	50/10	57/14
Min	10/50	6/43	1/34	5/41
Rainfall	69	68	60	61

	Sunshine	Rain Days	Frost Days	Wind	Gale Days*
Bay of Islands	2070	133	4	15	2
Auckland	2060	137	10	17	2
Napier	2188	91	29	14	3
Wellington	2065	123	10	22	22
Nelson	2405	94	88	12	2
Christchurch	2100	85	70	15	3
Queenstown	1921	100	107	12	2

* Gales defined as mean speed over 63km/h)

GETTING THERE

New Zealand is a long-haul destination from almost anywhere except Australia's east coast. Sydney, Melbourne and Brisbane are a mere three hours away by plane. Although a number of cruise ships include Auckland on their itineraries, the only realistic way to get there is by air. While the tyranny of distance might deter some, others are attracted by the peaceful isolation in the South Pacific, far away from the world's trouble spots. The discomfort of the journey is soon forgotten as visitors start to experience a lifestyle that is the envy of many.

Tourism is big business in New Zealand, which means that travellers have a choice of a number of airlines that fly the route. Since Emirates added Australasia to its itinerary, travellers from Britain have the additional option of flying via the Middle East, as well as via North America or South East Asia. It is even possible to travel via South America, although in order to visit Argentina and Chile on the way, travellers will need to be prepared to fly for up to fifteen hours on each sector to get there. On a direct route the trip can be made in around 24 hours. From North America there are a number of stopover options in the South Pacific.

The airlines listed below fly directly to New Zealand or work with a partner airline that operates the service. Use the list to check schedules and timetables.

The intense competition between airlines means that destinations and routings can change at short notice. If demand is patchy a route may be scaled back or an additional stopover may be required. You are advised to contact the airline concerned or your travel agent for their most up-to-date information on routings and the number of flights per week. While airlines like Air New Zealand and Singapore Airlines have daily services on large wide-bodied aircraft, some other airlines may only fly three or four times a week in planes with less capacity.

Airlines

From Australia:
The competition amongst airlines that fly across the Tasman between Australia and New Zealand is intense. When Emirates moved into this market, with its brand new planes and excellent service, it was a wake-up call for Air New Zealand and Qantas to improve their standards..Customers have benefited from even cheaper prices since the no-frills operators have entered the market.

Air New Zealand: (Brisbane Travel Centre ☎ 07 3007 1500; Melbourne Travel Centre ☎ 03 9613 4850; Perth Travel Centre ☎ 08 9326 0910; Sydney Travel Centre ☎ 02 8235 9999; www.airnz.com)

Emirates: (☎ 03 9940 7807; www.emirates.com) Emirates fly to Auckland from Brisbane, Melbourne and Sydney as well as Christchurch to Sydney.

Freedom Air: (☎ 1800 122 000; fax 1800 122 223; www.freedomair. com) the no-frills budget airline flies between Brisbane, Gold Coast, Melbourne and Sydney to Auckland, Christchurch, Dunedin, Hamilton and Wellington.

Pacific Blue: (☎ 136789; www.flypacificblue.com) Pacific Blue, owned by Virgin Blue flies between Brisbane, Melbourne, Sydney to Auckland, Wellington and Christchurch. Passengers from regional Australian destinations can link up with Virgin Blue's extensive regional network.

Qantas: (☎ 13 13 131; www.qantas.com.au)

From the UK:

Aerolineas Argentinas (☎ 0845-601 1915; www.aerolineas.com,ar) fly from London Gatwick via Madrid and Buenos Aires to Auckland.

Air New Zealand (☎ 0800-737 000; www.airnz.co.nz) fly from London Heathrow to Auckland via LA or San Francisco, or various Pacific Island destinations.

British Airways (☎ 08750-850 9850; www.britishairways.com) fly from London Heathrow to Auckland and Christchurch via America and Australia.

Cathay Pacific (☎ 020-8834 8800 ; www.cathaypacific.com) fly from London Heathrow to Auckland via Hong Kong.

Emirates (☎ 0870-243 2222; www.emirates.com) fly from London Heathrow to Auckland and Christchurch. Auckland via Dubai or major centres in South East Asia. Christchurch is via Dubai and Melbourne.

Garuda Indonesia (☎ 0807-1 GARUDA427832; www.garuda-indonesia.com) fly from London Gatwick to Auckland via Jakarta, Bali and Brisbane.

Korean Air (☎ 0800-413 000; www.koreanair.com) fly from London Heathrow to Auckland and Christchurch via Seoul.

Jal (☎ 0845-7747700; www.jal.co.jp) fly from London Heathrow via Tokyo connecting with a codeshare partner to Christchurch and Auckland.

Lan Chile (☎ 0800-917 0572 www.lan.com)fly from London Heathrow to Madrid then via Santiago to Auckland.

Malaysia Airlines (MAS) (☎ 0161-835 3020; www.mas.com.my)fly from London Heathrow to Auckland via Kuala Lumpur.

Qantas (☎ 020-8846 0466; www.qantas.com.au) fly from London Heathrow to Auckland and Christchurch via Bangkok, Singapore, Sydney or Melbourne.

Singapore Airlines (☎ 01784-266122; www.singaporeair.com)fly from Manchester and London Heathrow to Auckland and Christchurch via Singapore.

Thai Air (☎ 0870-606 0911; www.thaiair.com) fly from London Heathrow via Bangkok.

United Airlines (☎ 0800-0656 2001; www.united.com)fly from London Heathrow connecting into various destinations in the US with a code-share partner to Auckland.

From Canada and the USA:
Air New Zealand and Qantas are the two carriers that operate across the trans-Pacific route. Air New Zealand fly from San Francisco or Los Angeles. Qantas fly from LA. In March 2006 a new service linking New York to Auckland is due to start with Air Tahiti Nui, the airline of French Polynesia.

Air New Zealand: (☎ 1-800-262-1234; www.airnewzealand.com).

Air Tahiti Nui (☎ Toll Free 877-824-4846).

Qantas: (www.qantas.com.au).

From South Africa:
Qantas (☎ 11 441 8550 www.qantas. com.au) flies to New Zealand from Johannesburg via Australia.

South African Airways (☎ 0861 359 722 www.3.flysaa.com) fly from Johannesburg as far as Australia where you can connect to New Zealand with the code share partner Qantas.

Travel Advice

Once you've checked the timetables and schedules and the length of stopover between flights, the cheapest way to book is to contact the agents or online booking companies below. In low season some of the deals can be incredibly good value given the distance. Low season is generally from

April to June in the UK and you can fly from around £700 return. Avoid the lead-up to Christmas as not only will you have to book months in advance, but the amount you'll end up paying even for an economy seat could be up to three times the price you would pay in low season for the same seat. If you booked in advance you might get a flight from the UK for £1700 at Christmas.

Book early enough from Australia using a budget airline like Freedom Air or Pacific Blue and you could get there for as little as A$500 return from the east coast cities, even in summer. Peak times such as Christmas and school holidays could see you paying as much as $1000 return using a scheduled airline. From the west coast in the USA you could get a cheap fare in low season for as little as $1200 which can go up to $2000 in peak season. Flights from South Africa are advertised from ZAR13,305 in the low season to as much as ZAR 14,065 in the high season. Bargains may be hard to find on the route as SAA and Qantas are the only two carriers that fly direct to Australasia.

Direct flights with the shortest refuelling stops are always the first to be booked out, no matter when you travel. Dates for low, shoulder and high season vary between airlines. For those with more time, a round-the-world ticket may be the best option for travellers keen to see as much as they can of the world on the way. The ticket may not be much more expensive than a standard return, although the cost of the stopovers should be taken into account.

Travel Agents and Online Booking

Austravel; ☎ 08701-662 130; www.austravel.net.
Bridge the World; ☎ 0870-4447474; www.b-t-w.co.uk.
Cresta World Travel; ☎ 0161-927 7177; www.mytravel.co.uk.
Expedia; www.expedia.msn.com
Flightbookers; ☎ 0870-010-7000; www.ebookers.com
Lastminute.com; www.lastminute.com.
London Flight Centre; ☎ 020-8879 6789; www.topdecktravel.co.uk.
Quest Worldwide; ☎ 0870-442 542; www.questtravel.com.
STA Travel; ☎ 08701-600 599 www.statravel.co.uk.
Trailfinders; ☎ 020-7292 1888; www.trailfinders.com.
Travel Bag; ☎ 0870-890 1456; www.travelbag.co.uk.

Airports. Auckland and Christchurch are the two major international airports. Wellington Airport can't handle anything bigger than short-haul aircraft because of the length of its runway. Regional airports such as Hamilton, Dunedin and Queenstown operate flights to and from Australia. Rotorua Airport which is undergoing a runway extension in 2006, is due to start operating transtasman charter services by Christmas 2006.

GETTING AROUND

The best option for house hunters to get around the country is to fly to a regional centre and then hire a car. There is no long distance train service for commuters and train travel is for tourists who have time to enjoy the scenery.

Domestic Air Travel. The major domestic airline is Air New Zealand, which through the Link service, offers connections to many of the smaller centres. Qantas flies a domestic route in New Zealand and is the national airline's main competitor.

Car hire. On a shorter inspection visit hiring a car is the best option. International companies such as Budget, Hertz and Avis all have offices or agents in most of the bigger cities and towns. The larger firms may also offer one-way rentals. Some do not allow you to take their car on the ferry across the Cook Strait or charge you a premium to do this. A car will normally be dropped off in either Picton or Wellington and another vehicle will be ready for collection after you've crossed the strait.

Local car hire companies offer much better rates than the big firms but without a network of countrywide branches, if a car breaks down there could be delays in finding a replacement vehicle. Smaller firms may not provide Collision Damage Waiver Insurance.

On the Road

Negotiating the sometimes narrow and twisty roads can be a challenge for international visitors who can underestimate driving times between the various centres. There is no long distance motorway network and there are no toll roads either. Auckland has a limited motorway system that extends south as far as Mercer and north only as far as the North Shore.

State Highway One, the main road between Auckland and Wellington would be considered an A road in the UK. Mainly single or dual carriageway, the further south you travel, the highway detours through town centres, which can add to the journey time. Roads are not as smooth and can at times be very uneven so exercise care when overtaking.

Speed limits. The speed limit on the open road is 100 kph (62 mph) and 50kph (31 mph) in most built-up areas. The Limited Speed Zone or LSZ sign requires drivers to make their own assessment on when it is safe to travel at 100 kph or when to slow down to 50 kph.

The right hand rule. Although New Zealand drives on the left and most of the road rules are similar to those in the UK, the right hand rule is one exception. Drivers turning left must give way to oncoming traffic turning right. This is the one rule that causes more problems with international visitors than any other. Confusion arises in built-up areas when there are two lanes and there is another driver that wants to go straight on. While the car turning right must wait, the car turning left usually doesn't bother to wait and turns left anyway.

Driving Standards

The standard of driving is generally lower compared to the UK or the USA. New Zealanders are usually courteous – until they get behind the wheel. When two lanes become one, instead of merging 'like a zip' , drivers often barge in front, with no consideration for the person behind them, who may be forced to brake. On the urban motorway network each lane is treated as a separate entity, therefore the principle of keeping left does not apply. Slow drivers can hog the outside lane, holding up all the traffic, exacerbating urban congestion. Impatient drivers will overtake on the inside lane and weave in and out of the traffic. Tailgating and an aversion to indicators is another factor of driving on New Zealand roads. Stop signs are treated like Give Way signs and Give Way generally means go if you can sneak in.

Traffic Management. The straight empty roads in Canterbury's South Island can be so tempting – they even caught out the Prime Minister's motorcade – resulting in an embarrassing court case. Getting caught speeding can result in a hefty fine and police make good use of hidden speed cameras. As drink driving is a contributory factor in a great many road accidents, a rigorous system of random breath testing is enforced.

Driving Hazards. Drivers get stuck behind large logging trucks and slow camper vans on country roads and the lack of passing bays can lead to reckless overtaking manoeuvres by impatient drivers. Do not drive too close to the edge on rural roads as cars can skid on loose chippings. The rule, as it is driving anywhere, is to drive to the conditions. In winter icy roads can be a problem particularly in more remote areas which may not be accessible to gritting trucks. Driving at night can be a challenge at first as only roads in the cities are lit and marker posts at the side of rural roads can be difficult to adjust to if you are used to the 'cats eyes' system.

A number of rural bridges in New Zealand have weight restrictions and are single lane only. A red arrow indicates that you must give way. Even if it is your right of way, if two cars are approaching a one-lane bridge at the same time, slow right down and pull to the side if necessary.

The use of hand-held mobile phones in cars is not yet banned, even though their use has contributed to a number of road fatalities. In the cities it pays not to be hard up against the intersection when turning right in case a careless driver fails to take the corner correctly and clips the right wing of your car. SUV drivers who steer with one hand and look down at their phones to send or receive a text message are particularly frightening.

Road Accident Statistics. New Zealanders love their cars. There are 3.7 million car owners out of a population of 4.1 million. Unfortunately New Zealand rates poorly in the fatal accident league table with 1.3 people dying in 10,000 cars. Out of every 100,000 there are 10.30 fatalities and New Zealand is the second highest, after the USA at 14.66 in a selective table of countries known for safer driving – including in descending order – Germany, Japan, Australia (8.21), Canada, Britain (the second safest at 6.10) and Sweden, the safest at 6.00.

Excessive speed is to blame for 32 percent of the fatal accidents with drink driving blamed for 29 per cent and failure to wear seat belts contributing to the rest of the fatalities.

Safety Belts and Child Restraints. Safety belts must be worn by the driver and the passengers unless you have a doctor's certificate. Children under the age of five should be properly restrained in an approved child restraint unless travelling in a taxi. Children aged between five and seven years should use a child restraint if available or use a safety belt. Approved child restraints can be hired from the Plunket Society, a child health organisation unique to New Zealand. (☎ 04 471-0172; www.plunket.org. nz) Plunket has branches throughout the country.

Driving Licences. New Zealand allows overseas drivers up to one year to drive with their current licence before they have to pass the driving theory test, a series of multi-choice questions. Sample question and answers sheets can be purchased prior to the test. Anyone who has sat the demanding British driving test should sail through.

COMMUNICATIONS

Postal Services

New Zealand Post through its network of Post Shops operates postal services, bill payment and banking services through their subsidiary, Kiwibank. Standard post can take up to four days within New Zealand and FastPost has a target of next-day delivery between the larger centres. Standard post costs start at 45 cents and FastPost 90 cents. Stamps can be bought at supermarkets, dairies, petrol stations and stationers as well as at Post Shops which are open six days a week in larger centres, keeping the standard office hours of 9am-5pm during weekdays and until 12.30pm on Saturdays.

Posties deliver to household letterboxes, situated in front of each house, rather than pushing letters through front doors like they do in the UK. In New Zealand the boxes are so poorly designed, especially the wooden ones, they seem expressly designed to let rain in. Metal provides the greatest protection from the elements.

In rural areas each house has a collection as well as a delivery. A red flag indicates you have letters to post. In towns and cities, finding an official New Zealand Post mailing box may entail a bit of a hike – unless you have a small shop or dairy close by.

General Delivery (Poste Restante). This is available in the main post shop in each large town. Passports or another form of photo identification is required to pick post up. Post is held for up to three months and then returned to sender. Redirection is available at a cost.

Telephones

Telecom is a privatised monopoly and all new phone connections have to go through the company even though the calls can be made at cheaper rates from other providers. Rural customers now have to pay the actual cost of phone installation for a new line, which can be hugely expensive in the remoter areas. Telecom's main competitor is TelstraClear but until the telecommunications market is de-regulated Telecom will make the most of its monopoly.

OFF-PEAK CALLING
From 6pm-8am Monday to Friday and all weekend

Calling Costs. Although local calls from land lines are free to other land lines, the price of fixed to mobile calls are prohibitive. This is a direct result of Telecom's monopoly, see below.

Effect of Telecom's Monopoly. New Zealand historically was an early adopter of new communication technology and was constantly used as a test-bed for new services. It still has among the world's highest internet and mobile phone use but since the de-regulation of telecoms in the 1980s there has been an effective monopoly of key areas of telecommunication by Telecom. The result has been a disappointing version of third generation mobile technology and broadband internet, which lag behind international best practice. TelstraClear, Telecom's smaller competitor is now permitted to provide line rental services to Christchurch and Wellington residents. Telecom's prices in these cities have come down as a result.

Broadband Internet. Telecom has the broadest coverage of broadband internet but it is slow by international standards. The wireless operator Whoosh is too small with only main city centre coverage to be a significant player yet. In January 2006 Telecom and TelstraClear signed a deal which will enable TelstraClear to have access to Telecom's unbundled bitstream (UBS) internet service. 100,000 TelstraClear customers will be offered this service.

Unfortunately, the deal agreed between the two companies was done so that TelstraClear could steal a march on the smaller players in the market and thus deliver more revenue to its shareholders. Consumers will, once again miss out on a better and faster broadband service.

Calling via the Internet. VoIP or Voice over Internet Protocol is a system that strikes fear within traditional telecommunications companies. In New Zealand in 2005 over one third of all broadband subscribers were Skype users at www.skype.com. Offered as a free download over the internet any computer with a microphone/headset can be used as a telephone calling others with the Skype software.

Skype launched two other upgrades in 2005 – Skype Plus which enables voice mail and calls from standard phones and SkypeOut – going further and allowing those with Skype to call standard phones and cell phones via a pre-paid account. The drawback with the system is that users cannot receive calls from either landlines or mobile phones and are unable to dial the emergency services. And some analysts say that although Skype rates are very competitive they are in some instances beaten by the easy to use low-cost calling cards, available from local shops.

Mobile Phones. If the landline telephone market is virtually a monopoly then the mobile phone market is a duopoly with Telecom and Vodafone controlling the market. Mobile phones can be purchased from other retailers selling electronics as well as directly from Telecom and Vodafone. There is as yet no number portability so users can't retain their old numbers when switching networks. The regulator though is addressing this and has given Telecom and Vodafone a deadline of April 2007 to provide this service. If you receive poor service from your provider you are stuck with them and there is no real incentive to improve customer service. If you have brought your phone with you from overseas then the cheapest option is to buy a New Zealand SIM card. Like mobile phone providers both Telecom and Vodafone have a system of complicated price structures for payment of airtime as well as a range of payment options.

Making and Receiving International Calls. To call New Zealand dial the international access code 00 from the UK, 011 from the USA, and 0011 from Australia then 64, the area code minus the initial zero and then the number. To call the UK dial 00 then the country code 44 then the rest of the number, omitting the first zero in the area code. If dialling the USA the country code is 1, for Ireland it is 353.

Keeping Track of the Time Difference. New Zealand Standard Time is 12 hours ahead of Greenwich Mean Time, making the time difference a breeze to calculate. At 12 noon in New Zealand it will be 12 midnight the day before in the UK. There are barely more than a few weeks in any year when there is 12 hours time difference as both countries change their clocks for Daylight Saving. In New Zealand the clocks go forward on the first Sunday in October until the third Sunday in March. In summer time in New Zealand the clocks will be 13 hours ahead of GMT and in winter the time difference will be 11 hours. International directory assistance will assist you in clarifying time differences with other countries or go to www.whitepages.co.nz/world-directories.

Dialling Within New Zealand. There are only four area codes throughout the country and the entire South Island only has one. Within a large geographical calling area like Auckland or if calling Nelson from Christchurch, you will need to dial the area code first.

AREA CODES	
Auckland	09
Bay of Islands	09
Christchurch and the South Island	03
Hamilton	07
Napier and Hawkes Bay	07
New Plymouth	06
Tauranga	07
Wanganui	06
Wellington	04
Emergency & Useful Numbers	
Emergency services – ambulance, police and fire	111
National Poisons Centre (urgent enquiries)	0800 764 766
International directory assistance	018
National directory assistance	0118

FOOD AND DRINK

Food

Food cooked at home rather than served in restaurants reflects how the nation really eats. New Zealanders have adventurous tastes and like to embrace the best of other food cultures. The roast *kumara* (sweet potato) was brought by Maori, the lamb from Britain but how that North American staple, the pumpkin came to be served with roast lamb – is anyone's guess.

Where once lamb would have been so over cooked that it had the texture of an Ugg boot, now it is as likely to be served rare as lamb racks or baked slowly as meltingly moist lamb shanks.

In an emerging nation, where there are no ancient food traditions to have to live up to, cooks have the freedom to creatively combine ingredients without fear of breaking inflexible food rules.

Just as the best meal of the day in the UK was supposed to be breakfast; in New Zealand in the 1950s and 1960s it was morning or afternoon tea. A legacy from the English and the Scots :- club sandwiches, pinwheels, pikelets (drop scones), ginger crunch, Anzac biscuits, cream sponge and copious cups of tea were served up in village halls up and down the country. And which side of the Tasman Sea the first pavlova was made matters less than the fact that New Zealanders (and Australians) still care enough to continue baking them at home.

While the cafes in the tonier parts of town are busy being pseudo-French, serving *friands* (a word you'll only ever hear in Australasia and probably a mis-spelling of *friandise*, the French word for small cake) – in the suburbs they've embraced good old Uncle Sam. Going out for an enormous plate of Eggs Benedict for brunch, is a weekend ritual.

Whether or not the global influence of American culture is entirely responsible for our enthusiasm for all things coffee is debatable. The Dutch who emigrated in large numbers in the middle of the last century brought with them the taste for freshly ground coffee. A number of Dutch coffee houses sprang up around the country, bringing a touch of European flair to the culinary scene.

Set up originally as a place where the homesick new arrivals could meet and speak their language, the friendly atmosphere and delicious strudel soon found favour with the locals. Sitting in Chez Eelco or Suzy's Coffee Lounge listening to Dutch being spoken felt more like the Singel in Amsterdam than it did downtown Nelson or Wellington.

With the arrival of a new group of migrants in the 1980s, this time from South East Asia, the emphasis shifted from meat and dairy products towards a healthier style of eating and cooking. Combining food from East and West may have given rise to Pacific Rim cuisine but done badly it's a case of too many competing flavours. When confectionery manufacturers start producing green tea flavoured chocolate wafer biscuits, it's time to move on.

The innovative and talented chef and restaurateur Peter Gordon has gone much further than merely copying imported trends by showcasing the best local ingredients and combining them to create a distinct and exciting style of fusion food, which has found favour in London and beyond.

Food fashions come and go but for people who love to cook, New Zealand offers some of the world's freshest produce. Tell an expat Kiwi in London that you spent Christmas eating snapper caught that day and then cooked on a barbecue, washed down with a Marlborough sauvignon blanc, and that might be enough to persuade him to return home.

While lamb and beef have always been staples, what most New Zealanders take for granted is that the animals are not only free range but fed a natural diet of grass, producing delicious and succulent meat. Thanks to the market gardening skills of recent immigrants from Asia you never need to eat another boring Brussels sprout again.

Even though supermarkets are where most New Zealanders shop for food, the key to eating well and cheaply is to buy in season. While the 'upside down' seasons can take a while to get used to, it's worth persevering. You can still find tomatoes in winter but they'll be grown in a greenhouse and twice the price of the outdoor ones available in the summer.

Fish and seafood lovers have the opportunity of buying freshly caught, delicately flavoured fish and a number of different varieties of seafood. While the different Southern Hemisphere fish species may have unfamiliar names, for firm white fish try *snapper, hapuka, tarakihi* and blue cod. Try serving *pipis* – a clam-like shellfish, with spaghetti to create an Italian style pasta dish.

If your only experience of New Zealand's green-lipped mussels has been the tough frozen sort found in UK supermarkets, you will find they are tender and sweet when fresh. The best place to try them are the Belgian beer chains in the main centres where that winning combination of mussels and chips is as popular here as it is in Belgium. Crayfish (rock lobster), although expensive, is a winner for special occasions and oyster-lovers can't go past the fine Bluff oysters from the southern most part of the South Island. Whitebait (a tiny sweet-tasting fish) are usually served in a light pancake batter called a fritter.

Tamarillos (tree tomatoes) taste great poached in a vanilla-infused syrup while you will either love or loathe the perfumy *feijoas*. Originally from South America, these fruits are as much part of Kiwi food culture as the new season's cherries from Central Otago at Christmas or the first succulent apricots from Hawke's Bay.

With those delicious stone fruits you'll want to add a scoop of creamy ice cream. For those with a sweet tooth the hokey pokey (crunchy butterscotch), boysenberry or plain old vanilla flavours still maintain their hold over the nation's taste buds. Cheese has been another dairy success story with a great many more locally made European-style cheeses available now. Thirty years ago the three varieties were tasty cheddar, medium cheddar and mild. Bread though has always been good in New Zealand with Swiss-style mixed grain bread a favourite. Hand-finished Italian style bread is becoming increasingly popular.

New Zealanders have taken to drinking and sometimes even slurping great bowls full of freshly made coffee – whether that is lattes, long-blacks, flat whites, machiatti or capucchini. But unlike the Italians, they'll drink coffee at any time of the day (or night.) 'Just another latte sipping Aucklander' is a derogatory term used by those living in the provinces to refer to the inhabitants of the nation's largest and most powerful city.

Despite the availability of sushi at lunch-counters, Kiwis still consume around 60 million pies a year. For the last few years the Supreme Pie Award has been dominated by bakers that hail from Asia cooking up such fillings as mince and cheese, steak and vegetable or bacon and egg.

Generations of Kiwis have enjoyed cooking simple food on their summer holidays at their *bach* (holiday house) or crib, as it's known in the South Island. There's an entire magazine dedicated to the bach and beach lifestyle but for anyone arriving here now the price of coastal property puts owning a beach house as well as a main residence out of reach for most. However, renting is still an option and the country still has a long way to go before the bach lifestyle disappears, as sitting round an open fire in the Outback eating damper and drinking billy tea has for most urban Australians. Even for city families that don't have much outdoor living space, cooking a meal outdoors is still possible. In local parks there are gas barbecues enabling the different generations to gather en masse for a weekend lunch.

Markets. It might seem to visitors that New Zealand is just one big farm-ers' market and up until the last twenty years there was some truth in this. Supermarkets were still a novelty and a great many more people, even in the suburbs had access to a patch of dirt where they could grow their own lettuces and tomatoes.

As gardens have shrunk and apartment living has been embraced by those looking for a lock-up and leave lifestyle – that convenience comes at a price. In some cases those apartments don't even have a balcony big enough to hold a few pots of herbs. But now artisan producers bring their delicious organic produce direct to the city consumer in weekly or monthly markets up and down the country. New Zealand it seems has come full circle.

The monthly glossy *Cuisine* will help you make the best of the local produce. It's an award-winning publication dedicated to New Zealand food and wine and is a great source of information on the latest food developments. One exciting recent trend has been the growth of avocado oil as an export industry. If the optimistic avocado industry has its way then soon even Italian consumers could be dressing their salads with extra virgin avocado oil from Kerikeri.

Drink

Wine. From the oldest established vineyards to the west of Auckland to the newly planted vines in mid Canterbury, there are currently over fourteen wine regions in New Zealand. A Scot, the British Resident, James Busby made the first wine in Northland, in the 1840s. With its high humidity and rainfall, the region is not really suitable for grape cultivation on a mass scale and is now only home to a handful of commercial vineyards.

Urban sprawl has encroached on the vines in Henderson, west Auckland making it less appealing for wine tourism than horse country in South Auckland around Clevedon. With a developing wine trail it is a picturesque destination for an afternoon's outing. Out east in the Hauraki Gulf, Waiheke Island has its own microclimate, perfect for growing the full-bodied red wines produced by the Goldwater Estate and Stonyridge. In the last ten years new vineyards have sprung up on the island attracting many more day-trippers from Auckland who find the laid-back ambience a world away from the city vibe.

An hour's drive north of Auckland the Matakana Valley is the perfect place for a leisurely lunch amongst the vines.. Further down on the east coast, chardonnay grapes have been grown commercially in and around Gisborne for many years. The first place in New Zealand to see the sun, the drier climate makes it perfect for viticulture.

Hawke's Bay is New Zealand's premier area for wine and food tourism. With over 40 vineyards, some of the names to watch out for are Black Barn, Sileni Estates, Te Mata and Kim Crawford. Hawke's Bay even has its own appellation – 'Gimblett Gravels' named after the unique local soil. Just as the wine and food regions of France and Italy are inextricably linked, so too in Hawke's Bay where a handful of stylish eateries mean that you have a choice between a more casual way of enjoying the food or going for the more formal fine-dining experience.

There are standout white wines in the Wairarapa and in the top half of the South Island from Siegfried in Nelson and Cloudy Bay in Marlborough. But it is in Central Otago and now Canterbury where really exciting developments have been taking place. For a country known for its first class Sauvignon Blanc, making a success of the much more fickle and labour-intensive Pinot Noir grapes proved an irresistible challenge to ambitious pioneering wine-makers.

The new wine hope of the future, according to Bob Campbell of Cuisine, is along the Waitaki River in Canterbury and pinot noir is still the favourite grape to plant. What's all the excitement about? Canterbury is sunnier during the crucial summer fruit ripening months and so has the edge on its Central Otago neighbour. You might want to raise a glass to that.

Beers. New Zealand has come a long way since the days of the 'six o'clock swill' – when it was a race to down as much beer (sold by the jug rather than the glass) between the time you finished work and when the pubs shut at six. Boutique breweries have sprung up in the hop-growing regions in the South Island. Look out for brands such as Speights, Macs and Monteith all of whom offer a range of pilsners, white beer, ales, lager and seasonal specials.

Spirits. 42 Below is the brand to watch out for, producing a highly rated vodka and gin. Locally made whisky or kiwifruit liqueur is to be avoided.

SCHOOLS AND EDUCATION

School attendance is compulsory for children aged from six until sixteen although most children start school at five. Parents and caregivers have the choice of a range of schooling options from private and integrated (religious schools integrated into the state system or schools of special character) to state schools, with the majority of children being educated at state schools.

- ◘ Primary schools take children from the age of five – Year 0 to the end of Year 6.
- ◘ Children in Years 7 and 8 may go to a separate intermediate school if

there is one in the area or continue at their primary school.

○ Secondary schools take students from Year 9 to the end of Year 13.

There is no school meal service at primary or secondary school level and children take a packed lunch. Classroom sizes vary and in some cases may be larger in the state schools compared with the home country. Schools even in the cities have a grassed area or playing fields for children to enjoy. And the universities are either situated in the older, leafier neighbourhoods or on a green field site just out of town. The campus at the University of Waikato is particularly pleasant with a lake, trees and extensive landscaping.

Zoning

For parents with school-age children the decision about where to send your child to school can have a strong influence on where to buy a house. Around 25% of the state schools in New Zealand are zoned. Zoned schools are concentrated in the areas of highest population density. If you live at an address in the zone then the school is legally obliged to enrol your child. The system was designed to prevent overcrowding but if housing density in the central city areas continues at the pace it has been running at in recent years, then zone boundaries may have to be looked at again. In some outer suburbs rolls are falling, as parents, fed up with the long commute move closer into town, thus putting further pressure on schools closer to the CBD (central business district).

Zoning and house prices. The zoning system has a marked effect on house prices with houses in zone having a higher premium than those just out. Parents who want the best education for their children will move house just so that they can get in to the top school in the area. There are many other factors to take into account when choosing a school and just because a school in your area is not zoned doesn't mean that you should avoid it.

Ranking System

An informal ranking system operates in New Zealand schools that allows parents to rate one school against another. What it measures though is the income of the parents and not the quality of the education. Decile 10 is the highest with Decile1 reflecting the lowest socio-economic ranking. Low decile schools receive more funding from the government while the higher decile schools rely more on the parents to fundraise. This system of ranking schools by decile highlights the notion that when it comes to the education of children, New Zealand is not the classless society it claims to be.

NCEA

One of the issues facing schools is the success or otherwise of the new standards-based qualification system introduced in 2002. The National Certification of Educational Achievement (NCEA)replaces School Certificate, Bursary and Sixth Form Certificate where students were awarded marks and assessed against each other. The NCEA breaks down subjects into units with grades of Excellence, Merit, Credit or Incomplete given. In a subject like English individual grades could be given for comprehension, formal writing and oral skills.

Critics of the NCEA say that while for the average student, being marked against standards might be a fairer system, this holistic approach does not prepare young people for the inevitable – that once they leave the cocoon of school, they will have to compete against their peers for places on sought-after courses at university and eventually for jobs.

The New Zealand Qualifications Authority (NZQA), the body charged with implanting and running NCEA were awarded 'nil points' by parents and educators alike when what they described as 'teething problems' in 2004 turned into wild fluctuations in pass rates in the Scholarship exams. But the variations in pass rates from previous years were not confined to Scholarship as NCEA Levels 1 and 2 in 2004 also had to be investigated. 2005 will see the second group of secondary students graduate with NCEA Level 3 (Year 13). Only when the first year's intake from 2004 graduate from university can any real judgement be made on how the old and new systems measure up against each other.

Comparing Schools. In their desire to do the best for their children, parents can sometimes forget that dedicated and gifted teachers may not want to work in the top decile schools but may choose more challenging environments. The Education Review Office, part of The Ministry of Education, reports on schools on a regular basis. The findings are published at www.ero.govt.nz.

As well as these reports, the Ministry publishes academic results for schools. One of the issues about NCEA is that a standards based assessment system no longer allows schools to be compared. Only if they offer alternative qualifications like the Cambridge (CIE) system or the International Baccalaureate (IB) can the results be measured.

CIE and IB

Parents who don't wish their children to be the 'guinea-pigs' of an as yet unproven assessment system have an alternative in the Cambridge International Exams (CIE). Over fifteen state schools offer Cambridge in some subjects alongside NCEA. And about the same number of independent schools offer Cambridge as well. A further five offer the highly portable and more rigorous qualification, the International Baccalaureate (IB) course.

Critics of Cambridge question the relevance of a qualification with no New Zealand content. But elitist or not, as competition for jobs across the globe increases, anyone who strives to attain an internationally recognised qualification and is capable of doing so deserves to be encouraged. The lack of New Zealand content argument does not really stack up if the child is educated at a state school as they can only offer Cambridge alongside NCEA. For expatriates who don't plan to remain in New Zealand or who wish to give their child the option of being educated in their home country, providing the student has achieved the necessary academic standard then the Cambridge or IB courses may be the best option.

The schools listed below are registered to offer the Cambridge (CIE) international qualifications, although some have yet to do so, or offer a very limited selection at present, sometimes no more than an AS Level in Mathematics. But the private schools that originally backed the NCEA may see their popularity waning if they do not offer an alternative system alongside NCEA. Whether or not the problems with NCEA are resolved in the near future, the demand for either Cambridge or IB from parents of the more able students will continue.

ACSNZ Association of Cambridge Schools in New Zealand

The number of schools offering the Cambridge exams has grown in recent years. Some of the schools listed offer a limited choice of subjects but may be planning to add new subjects in the future so check with the individual school.

The Academic College Group (ACG) is the umbrella organisation for four schools that offer pathways into the Cambridge system as well as the exams. The four schools are: *Junior College* (Years 7-10), *International College*, as well as *Senior College* and *Strathallan,* The Academic College Group schools are independent fee-paying co-educational schools.

Senior College: Level 1, 2-14 Wakefield Street, Auckland 1036; ☎ 09-307 5399; fax 09-377 7125; e-mail admissions@acg.ac.nz; www.acg.ac.nz/seniorcollege.

ACG Strathallan College: Hayfield Way, RD1 Papakura; ☎ 09-295 0830; fax 09-295 0833 e-mail strathallan@acg.ac.nz; www.acg.ac.nz/strathallan

Auckland Grammar School: Mountain Road, Epsom, Auckland; ☎ 09-623 5400; fax 09-623 5401 e-mail admin@ags.school.nz; www.ags.school.nz. Auckland Grammar is a traditional boys only state school. Properties within the 'grammar zone' command a premium price tag.

Carey College: Carey College, 21 Domain Road, Panmure, Auckland 1006; ☎ 09-570 5873; fax: 09-570 5877 e-mail info@carey.school.nz; www.carey.school.nz. Carey College is a Christian co-educational school.

Christ's College: Rolleston Avenue, Christchurch; ☎ 03-366 8705 fax: 03-364 5295; e-mail headmaster@christscollege.com; www.christscollege.com. An independent day and boarding school for boys.

Columba College: 421 Highgate, Dunedin; ☎ 03-467 5188; fax 03 464 0418; e-mail admin@columbacollege.school.nz; www.columbacollege.school.nz. An independent Presbyterian day and boarding school for girls.

Corelli School: 50 Anzac Road, Browns Bay, Auckland; ☎ 09-476 5043 fax 09- 479 8789; e-mail admin@corelli.school.nz; www.corelli.school.nz. An independent co-ed school specialising in performance arts subjects with entry/audition requirements in specialist subjects.

Corran School: 514 Remuera Road, Auckland 1005; ☎ 09-520-1400 fax 09-524 7657; e-mail info@corran.school.nz; www.corran.school.nz. An independent girls' school.

Hagley Community College: Hagley Avenue, Christchurch; ☎ 03-364 5156 fax 09-379 3134; e-mail info@hagley.school.nz; www.hagley.school.nz. A state co-educational day school.

Hamilton Boys'High School: Peachgrove Road, Hamilton; ☎ 07-853 0440 fax 07 853 0433; e-mail smorley@hbhs.school.nz; www.hbhs.school.nz. A state zoned boys' school.

Hillcrest High School: Masters Avenue, Hillcrest, Hamilton; ☎ 07-857

0297 fax 07-856 5125; e-mail office@hillcrest-high.school.nz; www. hillcrest-high.school.nz. A state co-educational zoned school.

Immanuel Christian School: 63 St Georges Road, Avondale, Auckland; ☎ 09-828 4545 fax 09-828 4250 e-mail admin@immanuel.school. nz; www.immanuel.school.nz. An independent Christian school.

King's College: Golf Road, Otahuhu, Auckland 1133; ☎ 09-276 0699;fax 09-276 0670; e-mail reception@kingscollege.school.nz; www.king-scollege.school.nz. King's is an Anglican independent school, resembling a traditional British public school. Girls are admitted in Years 12 and 13.

Lindisfarne College: 60 Pukpowhai Road, Hastings 4201; ☎: 06-878 8182; fax 06-878 8182; e-mail:office@lindisfarne.hb.school.nz; www. lindisfarne.school.nz An independent boys school.

Macleans College: Macleans Road, Bucklands Beach, Auckland; ☎ 09-535 2620; fax 535 2621; e-mail office@macleans.school.nz; www.ma-cleans.school.nz. A co-educational state school with a strong emphasis on academic success.

Napier Boys' High School: Chamber Street, Napier; ☎ 06-833 5900; fax06-833 5909; e-mail nbhs@nbhs.school.nz; www.nbhs.school.nz. A state boys school. The school has CIE status but has not delivered any courses apart from NCEA to date. The curriculum and assessment was being reviewed in 2005.

Onehunga HS Business School: Pleasant Street, Onehunga, Auckland; ☎ 09-636 6006; fax 09-636 4465; www.ohs.school.nz. A co-educational school where seniors study all aspects of starting and running a business.

Palmerston North Boys' High School: Featherston Street, Palmerston North; ☎ 06-354 5176; fax 06-354 5175; e-mail admin@pnbhs.school.nz; www.pnbhs.school.nz A boys' state school.

Pinehurst School: Bush Road, Albany, Auckland; ☎ 09-414 0960; fax 09-414 0964; e-mail: reception@pinehurst.school.nz; www.pinehurst. school.nz. A co-educational independent school.

Rodney College: Rodney Street, Wellsford; ☎ 09-423 6030; fax 09-423 7555; www.schools.roadshow.org/rodneycollege. A co-educational state school.

Rotorua Boys' High School: Pukuatua Street, Rotorua; ☎ 07-348 6169; fax 07- 346 1270; e-mail: rotoruabhs@xtra.co.nz; www.rbhs.school.nz. A boys' state school.

St Peter's College: 23 Mountain Road, Epsom, Auckland 1003; ☎ 09-524 8108; fax 09-524 9459; e-mail admin@st-peters.school.nz; www.st-peters.school.nz. A Catholic integrated boys' school.

St Thomas of Canterbury College: 69 Middlepark Road, Upper Riccarton, Christchurch; ☎ 03-348 7010; fax 03-348 2621; e-mail info@stthomas-coll.school.nz; www.stthomas-coll.school.nz An integrated Catholic all-boys college.

Samuel Marsden Collegiate School: Marsden Avenue, Karori, Wellington; ☎ 04- 476 8707; fax 04-939 8934; e-mail: enrol@marsden.school.nz; www.marsden.school.nz. An independent girls' school.

Takapuna Grammar School: 210 Lake Road, Takapuna; ☎ 09-489-4167; fax 09 486-7118; e-mail office@takapuna.school.nz; www.takapuna.school.nz. A co-educational state school.

Wainuiomata Christian School: 106 Mohaka Street, Wainuiomata,6008, Hutt Valley; ☎ 04-564 8552; fax 04-564 9305; e-mailwainuiomata-christian@clear.net.nz; www.wellingtonnz.com/Education/WainuiomataChristianCollege. A co-educational independent school with a reformed biblical Christian perspective.

Wanganui Collegiate School: Liverpool Street, Wanganui; ☎ 06-349 0210; fax 06-349 0280; e-mail registrar@collegiate.school.nz; www.collegiate.school.nz. An independent co-educational day and boarding school.

Western Heights High School: Old Quarry Road, Rotorua ☎: 07 349 5940 fax: 07 343 1029 www.whhs.school.nz; email info@whhs.school.nz. A co-educational state school.

Westlake Boys' High School: 30 Forrest Hill Road, Forrest Hill, Auckland; ☎ 09- 410 8667; fax 09-410 7717; e-mail enquiries@westlake.school.nz; www.westlakebhs.school.nz. The only all-boys state school on the North Shore.

Westlake Girls' High School: 2 Wairau Road, Takapuna Auckland; ☎ 09-489 4169; fax 09-486 1860; e-mail enquiries@westlakegirls.school.nz; www.westlakegirls.school.nz. The only all-girls state school on the North Shore.

Whangarei Boys' High School: 130 Kent Road, Regent, Whangarei; ☎: 09-430 4170; fax 09-430 4172; e-mail I.ward@wbhs.school.nz; www.whangarei-boys.high.school.nz. An all-boys state school

Woodford House: Iona Road, Havelock North; ☎ 06-873 0700; fax 06-873 0719 e-mail enquiries@woodford.school.nz; www.woodfordnz.com. An integrated day and boarding girls school situated in the countryside.

Schools that Offer International Baccalaureate (IB)

Auckland International College: 85 Airdale Street, Auckland; ☎ 09-309
4480 fax 309 4484; e-mail info@aic.ac.nz; www.aic.ac.nz. A co-educational private school.

John McGlashan College: 2 Pilkington Street, Maori Hill, Dunedin; ☎
03-467 6620; fax 03-467 6622; admin@mcglashan.school.nz; www.
mcglashan.school.nz. An integrated boys' school.

Kristin School: 30 Albany Highway, Albany, Auckland; ☎ 09-415 9566;
fax 415 5094; e-mail kristin@kristin.school.nz; www.kristin.school.nz.
A co-educational private school.

St Margaret's College: Winchester Street, Christchurch; ☎ 03-379 2000;
fax 03- 365 5748; e-mail admin@stmargarets.school,nz; www.stmarga-
rets.school.nz. A private girls' school.

Wellington Diocesan School for Girls: – Nga Tawa Marton; ☎ 06-327 6429;
fax 06-327 7954; e-mail admin@ngatawa.school.nz; www.ngatawa.
school.nz. An integrated girls' school.

State versus Private. Some of the top schools in the country are in fact
state schools and New Zealand's Prime Minister Helen Clark is a stand-out
example of a former state school pupil (Epsom Girls Grammar) who went
on to excel. As you will note from the list of schools offering Cambridge
system in conjunction with the local qualification NCEA, fifteen of those
were state schools. The problem for parents is that as many of the top state
schools operate a strict zoning policy, if the family home is out of zone,
they may want to choose a fee paying independent school if the local secondary school they are zoned for does not meet their expectations.

Private education comes at a price, which seems to be increasing at an
alarming rate every year. Fees start at around $12,000 per child but that
is just the start. Add on the cost of the uniform and a laptop computer
(which one or two schools insist upon), as well as the money for school
trips and it is clear why parents are having to plan ahead in order to fund
their children's education.

Catholic schools, which have now been incorporated into the state system
and are known as integrated schools, charge modest fees of a few hundred
dollars a year per child over and above the cost of uniforms and school
trips. Catholic schools select their pupils and generally ask for references
from a priest.

Universities

Whether or not former secondary students arrive at a New Zealand university from an expensive independent school or a state school makes little difference once they become undergraduates. Unlike just about everywhere else in the world, apart from courses such as medicine and law, provided a student has attained the necessary entrance standard, entry is open to anyone.

Although one or two of the universities market themselves as better than the rest, with less than ten universities in total, New Zealand is too small to have a two-tier university system. The elite may choose to do their undergraduate degree in New Zealand or to try their luck against fierce international competition for places at Oxbridge or the Ivy League institutions in the USA.

Each university has strengths in individual subjects and biggest does not necessarily always mean best. A bachelor's degree can be completed in three years an honours degree takes four. Specialised courses such as teacher training, medicine, law or veterinary science will take longer.

Fees. The University of Otago's tuition fees guide for 2006, which is a useful benchmark, offers a cost comparison between various subjects using an example of the cost of a year's study for one full-time undergraduate course selecting from papers in Computer Science, Design, Geography, Information Science, Music and Science which comes to $4,432.65. Many students can only afford to study by taking out a student loan or holding down a part-time job. The average student loan debt for a student on a three-year degree course is around $15,000 -$20,000.

Textbooks are expensive in New Zealand so many of the universities ensure that multiple copies of the required texts are available on short-term loan from the university library. Prior to the election campaign in 2005 the government unveiled plans to ease the student debt burden by curtailing interest on loans for graduates that remain in New Zealand for a number of years after their courses finish. This move pleased not just students but their voting parents and grandparents.

Course fees for non-residents start at around $20,000 per year and accommodation costs are on top of that. Despite these fees, New Zealand's universities (as well as schools) attracted over 77,500 international students in 2005, representing more than 150 nationalities. The majority of students come from China although their numbers have dropped recently because of the strength of the New Zealand dollar while overseas students from the UK and the USA have been taking their place. International students regard New Zealand as a relatively cheap place to study, compared with other OECD countries.

HEALTH

The standard of healthcare in New Zealand is good but there is no comprehensive free health system like the National Health Service in the UK although there are some free core health services. These are available to residents or those people in New Zealand with a work permit and who are regarded as temporary residents. Public hospitals are unlike the depressing Victorian institutional buildings still found in parts of Britain and Europe. Although you have to pay to visit a GP, queues are shorter and patients are seen promptly. But for people living in rural areas away from the main centres, serious illness may require that they travel long distances to receive regular treatment. Specialist medical services, which are costly to provide, are concentrated in areas of greatest need, near a larger population centre.

Publicly Funded Health Services

The core services provided free to residents and citizens are as follows:

- Free treatment at a public hospital,
- Free treatment at a public hospital accident and emergency clinic (includes visitors as well), subsidies on some prescription items.
- Subsidised fees for GP referrals to physiotherapists and osteopaths
- Free or subsidised health care for those suffering from acute or chronic medical conditions.
- No charge for laboratory tests and x-rays unless carried out at a privately operated clinic
- No charge for health care for pregnant women
- Free prescriptions for patients at public hospitals
- Subsidised GP visits and prescriptions for children under six
- Free basic dental care for all school children
- Breast screening for women aged between 50-64

Costs

GP Visits. The average cost of visiting a GP varies from $45 to $55 a visit. For children aged between six and seventeen the cost is around $20-$30. Only for children under six are visits free. For weekend and evening appointments, add on a further $10 to $15 per visit.

Prescription charges. Expect to pay up to $15 per prescription item for up to 20 items a year. If you are a heavy user of prescription items, using more than 20 prescriptions a year then further items are free. For children under six prescriptions are free. Pharmac, the government agency responsible for drug purchases will only fund certain drugs, based on cost, even if there are newer and better treatments available. The costs of those medicines, which do not receive the full or partial subsidy from the Government, are passed on to the consumer.

Cost of Visiting a Dentist. The only pain you'll feel after visiting a dentist in New Zealand is in the wallet. While for primary school children a basic free service is available through the School Dental Service, the situation is more complex for 13 to 18 year olds. Although the treatment for secondary school age children is meant to be subsidised, dentists are not obliged to sign up to the scheme and many choose to opt out. For everyone else, expect to pay anything from $50 to $90 for a routine check-up. Dentists are more than happy to add a sparkle to those pearly whites with a range of expensive cosmetic dental treatments but for those who just want to repair crumbling fillings, the cost of a crown is around $1000.

No Fault Accident Insurance

If you are injured in an accident you cannot sue anyone for damages but the government runs a no-faults claims system administered through the Accident Compensation Corporation (ACC). ACC provides free treatment for both residents and non-residents involved in accidents, whether a motor vehicle accident or an accident in the home. Designed to avoid expensive and drawn out litigation, the Accident Compensation system guarantees those on low incomes access to the justice and compensation often denied them in countries where such claims have to be pursued through the courts.

The amount of money awarded through ACC might seem modest but as claims are processed relatively quickly, claimants can at least then get on with the business of recuperation and recovery, instead of being forced to put their life on hold for what can be many years, with no guarantee that they will win their case.

> The case of a British couple who were hit by a drunk driver in 2002, causing permanent injury, highlights the need for visitors to take out comprehensive travel insurance. According to a report in the New Zealand Herald, Tony and Jenny Legge, who live in Wales, were offered just £4200 when Mr Legge estimated that the crash had cost him £400,000 in lost earnings.

Private Health Insurance

Although the ACC system covers individuals after an accident and treatment is swift, routine surgery in the public health system is subject to a waiting list. For some operations it can take up to two years to get to the top of the queue. Private health insurance allows those with non-urgent conditions to be treated immediately and gives them access to private hospitals that provide a range of procedures.

Given that medical insurance premiums have risen as much as 10% or more a year recently, policies with voluntary excesses or those that offer no-claims discounts may be the best value.

New Zealand Medical Insurers

Sovereign, Private Bag Sovereign, Auckland Mail Centre 1020; ☎ 09-487 9000 freephone 0800-500 103 e-mail enquire@sovereign.co.nz; www.sovereign.co.nz.

Southern Cross Healthcare, Private Bag 99934, Newmarket, Auckland ; ☎ 09-356 0900 freephone:0800-800 181;fax 0800 379 844, e-mail-info@sxhealth.co.nz; www.southerncross.co.nz.

UniMed, UniMed House, 163 Gloucester Street, PO Box 1721 Christchurch ☎ 03 365 4048; fax 03 365 4068 freephone 0800-600 666 e-mail sales@unimed.co.nz www.unimed.co.nz.

International Health Insurers

BUPA: Russell House, Russell Mews, Brighton BN1 2NR; ; ☎ 01273-208181; fax 01273-866583;e-mail advice@bupa-intl.com; www.bupa-intl.com.

Expacare Insurance Services: Columbia Centre, Market Street, Bracknell, Berkshire RG12 1JG; ☎ 01344-381650; fax 01344-381690; e-mail info@expacare.net; www.expacare.net.

Medicare International: Matrix House, 9 Aldgate High Street, London EC3N 1AH; ☎ 020-7816 2033 fax 020-7816 2188;e-mail medicare@ medicare.co.uk; www.medicare.co.uk.

SHOPPING

Car culture and the demise of the public transport system saw shoppers flee the city centres in favour of the out-of-town malls, forcing the closure of the smart department stores in the city centres. Wellington, which does have a halfway decent public transport system is the honourable exception. Kirkcaldies and Stains is the closest you'll get to a Selfridges or a Macys. 'Kirks', as it is known, delivers a very high standard of customer service and is situated in the heart of the downtown area of New Zealand's premier walking city. Where once Queen Street had the stylish Milne & Choyce, now Auckland's department stores seem like provincial Britain's were 30 years ago – dull and unsophisticated with unimaginative window displays.

Ballantynes in Christchurch, at least is trying to appeal to the younger, trendier crowd with its Contemporary Lounge. But if you really can't do without a regular department store fix, then save up for a trip across the Tasman to Sydney or Melbourne where you can make up for lost time in David Jones and Myer. The nearest branches of Marks & Spencer are in Singapore and Bangkok.

Teenagers or the young at heart are better catered for with surf wear ranges like Billabong and Quicksilver, Max and Glassons for casual ware. Their older and better off peers search for designers such as Karen Walker, Carlson, Zambesi, Trelise Cooper and World. In city centres Australian labels like Country Road try to bridge the gap between casual and formal wear for both men and women. For kids clothes try Pumpkin Patch.

Expats comment that there's little middle ground between the cheaper chain stores and the expensive New Zealand designers. Even in the bigger cities there's a limited range of well-made stylish shoes for women. Briarwood is the one local exception but their shoes are pricey, otherwise shop for Italian-made imports at sale time. The biggest out-of-town shopping centre in the country is at Botany Downs, south east of Auckland.

Prices. As the average wage is only around NZ$41,000 per annum it seems logical that retailers can't charge too much for everyday items as nobody would buy them. And given that New Zealanders have enthusiastically embraced the consumer lifestyle, there's no evidence yet to suggest the passion for shopping has waned even though the impact of rising fuel prices will force prices up.

Books are expensive and the price of a weekly supermarket shop is no bargain either, but that's because food is subject to the local equivalent of VAT, Goods and Services Tax (GST) at 12.5%. But there are ways to reduce the weekly grocery bill, if you shop around, are prepared to pack your own shopping and only buy fruit and vegetables in season.

Electrical goods and cars are cheaper in New Zealand and for where to find the latest prices on these items see the websites below. Briscoes and the Warehouse stock cheap homewares. Freedom Furniture is the closest thing to Ikea in New Zealand but they have a limited range of furniture, home furnishings and accessories and don't stock the big-ticket items like kitchens. DIY is a national passion and there are a number of chains like Bunnings and Mitre 10 that cater for home renovators.

Discount Shopping Centres. There are two discount centres selling cut-price homewares, clothes, shoes and sports gear – DressSmart in Onehunga and The Fox Retail Centre in Northcote.

Shopping Hours

In the main centres shops are open seven days a week. From Mondays to Fridays opening hours are from 9.00am until 5.00pm and until 4.00pm on weekends. Expect reduced hours in smaller towns.. Late-night shopping until 8.00pm or 9.00pm on a Friday or Thursday night gives teenagers the excuse they need to hang out with their mates. Supermarkets in the main centres that open seven days a week, 24 hours a day charge a premium for this convenience. Dairies which sell basic provisions like milk, bread, papers and grocery items open early and close later in city centres.

Useful Websites

Farmers: www.farmers.co.nz. A middle of the road family-oriented department store. The on-line catalogue gives prices and the range and styles on offer.

Woolworths: www.woolworths.co.nz. Woolworths is a grocery chain in New Zealand and this site gives the latest prices on grocery items.

Pumpkin Patch: www.pumpkinpatch.co.nz. For kids clothes.

Noel Leeming: www.noelleeming.co.nz. Electrical goods for home and office.

Autotrader: www.autotrader.co.nz. Gives current prices for used cars and links to new car sites, otherwise search under the brand name.

Trade Me: www.trademe.co.nz. On-line site for pre-loved anything.

MEDIA

Newspapers

There is no national daily broadsheet newspaper in New Zealand although *The New Zealand Herald* tries to lay claim to that title. It might have the largest circulation of any of the newspapers at around 200,000 but it's really an Auckland regional paper. *The Dominion Post* is Wellington's daily, with a circulation of around 95,000 and Christchurch's *Press* is 90,000. On Sundays *The Sunday Star-Times* is the only national Sunday paper. There is nothing to match the UK tabloids in New Zealand with their tongue-in-cheek headlines. The only scandal sheet is the *New Zealand Truth and TV Extra* but its low circulation means that it is an insignificant player in the market.

All the broadsheet newspapers have extensive property sections with colour photographs (paid for by the vendor),advertising houses and land for sale. Newspapers advertise the weekly 'open homes' where houses are open for inspection mainly on weekends (Saturdays and Sundays) to all-comers without an appointment.

Property Press, published by ACP Media Cnr Fanshawe and Beaumont Streets, Westhaven, PO Box 90106, AMSC Auckland, is a free weekly colour publication delivered to homes in the local area or can be collected from real estate agents. For the on-line version got to www.propertypress.co.nz.

While coverage of the Auckland region is extensive with seven different editions for greater Auckland alone, there are large areas of the South Island that have no individual magazine. Bay of Plenty, Manawatu, Wellington, Otago and the Lakes District each have their own edition and there is a link on the site to property listings in Rotorua, Taupo and Taranaki.

For Christchurch, Canterbury, Nelson and Marlborough you'll have to rely on *The Press, The Nelson Mail* or *The Marlborough Express.*

Where to Find International Newspapers. *The Telegraph* and *The Express* distribute their weekly versions, printed locally to save costs. They're news-intensive, without the add-ons of colour supplements. And even if they weren't your paper of choice back home their international coverage is generally better and the standard of journalism higher than the local product.

In the main centres, bookstores such as Whitcoulls, Borders and Magazzino have UK and US broadsheets such as. *The Sunday Times, The Guardian, The Independent on Sunday* and *The Observer* flown out at great expense. Be prepared to pay up to $27.00 for a three-day-old newspaper or else find an expat friend to pass the paper on to and share the cost.

Radio

The public broadcaster is Radio New Zealand, which operates two radio stations that are advertiser free. National Radio has much in common with the BBC's Radio 4 and *Morning Report* from 7-9am, is the definitive morning news and current affairs programme. Concert FM is the classical station. For frequencies for Radio NZ go www.radionz.co.nz. By the end of 2006 all but the remotest regions should be able to receive these stations on the FM frequency, which is also available on the Sky Digital network.

The commercial radio station Newstalk ZB attracts those listeners looking for an alternative to National Radio. The downside to Newstalk or any of the other commercial radio stations, including the youth oriented station, The Edge, is the repetitive advertising.

Sports fans are well catered for with Radio Sport, while students get to hear about what's going on through the student stations, the bNet. The Auckland student station 95bFM is reputed to be the best. And the nationwide coverage of iwi (tribal) stations include the influential Mai FM in Auckland which attracts younger listeners. A Pacific Island station Niu FM and a dance station George FM complete the picture.

BBC Radio. New technology has meant that the BBC can now offer far more than the World Service to overseas listeners. While drama and comedy is now streamed over the internet, where you can listen to that week's episodes of a show like *The Archers*; radio-on-demand is the new development. This is a system whereby programmes can be downloaded via the internet and then recorded onto portable devices such as an i-Pod and an MP3 player for playback at a later time. Only talk programmes were available during the podcast trials in 2005 as there are still rights issues to be negotiated for the use of drama and comedy. Go to www.bbc.co.uk. for further information.

Television

There are five terrestrial channels in New Zealand, two of which are run by the state broadcaster. Television New Zealand operates TV ONE, a mainstream channel and TV2, which is aimed at a younger audience. Their biggest competitor is TV3 owned and operated by the Canadian broadcaster Can West who run a number of radio stations as well as the youth-oriented music channel C4. The recently revamped Prime Television, (recently bought by Sky) is looking to increase market share. It broadcasts prestige imported dramas and documentaries as well as other more commercial products. Maori Television was set up to offer programmes in the Maori language, *te reo* as well as English so that Maori speakers would have easy access to their living language.

Television New Zealand is state-controlled and governed by a charter but has to provide a substantial proportion of its revenue from advertising. There is no longer a licence fee but viewers have to put up with a constant stream of advertisements on all the terrestrial channels. And if you thought there was too much advertising on commercial television back home, there's one more advertising slot per hour at peak times than there is in the UK. You cannot watch either a film or sports coverage uninterrupted and a film that has a running time of one and a half hours will take two hours to watch.

When TV ONE does secure live sports coverage, as it did during the 2002/3America's Cup yachting series, much of the dramatic impact of the event was lost as at crucial moments the coverage cut out and went to a commercial break. TV ONE offers a selection of imported reality series as well as series drama from the US and the UK.

Locally produced television is mainly current affairs, news and a limited amount of local soap and series drama. Limited production budgets mean that extensively researched and thought-provoking documentary rarely gets made for New Zealand terrestrial television.

The New Zealand Natural History Unit, once the flagship of the state broadcaster and a production unit that New Zealanders were justifiably proud of, was sold off in the 1980s during the period of intense deregulation. Its high quality programmes are rarely shown on terrestrial television.

Satellite Television. Satellite television is the only way to guarantee access to live sports coverage. Dedicated night owls can cheer on their favourite English Premier football league team or keep up with the play at Wimbledon. While BBC World and CNN provide coverage of international news, CBS News from the US is broadcast as part of the Sky News package as is live coverage of Sky News Australia and Sky News UK. Viewers in New Zealand can watch the morning news in Britain at night and may know where it's raining or which junction on the M6 to avoid, before many Britons have even got up.

Sky offers a range of different options, which are, as in Sky's other territories, bundled together to suit the company rather than the subscriber. To have both the sport and the movie channels together is the most expensive of all the combinations. Sky also offers radio channels with FM frequencies, which may be the only way that these are available in some of the remoter parts of the country.

CRIME

New Zealand is a very safe country as the crime statistics below underscore. There is no Mafia, or other organised large-scale criminal operations that operate at the margins of society the way they do in nearly all of the other OECD countries. There are bike gangs who control the manufacture and supply of certain drugs but they keep to themselves. Occasionally a territorial dispute will turn nasty and lead to revenge killings but generally the public are not involved. These gangs operate mainly in the larger population centres.

It's safe to walk around city centres at night, although you'd be silly to do so in bad neighbourhoods on the urban fringe. Car jackings and violent crimes are rare, and when they do occur they still make headline news, rather than being so commonplace that the item is quietly tucked away in the middle of the paper.

New Zealand is officially one of the world's least corrupt countries. And in local and central government there is a level of transparency that is matched only by the Scandinavian countries. Bribes, kickbacks and corruption in officialdom occur very rarely probably because with a population of just over four million it is too easy to get found out.

Visitors and locals alike need to be aware that robbery from parked cars is on the increase but as the police point out, this is largely preventable by the public being more vigilant about removing valuables from their cars or camper vans.

Numbers and Types of Recorded Crimes. The crime statistics for 2004/2005 saw a total of 396,018 recorded offences. Just over half of these at 223,713 were for dishonesty, which includes burglary and theft as well as fraud and receiving. Property damage and property abuse, including arms offences and trespass, as well as the more minor crime of littering was the second highest category at 59,965 recorded crimes.

Drug and anti-social offences came in third, accounting for 51,230 offences. This includes drugs, gambling and vagrancy offences. Drug crime linked to methamphetamine, amphetamines and ecstasy rose 8.1% over the year. In certain parts of the North Island, including Counties Manukau, Northland, Waikato and Bay of Plenty, robbery, often linked in with a rise in drug crimes also increased. But many of the robberies were carried out by teenage petty criminals, not necessarily drug users.

There were 45 murders throughout the country out of a total of 45,941 violent crimes, which includes homicide, assault and robbery. And many of those violent offences were inflicted on children and young people by family members. Immigration and racial offences and other administrative crimes were next at 11,982 and the smallest numbers of recorded crimes at 3187 were sexual offences including sex attacks and indecent behaviour.

While car crimes are less common in suburban neighbourhoods where houses come equipped with a garage or at least some form of off-street parking, in some of the poorer regions of the country, what might seem like an average car with average gear in it may prove to be too much of a temptation to someone less fortunate.

Isolated scenic spots where tourists visit, leave their cars to go and walk off into the bush to take photos of waterfalls, are the sorts of areas that can be targeted. If you plan to hire a campervan on your look-see visit be vigilant about keeping your passport and other valuables with you at all times. Bags left on neighbouring tables when dining out, particularly at night may be the target for petty criminals.

Those responsible are opportunist thieves either operating alone or in a group of three or four. It's usually a random act and nothing like the well-organised criminal operations in Italy, Spain or the Paris Metro, where you can be stripped of valuables by a gang, before you even know it's happened.

Unimaginative politicians with no real policies like to exploit the perception that people are not safe in their homes anymore. They will go on about 'law and order' being a problem which only their party can solve. Methamphetamine has been implicated in a number of recent senseless violent crimes but that doesn't mean that there is now an out-of-control 'P' epidemic. The reality is that there is less crime in New Zealand than in many other countries and a lot less violent crimes against strangers.

In the South Island in the smaller centres you can still find people who don't lock their doors at night. In the mountainous regions of the South Island watch out for the winged criminals that roam the skies. The mountain parrots or *keas* like to steal and chew through anything that's left lying around. They're partial to shoes left outside and the rubber seals on windscreen wipers.

The greatest risk that anyone in New Zealand can take is to step into a car as the most dangerous criminals are stupid, impatient and immature drivers that selfishly put the rest of the driving public at risk by their dangerous overtaking manoeuvres or sending or receiving text messages while driving.

MAORI PLACE NAMES

As you travel around New Zealand, particularly the North Island, once you have a few basic words of Maori, you will be able to make sense of a great many of the place names. If the clouds part long enough for you to see the jagged peak of *Aoraki*, you will know why its translation, 'Cloud Piercer' is so accurate. Or, for those visiting the little town of Te Aroha in the North Island, knowing that the words translate as 'the place of love,' may make you want to delve into the origins of the name.

A Maori vocabulary

ao	cloud	*ika*	fish
ara way,	path	*kai*	food
awa	river or valley	*iti*	small
hau	wind	*iwi*	tribe
heke	descend	*kainga*	home, village
hine	daughter, girl	*kaumatua*	respected elder

kauri	giant pine (*Agathis australis*)	*powhiri*	welcome onto a marae
kawakawa	a shrub (*piper excelsum*)	*puke*	hill
		puna	spring
kereru	wood-pigeon	*ra*	the sun
mana	prestige	*rangi*	sky
manga	stream	*raupo*	bullrush
tangi	lamentation	*runga*	top
marae	meeting house	*tahu*	light
mata	headland	*tane*	man
maunga	mountain	*tangata whenua*	people of the land
miti	speeches	*mana*	status, standing
moana	sea, lake	*manu*	bird
moko	tattooing; lizard	*taonga*	treasure
morepork	owl	*tapu*	sacred, forbidden
motu	island	*toetoe*	pampas-like grass
muri	end	*totara*	forest tree (*Podocarpus totara*)
nui	great		
ngati	tribe	*tui*	green song bird
o	the place of	*utu*	paying ones dues; 'revenge'
pa	fortified village		
pakeha	non-Maori New Zealander	*waiata*	song
		waka	canoe
paua	abalone	*whanau*	extended family
pipi	cockle	*whare*	house
pounamu	greenstone	*whare taonga*	museum

PUBLIC HOLIDAYS

Shops, supermarkets, banks, post offices, and cinemas are all closed all day on Christmas Day and Good Friday. Some shops re-open in the afternoons on ANZAC Day but most businesses will remain closed for the day.

PUBLIC HOLIDAYS	
1 January	New Year's Day
2 January	Public Holiday
6 February	Waitangi Day
Good Friday	

Easter Sunday	
Easter Monday	
25 April	ANZAC Day
Queen's Birthday	First Monday in June
Labour Day	Fourth Monday in October
25 December	Christmas Day
26 December	Boxing Day

REGIONAL HOLIDAYS

Each region celebrates an Anniversary Day. In Auckland, Bay of Plenty, Coromandel, Taupo and Waikato the holiday is in late January. Wellington and the surrounding areas take theirs on a different day in the same month. Taranaki and Otago wait until the end of March, while Hawkes Bay and Marlborough celebrate theirs in November while Westland and Canterbury's is in December.

STARGAZING

Astronomy is one of the oldest sciences and was studied by the founders of Ur of the Chaldees and the Ancient Greeks, in India and Egypt, and has played an important part in many cultures around the world, including those of Polynesia. The early Polynesians were so proficient at celestial navigation that long before Western navigators thought it was possible, they set out fearlessly, across the Pacific to reach the land we call New Zealand. And hundreds of years later, it was because Captain Cook was on a scientific mission to observe the Transit of Venus that his voyage brought him to New Zealand.

Astronomy is one of the few remaining sciences left that allows amateurs to make important discoveries, proving that you don't have to have the resources of NASA to contribute to scientific research.

The ideal place to see stars is out in the back country where there is no light pollution. On a clear night you should be able to see satellites passing overhead as they orbit the earth. But if you don't manage to find a get-away-from-it-all vantage point, you can still get a superb view of the night sky from a suburban garden. All you will need in the way of equipment is a pair of binoculars.

What's in The Southern Sky? In summertime (December to February) you can get a good view of the Southern Cross just before 10.00pm. If you haven't seen the Southern Cross before, beware the 'false cross', which is high in the sky early on in the evening. The Southern Cross can be identified by the two brightest stars known as the Pointers. The nearest and brightest of the two Pointers is *Alpha Centauri* and is one of our nearest neighbours in the galaxy. There are five stars that make up the Southern Cross constellation – the false cross only has four.

Once you've located the Southern Cross, finding True South is easy: Extend an imaginary line through the long axis of the Southern Cross and then look for the Pointers. Imagine a line between the two Pointers and another line crossing it at 90 degrees. If you were to look downwards where the two lines meet, this is the direction of True South.

Although you'll be familiar with the three bright stars of Orion's Belt, you may not realise that it looks rather different in the southern sky as it will appear to be upside down. Instead of Orion's sword hanging down, it appears to be raised in the air. The Pleiades or *Matariki*, also known as the Seven Sisters plays a very important role in Maori culture as the Maori new year is marked by the sighting of the new moon and the rise of Matariki. It was thought that the brighter the stars the better the harvest that year. Matariki falls in and around the shortest day in June when some New Zealanders use it as a convenient time to celebrate an informal mid-winter Christmas.

You'll get a great view of a number of the planets, including Venus, Mercury, Mars, Jupiter and Saturn. Because Venus is our closest neighbour in space, apart from the Moon, it will appear as the brightest star in the sky. Venus can be observed even at twilight as well as at dawn as it is both the evening star and the morning star. Mars, the red planet is easily identified by its distinct colour. If you are lucky you may be able to see Saturn – but to see the Rings of Saturn as well as the most distant planets of Neptune, Uranus and Pluto you'll certainly need a telescope or better still, a trip to an observatory.

While you may be familiar with the Northern Lights – the *Aurora Borealis*, the Southern Hemisphere version, the *Aurora Australis* puts on an equally magical light show. South Islanders will have the best chance of spotting the Aurora Australis. But the best view of all is down on the ice at Scott Base, Antarctica, between March and September. The extraordinary colour displays – green, pink, yellow and sometimes even violet are caused by electrons and protons from the sun colliding with gases in the outer reaches of the atmosphere.

Websites and References for Stargazers

www.antarcticconnection.com/Antarctic/weather In weather pages of this site there is a link to the Aurora Australis with photographs.

www.stardome.org.nz The website for the Auckland Observatory, known as the Stardome. Go to the link Skyguides and then Star Watch which will take you to www.heavens-above.com where you pinpoint your location and a star map will appear for that date in your neighbourhood.

www.nasa.gov. The site has a 'picture of the day' from space as well as all the information on launchings.

Naked Eye Wonders – A Short Guide to the Stars as Seen From Aotearoa New Zealand, by Paul Taylor. A handy little pocket book, written by an enthusiastic amateur, published by the author.

RESIDENCE AND ENTRY

CHAPTER SUMMARY

- You can obtain New Zealand residency in four main ways: as a skilled migrant, by starting or investing in a business, for family reasons or on humanitarian grounds.
- For the past two years over 30% of the migrants accepted for residency have been British.
- New Zealand is too small to be able to find all its work force at home and relies on many skilled, talented and well-educated people who were born overseas.
- Potential migrants must prove that they are in good health, are of good character and have a high standard of written and spoken English.
- The Immediate Skill Shortage List (ISSL) has vacancies in professions as varied as wine-making, ski and snowboarding instruction to the racing industry.
- There are a number of identified professions that are on the Long Term Skills Shortage List (LTSSL) which include a number of different vacancies in medicine and health.
- There are restrictions placed on applications for residency for those over the age of 55.
  - The Expression of Interest document is the first step in the application process for skilled migrants.
  - Applicants make many basic mistakes even at this early stage.
  - Information provided by you on this form is not only kept but the application then goes into a pool for possible selection for residency.
- New Zealand has to compete with countries such as Australia and Canada for its migrants.

- ○ It is seen as the third most popular destination for UK migrants after Australia and Canada.
- ○ A sign of the country's coming of age has seen New Zealand becoming choosier in granting permanent residency.
  - ○ The visitor Visa Waiver Scheme and Visitor's Visa means that you can still buy a house and live in your New Zealand holiday home for a few months every year.
- ○ **Temporary Work Permit.** Before you commit to such a big decision as emigrating, 'try before you buy' and work in New Zealand for a couple of years first.
- ○ **Experiencing life as a student.** Many of those people that want to emigrate have already lived in the country as a student.
- ○ **Working Holiday.** Those aged between 18-30 can come to New Zealand and live like a local on a working holiday.

OVERVIEW

New Zealand is a relatively young country and is still building up its key industries as well as innovating and developing new areas of excellence. The economy has been robust over the past few years and if the government is to be successful in keeping it that way, New Zealand needs to actively recruit beyond its shores for the skilled and well-educated workforce to sustain it.

There is much hand-wringing on talk-back radio and in the letters pages of the newspapers about what is termed as the 'brain drain'- that is, young New Zealanders educated in the country who leave as soon as their degrees are finished to gain the necessary skills and experience they might not be able to get back home.

What the talk-back hosts and many of the letter writers ignore is that although many younger New Zealanders do have to leave the country to further their careers, many of them, especially once they hit their 30s and start to want families, return. (a government campaign in 2005 was launched with the aim of luring them back.) And that although there are educated New Zealanders leaving the country there are a great many even better educated, qualified and skilled migrants willing to take their place. Rather than a drain, it would be more accurate to say that New Zealand has experienced a 'brain-exchange'.

Many potential migrants do not fully appreciate why New Zealand had to abandon its open-door policy of the 1960s and 1970s in favour of a more selective system. Sometimes too, seemingly perfectly good prospective migrants who have job offers but who do not pass on the other criteria are turned away. The world of work has changed drastically in the past 30 to 40 years and many jobs have disappeared. In their place have come those that involve new technology and those people who have kept up with the change in the workplace and have up-skilled are the people most in demand.

Trying to gain residency in any OECD country these days is tough as rules are constantly tightened and reviewed and New Zealand is no exception in applying even more rigorous criteria. The NZIS (New Zealand Immigration Service) has responded to recent criticism in the past few years by re-evaluating which people should be granted residency.

Under the now-defunct General Skills Category a situation occurred where many highly skilled migrants (mainly from developing countries who did not have English as a first language) were unable to get work in their profession and ended up driving taxis. This waste of human capital does not reflect well on a country that prides itself in giving everyone a chance. Unfortunately, migrants from labour markets which are not considered as comparable who did not get jobs were told that they lacked what is referred to as 'New Zealand experience', a term that many regard with suspicion. For people who have worked overseas in organisations that upheld values of equal opportunity, this came as something of a shock. Too often, 'New Zealand experience' became a requirement for anyone with accented English from a developing country. It is mainly smaller and more conservative businesses that were the companies who were openly asking for New Zealand experience in job advertisements. The more enlightened know that the country will lag further behind the rest of the OECD if it doesn't tackle such parochial attitudes.

In 2003 the Skilled Migrant category replaced General Skills. The emphasis has shifted to employability instead of just skills, experience and qualifications. Although a limited number of migrants can move to New Zealand to be reunited with family members, the majority of migrants from the OECD countries are granted residency through skilled migration.

Even though the changes implemented by the NZIS have largely met with public approval, by being seen to target people who can directly contribute to the work force, many good applicants will still miss out. The system is now seen to favour native English speakers as non English speakers must pass a language test and be what is termed as a 'competent user' of English. And applicants who are over the age limit will not be eligible to come in either as a skilled migrant or under work to residence. Unfortunately no selective system will ever be perfect.

In recent years New Zealand as a nation seems to have begun to shake off some of its collective low self-esteem and has started to see itself the way that others do – as a desirable destination to live and work. As the volume of enquiries from prospective migrants has risen, combined with the fact that the economy has picked up in recent years, the country can afford to be more selective.

Even if you are exactly the kind of person the New Zealand government is looking for (see skills shortages below) before you take the plunge and apply to move there permanently you should consider going there on a temporary basis first – either as a student, on a working visa or working holiday visa, or as a visitor. Your chances of a successful relocation will be greatly enhanced.

When you stay a little longer and experience the work place and the business culture, sit in rush hour traffic, rent a house or apartment and enjoy Christmas Day at the beach, you really will have sampled the highs (as well as the lows) of living in New Zealand.

When the novelty of the new country has worn off and you have had a chance to assess what it is really like to be away from friends and family for long periods – if you still like it enough to want to make a permanent move then that will be the time to apply for residence.

Immigration is a sensitive issue in New Zealand but only because the media seldom highlight the positive benefits of immigration. The government is criticised for being too lax on who it lets in by its own citizens. But from the point of view of those people from overseas who are excluded on age or health grounds the system can seem unfair. But many New Zealanders resent supporting citizens of other countries access the health system when the country is already overstretched in providing health and social welfare services for its own people.

And the New Zealand government wants the migration experience to be equally positive and successful and not one where those that move find themselves worse off than they would be in their home country. In recent years the number of applications from overseas students from China to study in New Zealand on student visas dropped as bad publicity surrounding the collapse of a few English language schools filtered back through the media. But the New Zealand media in turn are quick to publicise any wrong-doing by foreign nationals – wherever they come from.

One inspiring story about the positive contribution made by migrants is the recent gifting of a substantial tract of land in the Kaipara Harbour for a new national park by a European couple, Pierre and Jacqueline Chatelanat. The 834 hectare farm is valued at $10 million and will become a regional park. Their generosity to the nation is one of the country's most significant acts of philanthropy in its history.

Minimum Entry Requirements

Potential migrants have to provide medical certificates and police checks to prove that they are: a) in good health b)are of good character and c) have a high standard of written and spoken English.

APPLYING FOR NEW ZEALAND RESIDENCE AS AN EMPLOYEE

One frustration for those that live and work in the Asia/Pacific region is that there is no free movement of labour across borders the way there is in the EU. As many countries in Asia and the Pacific do not even share borders and are at odds politically and socially, it has been difficult to see how they could ever find common ground. A country as small as New Zealand could really benefit if it was part of an economic region that allowed free trade, exchange of human capital and had a single currency. But this may be a long time coming.

Only New Zealand and Australia currently have any official form of labour exchange that allows citizens of both countries to move between the two to live and work. Citizens of EU countries and North America can come to New Zealand and obtain either permanent or temporary residence.

Skilled Migrant

The main criteria to qualify under the Skilled Migrant category are that you are less than 56 years old, have a job offer in New Zealand with at least two years work experience along with a tertiary or trade qualification. The Skilled Migrant category is the best way to enter New Zealand permanently as there are no restrictions placed on your visa and you cannot have your residency revoked if you change jobs.

The New Zealand Immigration Service website has a user friendly checklist called The Skilled Migrant Points Indicator that will calculate eligibility points to help you determine whether or not it is worth putting in a formal application. Potential migrants fill in the dozen or so questions relating to skilled employment, qualifications, work experience, (for themselves and their partner) and whether or not the applicant already has a close family member living in New Zealand.

You will notice that the Skilled Migrant Points Indicator has questions on whether your offer of employment, qualifications and work experience are in: a) future growth areas – currently biotechnology, creative industries and information communications technology b)in an identified cluster (a cluster being a group of employers in a particular industry who work together co-operatively to gain a business advantage) or c)an area of absolute skills shortage – that is in any of the industries listed in the Long Term Skills Shortage List.

In December 2005 the employers identified as belonging to a qualifying cluster were companies involved with industries associated with the future growth areas. One final question the Points Indicator asks is whether or not your offer of employment is outside the Auckland region and you will get extra points if you can prove this. The rationale behind this is that it is important that there is a trickle-down effect of continued economic prosperity to the regions and not just to the nation's largest city.

Anecdotal evidence suggests that world events have a big impact on the numbers of potential migrants registering their interest in moving to New Zealand.

The Skilled Migrants Points Indicator is not part of the formal application process and no personal details are retained. You can take the test as often as you like, using different combinations to maximise your points, providing you fulfil the necessary criteria.

In late December 2005 the pass rate to proceed to the next step was raised. It had been at 100 points for some months and there was speculation as to how long it was going to remain at such a low pass mark. The mark has been much higher in the past. The new selection passmark for Expressions of Interest from 22 December 2005 was 140. Anyone with point scores between 100 to 139 with a job offer from a company recognised by the NZIS will be ranked and scored subject to both the number of slots left that the government needs to fill and the strength of the applicant's case.

The third tier for selection will now be those with point scores of 100 to 139 without a New Zealand job offer. At the time of writing, NZIS had not defined its criteria for this selection.

The last selection under the 100 point passmark was on 21 December. The first selection under the new criteria was due to take place on 1 February 2006.

Applying under the Skilled Migrant Category. Once you have scored the pre-requisite points after taking the Skilled Migrants Point Indicator test the next step is to register an Expression of Interest. Take your time filling in the Expression of Interest, as unlike the Skilled Points Indicator, the information is retained. It is then scored, put into a ranking system and pooled along with all the other applications. Only the highest-ranking applicants are invited to apply for residency. Skilled migrants are much more likely to be successful if they have a New Zealand job offer first. Medical personnel and any other occupations that require New Zealand registration must ensure that they complete their registration before applying for residency.

Expression of Interest Statistics. Immigration New Zealand issues a useful fortnightly set of statistics, which makes interesting reading for potential migrants. As well as reporting on the numbers of Expressions of Interest received and the most up to date selection point, the statistics are shown as two pie charts – one of which shows which country the applications came from and the other, how many applying had job offers against the numbers that didn't.

For the 7 December 2005 selection group a total of 450 applicants with job offers compared to 485 without, were then due to be processed to undergo preliminary verification to determine whether or not they would be invited for residency. N.B. As there is one application per family these figures can represent several people.

One of the dilemmas potential migrants face is whether to apply for residency first and then look for a job or to find a job first and risk not getting their residency. The anecdotal evidence suggests that, providing those with job offers fulfil all the other criteria that they are more likely to be accepted. And if you do have a firm job offer with a specified start date, providing of course that the deadline is realistic, the NZIS are generally quite helpful in trying to assist you to meet your obligations.

You only have to compare the EIO statistics with those of actual residence approvals to see how much emphasis is put on the skilled/business criteria. In the 2005/6 financial year a total of 5,573 residency applications were approved, representing 13,093 people under the skilled/business stream. Less than half this number - 6,040 people were approved under the family/ sponsored category.

Those applicants without job offers may well have been better off going to the job link on the Immigration New Zealand website first, before they filled in the Expression of Interest application.

NetworkZOnline. This link on the NZIS website connects job seekers from abroad with New Zealand employers. If you do not have a job offer but want to apply for residency the website suggests that job-seekers create a profile on the site which will compare your skills and experience with the current set of job vacancies. The site will inform you of any matches which can then be followed up with an employer.

Expressions of Interest by Nationality. To the year end in 2005 roughly one quarter of the applications for Expression of Interest came from the UK and other EU countries with just over 6% from South Africa and 4.2% from the United States of America. Although a larger number of enquiries came from South East Asia, the raising of the bar for reading, writing and conversation skills has made it more difficult for anyone whose first language isn't English to move to New Zealand.

When it comes to translating the Expressions of Interest into successful residency applications though, the figures change. During the 1980s and 1990s interest from Britons and Americans slowed. But since the revival in New Zealand's economic fortunes in the early part of the 21st century the trickle has turned into a steady stream. In 2004 and 2005 30% of successful residency applications came from Britain.

Wanted – Skilled Professionals

New Zealand has the lowest unemployment figures in the OECD and as a result is facing an acute shortage of skilled, suitably qualified migrants to fill the growing number of job vacancies.

Medical Professionals – New Zealand Needs You. In December 2005 the Long Term Skills Short List included: anaesthetist, audiologist, dietician, GP (rural areas), laboratory scientist, midwife, nurse, radiation technologist, registrar (obstetrics/gynaecology), occupational therapist, pathologist, pharmacist, physiotherapist, psychiatrist, psychologist, radiologist, renal physician, palliative physician, surgeon, vet.

Whether you work in agriculture or film animation, engineering, IT or education, go to www.immigration.govt.nz for more information on the Long Term Skills Shortage List.

Immediate Skill Shortage List

New Zealand is not just looking for elite, highly skilled and educated professionals with degrees to fill job vacancies. Many vacancies exist in the trades – from plumber to cabinet maker or in industries such as horse racing. Recently Immigration NZ modified its Skills Shortage List and added ten new occupations to a list of over 100 different occupations. The new occupations were:

- Agriculture – Agricultural machinery operator, Assistant dairy farm manager, Herd manager, Poultry farm manager, Senior shepherd/stock manager.
- Draughting – Civil CAD (Computer Aided Draughting) designer, Engineering draughtsperson,
- Trades – Furniture polisher/finisher, Furniture upholsterer.

The Immediate Skills Shortage List – also available from Immigration NZ's website lists the qualifications it expects those applying to work in New Zealand should have.

Whether your occupation is on the LTSSL or ISSL the end result is the same – if you have the right work experience and qualifications then the likelihood of your obtaining a job offer will be greatly enhanced.

Employees of a Business Relocating to New Zealand

Along with the Entrepreneur category (see below) this is one of the few categories that doesn't place an age restriction on gaining New Zealand residency. It is only available to key talent in an organisation relocating to New Zealand. As the employee will be working in a New Zealand business environment, the applicant must meet English language requirements.

Work to Residence

If you work in a specialised or in-demand occupation, or are deemed to be an outstanding talent in sports or the arts, then you can apply for a work permit under the Work to Residence category. The applicant must either have an offer of full-time employment from a New Zealand accredited employer with a base salary of at least $45,000 per annum, or an offer of full-time employment in an occupation on the Long Termed Skilled Shortage list. Applicants cannot be over the age of 55 and must hold current registration if their occupation requires that. If applying as an outstanding sports or talent in the arts then this requires sponsorship from the appropriate New Zealand sporting or cultural organisation.

APPLYING FOR NEW ZEALAND RESIDENCE AS A BUSINESS INVESTOR

New Investor

New Zealand toughened its rules for business investors in 2005 when the New Investor category was introduced. There is an age restriction of 54 and applicants have to have five years business experience as well as meeting character, health and English language requirements.

But the big difference compared with the previous investor requirements is that the amount of money that new investors have to bring to the country to invest. Under the old rules investors needed to find NZ$1 million but that figure has been doubled to NZ$2million. New Investor's need not only a substantial amount of money to invest in New Zealand but these funds will be held by the New Zealand government for five years, during which time access to the money is very limited. Gaining permanent residence under this category is not without restrictions and conditions. These include: keeping the NZ$2million in an eligible investment for five years, that you make New Zealand your main home and that you co-operate with evaluation and monitoring as requested. Just having the requisite amount of money to bring in and invest in the country is not necessarily going to be enough to grant you residency.

The application procedure involves filling out an Expression of Interest in the same way that a skilled migrant would apply. The NZIS do not ask for any supporting documentation to go with the application at that stage but will assess the application from the information that you provide. Once the Expression of Interest has been checked the NZIS then invite suitable applicants to apply for residence. At this point applicants will need to provide their documents and once the application has been approved you will need to transfer your money to New Zealand.

The return on the invested funds is based on the rate of inflation as determined by the New Zealand Consumer Price Index. The return of the principal sum is guaranteed.

Business Visa

Since the standard was raised for business investors in 2005 many potential migrants have found the rules too tough. People wanting to establish a business in New Zealand do have an alternative – although it will take longer for you to qualify for residency. If you come to New Zealand with a three-year business visa you can apply for permanent residence as an entrepreneur.

Entrepreneur

One of the few categories that doesn't carry an age restriction or require the applicant to have formal qualifications, although English language standards must be met. The applicant must either set up a business working to an agreed business plan or purchase an existing business. The business must be one that will benefit New Zealand and must be run and operated successfully for a minimum of two years.

APPLYING FOR NEW ZEALAND RESIDENCE ON FAMILY OR HUMANITARIAN GROUNDS

The family category is open to those with immediate family or a de-facto partner who are either New Zealand residents or citizens. Generally only a spouse/partner, child, sibling or parent is eligible for sponsorship. Although there is no English language requirement under this category, entry is not guaranteed as some applications will be subject to either a quota or a lottery. New Zealand, like all other humanitarian countries accepts refugees under strict conditions.

TEMPORARY RESIDENCE

Temporary Residence through Work

- You can apply for a temporary work permit if you have a job offer from a New Zealand employer and are skilled in an occupation that is in demand.
- A temporary Work Permit may also be issued to those who need to work in New Zealand for a specific purpose or event – such as a film or television production, a tournament or other sports tour or for certain professional reasons.
- You are also eligible for a temporary Work permit if you are joining your partner in New Zealand.
- Students or trainees wanting to gain work experience in New Zealand are also eligible for a temporary work permit.
- Those aged between 18 and 30 who want to come to New Zealand for a working holiday can experience the lifestyle that way. The NZIS has the full list of countries that have a New Zealand Working Holiday Scheme. These include: Britain and a number of EU countries, the USA and Canada, countries in Latin America, including Argentina and Chile, countries in Asia including Singapore, Japan and Thailand. Australian citizens do not need temporary residence as they are freely allowed to work in New Zealand.

Temporary Residence through Study

International students can study in New Zealand providing they have an offer of a place from a school, polytechnic or university and their proposed course of study meets specific course requirements. International student fees are high and applicants have to prove that not only have they paid their course fees but also that they have enough money to support themselves during their temporary stay. For courses over three months students need to apply for a student visa.

In addition to the academic requirements students have to prove that they are of good health and good character. For stays longer than six months this may include a TB clearance as well as a medical and police certificate.

ENTERING NEW ZEALAND AS A VISITOR

New Zealand operates a Visa Waiver scheme with certain countries that allows visitors to travel to New Zealand and stay for up to six months for UK nationals and three months for nationals from certain other countries including the USA. A visitor's visa is perfect for home owners over the age 55 who do not qualify for residency by working or owning a business but who plan to spend the northern winter 'Down Under' in their holiday house. If you want to stay longer than your visa-free conditions permit you need to apply for a visitor's visa.

The usual maximum stay for a visitor is nine months in an eighteen-month period. Holiday homeowners visiting New Zealand on a regular basis need to keep track of the date they arrived in order not to exceed the time they are allowed to stay in the country. When travelling in and out, ensure that your flight bookings are organised well in advance as any breach of your visa conditions – even if they were unintentional and beyond your control could seriously hamper your chances of getting back in again without a hitch.

Students who are studying in the country for less than three months can come in as a visitor although they should check with immigration first to clarify whether or not that their country of origin has an agreement with the NZIS that will allow them in on the Visa Waiver Scheme, or whether they need to apply for a visitor's visa.

Health and Medical Requirements for Renewing a Visitor's Visa. Further information can be obtained about health requirements in the NZIS leaflet 1121. New Zealand is particularly concerned about the health of visitors who have been in countries where the incidence of TB is high. If you are approved for a nine-month visitor's visa you will need to complete a chest x-ray certificate.

Applying for Residency if You are Over 55

There are only two categories where applicants over the age of 55 can apply – one of which requires that the individuals are coming to New Zealand to work. These are the Entrepreneur category and the category of Employee of a Business Relocating to New Zealand. These are for key essential employees of companies moving their business to New Zealand.

IMMIGRATION CONSULTANTS

The big advantage of moving to New Zealand with a large company is that the biggest headache of all – the paperwork involved with obtaining visas and residency is carried out by a professional, freeing up your time to get on with all the other aspects involved in moving. As more and more companies are realising, in order to compete with other countries for talented individuals, they need to offer their relocating staff immigration assistance.

Immigration consultants take the hassle out of filling out all the forms but you still have to have to pass a medical, collect references from previous employers, pass the police checks and have all the other documentation available for them. And although a good immigration consultant can speed up the process of gaining residency they can only do this for those who fulfil the basic criteria.

But for those of you who are 'going it alone', without the support of an employer, the question as to whether or not it is worth your while consulting (and paying the fees) of an immigration consultant, without a New Zealand job offer first is a tricky one. Immigration consultants cannot influence decisions about whether or not you will gain residency if you do not meet the eligibility criteria. And you would be wasting your money if your qualifications, experience or your age do not match what the country has stipulated as a minimum requirement.

But an immigration consultant could help avoid the mistakes that many self-applicants make which occur at the Expression of Interest stage. Many potential migrants do not realise that their data is being recorded, that whatever they put down at this stage will have a lasting effect on whether or not they get selected for residency. A cheaper alternative is to consult the NZIS website and follow the link to: Tips for Lodging Expressions of Interest.

It could be worth your while engaging a consultant if you do not yet have a job offer and your skills, qualifications and experience are in one of the long-term skills shortage occupations and you have been able to secure New Zealand registration first. Immigration officers do have discretionary powers if the quota has not been filled and a person from a country with a comparable labour market such as the UK and the USA or Western Europe has a set of skills that are in demand by New Zealand employers. But you should do as much as you can on your own first, particularly by registering with NetworkZ (see section on Skilled Migrant category).

The best way to select a competent immigration consultant is to have a personal recommendation but if you do not know anyone that has previously used a consultant then ensure that the company is a member of NZAMI (New Zealand Association for Migration and Investment). There is no registration required for immigration consultants – anyone can set up in business and claim to be an expert.

The test of a good consultancy is their willingness to provide a referral from one of their clients. A good consultant should be working not just with individuals but also with corporates. If the company tries to fob you off by citing privacy or client confidentiality then find one that can provide you with the necessary references. It's a competitive industry, with many players in the market and you should shop around. If you are consulting an immigration consultant from the UK then this could cost you around £4,000. That is a substantial amount to pay particularly if you are funding your own move.

Immigration Consultants UK:

The Emigration Group: ☎ 0845-230 2526; www.emigration.uk.com.
Meridian Immigration Consultants: ☎ 0141-229 6140; www.meridianimmigration.co.nz.
Visa-Go Emigration: ☎ 0131-477 8585; www.visa-go.com.

Frequently Asked Questions

○ How much do the various visas and residency applications cost? Fees can range from $1700 for some business migrants to $80 for a visitor's visa. There is a comprehensive booklet produced by NZIS that goes into every possible fee combination. There are certain fee exemptions for visitors if your home country has a Visa Waiver Agreement with New Zealand.

○ How long will it take for my application to be processed? If you contact the main New Zealand Immigration Service question and answer section they refuse to be drawn on how long an application takes to process – stating that each case is different and will depend on such variables such as whether all the documentation has been provided and whether or not qualifications have been verified. However, on the Immigration New Zealand London link, they were game enough to suggest a time scale.

O How helpful is the NZIS website? Sometimes it can be difficult to get answers to some questions without going about it in a rather circuitous way. Some information is obtained via various links and may not always be the most easily accessed. Like all call centres the quality of the advice given out over the phone is variable. It can be hard to find an immigration official prepared to verify their informal advice in writing.

Useful Addresses

Immigration New Zealand Offices:
Auckland Central Branch: 450 Queen Street, Auckland; ☎ 09-914 4100; fax 09-914 4118; www.immigration.govt.nz.
Manakau Branch: 3rd Floor, Leyton House, Leyton Way, Wiri, Manakau City; ☎ 09-914 4100; fax 09-914 4118.
New Zealand Immigration Service: PO Box 3705 Wellington (for all paper correspondence including the sending of original documentation); ☎ 0508-558 855 (outside Auckland); www.immigration.govt.nz

Immigration New Zealand Offices UK:
Immigration New Zealand has offices in a number of countries including The Netherlands, the UK, the USA, Australia as well as South East Asia. The UK and US offices are listed below. UK callers should do as much as they can by e-mail and through the NZIS website first before they ring Immigration New Zealand in London. You may not appreciate having to pay the premium rate of £1 per minute just to listen to someone else_s record collection as you wait to be connected.
*Immigration NZ London:*Mezzanine Floor, NZ House, 80 Haymarket, London SW1Y 4TE; ☎ 09069-100100, fax 020-7973 0370.

Immigration New Zealand Offices USA:
NZIS: New Zealand Consulate-General Los Angeles, 2425 Olympic Blvd, Suite 600 East Santa Monica, CA 90404; ☎ 310-566 6555; fax 310-566 6556; e-mail nzcg.la@verizon.net.
New Zealand Embassy-Washington: 37 Observatory Circle NW, Washington DC 20008; ☎ 202-328 4800; fax 202 328 4836; e-mail nz@nzemb.org.
Residents living on the West Coast and in the South West should report to the Los Angeles office while Eastern Seaboard residents should contact Washington.

Australian Consular Office in New Zealand:

Australian Consulate-General: Level 7, PricewaterhouseCoopers Tower, 188 Queen Street, Auckland, Private Bag 92023; ☎ 09-921 8800; fax 09-921 8820.

British High Commission in New Zealand:

British Consulate-General: British High Commission, PO Box 1812, Wellington; ☎ 04-924 2889; fax 04-924 2822; www.britain.org.nz.

United States Embassy and Consular Office in New Zealand:

Embassy of the United States of America: PO Box 11900, 29 Fitzherbert Terrace, Thorndon, Wellington; ☎ 04-462 6000; fax 04 499 0490; www.usembassy.org.nz.

United States Consulate-General: Level 3, Citibank Centre, 23 Customs Street East, Auckland, Private Bag 92022; ☎ 09-303 2774; ☎ Duty Office Wellington 04-462 6031; fax 09-366 0870

Kiwis Come Home

As well as attracting the right kind of migrants, the New Zealand government launched a series of initiatives in 2005 to entice some of its 460,000 New Zealand born citizens back home. The government plans to assist expats to link up with potential employers and recruitment agencies with the promotion of job fairs. The idea is to keep expats up to date with the way that New Zealand has changed and to provide them with the right connections to smooth the way for their return. The initial focus will be to target the 58,000 expats living in the UK and then the 355,000 that live in Australia.

_____

Part II

_____

LOCATION, LOCATION

WHERE TO FIND YOUR IDEAL HOME

NORTH ISLAND

SOUTH ISLAND

WHERE TO FIND YOUR IDEAL HOME

CHAPTER SUMMARY

- Northland and the Coromandel Peninsula are the best locations in the North Island to choose if you're looking for sun, sea, sand and seclusion.
- The Warkworth area, one hour north of Auckland combines the best of the outdoor lifestyle yet with property prices that are more affordable than in the country's biggest city.
- Prices in Auckland are likely to remain buoyant because of the popularity of the city with migrants and with relocating New Zealanders who move there for the employment prospects.
- The South Island can seem like another country. Only one third of the population live in this island.
- Queenstown has become expensive and an apartment may be a better choice as a base for skiing holidays or else buy in the surrounding district.
- The West Coast of the South Island is one of the cheapest areas in the country to buy but the ruggedness and isolation of the area won't suit everyone.
- For a fishing lodge try either the Rotorua Lakes or Taupo.
- Christchurch may suit relocating families better than Auckland or Wellington as large family homes are more reasonably priced compared with either of the other two cities.

OVERVIEW

Once you've experienced New Zealand, it's hard to get it out of your system. Maybe it's the clarity of the light and the brilliant blues of the sky and oceans; but whatever it is, it's a country that draws people back. One UK visitor who first went there on a holiday in 1999 reports that like many British people his perception of the country had been formed long ago, as a small child tucking into New Zealand roast lamb at Sunday lunch or spreading New Zealand butter on toast. Seeing the Southern Cross and the Milky Way stretching overhead above a midnight beach at Golden Bay took his breath away. A year later, he was moving to Hamilton with a fulltime job.

But whatever brings you to New Zealand the choice about where to live can be tantalising. Out of all the 12 regions of New Zealand, every single one contains stunning scenery or the promise of an entirely different lifestyle. But which one to choose?

For some of you the decision about where to live may have already been made for you – through a job offer or to be near family. But much as you love your extended family, you could find yourself stuck with them in the middle of nowhere. So before you commit to living 30km south of Auckland at Drury or at the tip of the Whangaparoa Peninsula to the north, check out the following section to find your ideal place to live.

The decision to move to New Zealand could have come about from being on holiday and having the time to look at the world a little differently as the experience of that British holidaymaker illustrates. But when the bungy jump is over, where's the best place to come gliding back to earth?

You really do need to have an appreciation for the natural environment if you're going to thrive in New Zealand, no matter where you choose to live. Those looking for urban sophistication may tire of Wellington or Auckland rather quickly as they are small cities by international standards.

The smaller cities in the Sunshine Belt, such as Nelson or Marlborough, the Bay of Plenty or Hawke's Bay offer an enviable lifestyle yet have enough going on to ensure that residents can pursue cultural interests as well. The attractive little town of Napier in Hawke's Bay is noted for its Art Deco heritage as well as its wine and food tourism. Or if a more exclusively beach life style appeals then there's the go-ahead Bay of Plenty centred on the city of Tauranga. Or how about that most congenial of little cities, Nelson, a city that is passionate about artistic pursuits, values its heritage, yet has great beaches, a laid back lifestyle and excellent local wine.

Maybe you're looking for a second home – a holiday retreat in the mountains for skiing holidays or a base to catch fish from. You'll be able to afford more frequent visits to the snow if you avoid Queenstown and Wanaka and buy in Alexandra or Arrowtown. But be quick – these areas are fast catching up with the flashier Queenstown. Or if your ideal way of unwinding is fishing for trout, a weekend retreat on the shores near the Rotorua lakes or Taupo can be bought for $400,000 to $600,000.

If your one and only sailing experience was the Cross Channel ferry, it's unlikely you'll be buying a yacht just because you've moved to Auckland. But for anyone passionate about sailing, Auckland, the 'City of Sails' or the Bay of Islands would be two great options.

Parents raising a young family may choose an area because of the schooling as much as for the lifestyle. Then there's the dilemma of trying to find a house big enough to accommodate everyone yet in area that is affordable. If your job is based in Auckland then South East Auckland is a good compromise as it has good schooling, it's near the water yet the houses are around 15% to 20% cheaper than their equivalent in the more expensive Eastern Bays or Grammar Zone. Another child-friendly location is the city of Hamilton, a thriving little place, and an hour and a half south of Auckland but with cheaper property prices.

Or then there's the South Island's biggest centre, Christchurch. It has a dry climate with plenty of sunshine, great schools, superb skiing nearby and even a beach or two, and what's more you'll get a whole lot more house for the price you'd pay in Auckland. For holidays you can head south to the stunning regions of Queenstown and Central Otago or if you're seeking sun and sand it's a few hours drive to the delightful areas of Nelson and Golden Bay.

If you're prepared for a more bracing sea experience, you can still find properties, a block back from the beach for around $200,000 on the rugged coastline near the river city of Wanganui on the West Coast of the North Island. At the southern tip of the South Island in the beautiful empty spaces of the South Otago coast, a three bedroom un-renovated house on 6 hectares (15 acres) with rural and coastal views can be had for around $300,000.

Or if you'd like to build your dream house on the remote West Coast of the south island, a block of land on 2.3 hectares (5.68 acres) with mountain and native bush views could be yours for just over $100,000.

Christchurch is perhaps the only place in New Zealand where regional identity mattered because of its supposedly more genteel and ordered settlement in the 1850s. And as you'll see in the section on the area, echoes of this gentility still prevail. In the rest of the country regional identity only starts to matter during a sporting match – when regional teams play netball or rugby against each other. The further down the country you travel, provincial attitudes to city life become apparent. Tell a person from Invercargill that you're from Auckland and they'll shake their head and offer their commiserations.

Although we all supposedly speak the same language, there is a rich Kiwi vernacular, one of which is the language of real estate. This is a brief guide to architectural and real estate terms as used in the New Zealand context. You will find references to these terms used throughout the book.

Art Deco – This decorative style was named after an exhibition held in Paris in 1925 (the *Exposition Internationale des Arts Decoratifs et Industriels Modernes*). It was a style widely used in architecture of the 1930s, characterised by houses with angular or zigzag surface forms. Art Deco houses have flat roofs and are built of stucco or other form of solid construction. The city of Napier, which was rebuilt in the new style after the 1931 earthquake, has one of the most accessible collections of Art Deco architecture in the Southern Hemisphere.

bach – some say that the word is short for bachelor and that the term was shorthand for bachelor pad. But a bach today means a scruffy old holiday cottage, probably sitting on a piece of very expensive coastal land. When the old bach is pulled down what is built in its place will be grander and probably called a beach house.

Californian bungalow – a spacious bungalow, very suitable as a family home, made of wood dating from 1910 onwards with distinct features of the period including a river boulder verandah post on the exterior, window hoods, wide eaves and exposed rafters on gables. The interiors are characterised by extensive use of wood panelling, and sometimes a plate rail, which emphasises the horizontal aspect of the house, creating a feeling of space, which was reinforced by the open plan design. One important and practical design feature of some Californian bungalows is sliding wood panelled doors that close off the sitting room from the dining room.

cottage – a small, single-story building, generally with four rooms and without a hallway.

crib – the South Island term for the word bach, in common use south of Christchurch. The family crib might be near a lake, a river or the beach.

indoor-outdoor flow – describes the connection between the outdoor living space and the house and is a feature of open-plan houses.

kauri – *Agathis australis* The much prized timber felled extensively by the early settlers for house building. Fijian *kauri* is one remaining source of kauri grown specifically for the timber trade in sustainable forests. The most famous example of a living kauri in New Zealand is *Tane Mahuta* in the Waipoua Forest, Northland.

Lifestyle block – a two to three hectare hobby farm or small-holding.

Usually bought by city folk who have had enough of the rat race and who don't have to live off the income from their land.

matai – *Prumnopitys taxifolia* a native timber with grey/brown bark once used for flooring and interior joinery.

Monolithic cladding – a form of exterior cladding that became popular in the 1990s as a cheap way of making a house look like it was built of solid construction. (Monolithic cladding has an image problem now as incorrectly applied cladding of this nature was implicated in the Leaky Building Crisis – see *Section 3* where this is discussed in detail).

o.s.p. – an abbreviation for off-street parking, commonly found in real estate advertising.

relocated house – To British readers, living in solidly built semi-detached or terraced housing, the idea that a house could be relocated from one place to another might seem incredible. But it's been going on in New Zealand for years as old wooden villas have been removed from their original sites and moved elsewhere. It's only thanks to relocation that so many fine examples of villa housing still exist today. A relocated villa is easy to spot from the outside as it generally no longer has a brick chimney – unless of course the new owners have gone to the trouble of having replacement brick chimneys rebuilt.

Some buyers are hesitant about buying a relocated house but as most of them have had to be rewired, re-piled and sprayed for borer or termites before they can be moved, they may even be in better shape than a house on its original site.

rimu – *Dacrydium cypressinum* – a red pine native timber previously used in interior joinery.

section – the land that the house sits on and the size will be described in sq m or hectares.

sleepout – this describes an extra room for guests, usually away from the main house, which could be a summerhouse or even a converted garage.

Spanish Mission – Made of stucco, with a roughcast exterior, Spanish Mission style generally has arched doors and windows, balconies, an orange tiled roof, and long thin windows. The town of Hastings in the Hawke's Bay, which like Napier was flattened in the earthquake has a few surviving Spanish Mission buildings which weren't destroyed including,the Municipal Theatre built in 1914. Elsewhere the style is found in small low-level blocks of flats or in other examples of public architecture, such as theatres or school buildings. Auckland Grammar is one noted example of Spanish

Mission style.

Stripped classical – a design feature, used mainly in public buildings where elements of classical design have been pared back and ornate features replaced with simpler ones. The style was said to have originated in Melbourne and contained many features of the Chicago School. The Harbour City Centre (formerly the DIC building) in Wellington, the Wellington Railway Station, Broadcasting House in Napier and the NZ Guardian Trust building in Auckland are all of this design. The Guardian Trust building has a marked separation between the first and cornice levels and has a distinct Doric columned entrance way.

tandem garaging – where two cars are parked one behind the other, making access more difficult for the driver of the car in front.

townhouse – A house dating from around the 1980s, often replacing an original house which will either have been demolished or relocated. Developers will try to cram in three or even four of these high-density houses onto a site previously occupied by one house. The house occupies most of the site with just enough room to fit a small courtyard garden.

transitional style – Between 1908-1918 approximately, the fashion for the ornately decorative villa began to fade. During the transitional phase gradually house design began to incorporate elements of bungalow style. Verandah decoration was simplified, roof angles were flattened and casement windows began to replace double-hung sash windows.

villa – The first houses to be mass-produced in New Zealand were wooden houses built in the Victorian and Edwardian period. Villas are characterised by a central corridor with rooms leading off on both sides and high ceilings. Villas are often decorated with elaborate balustraded verandahs, which extends right around the house. The best examples were made of *kauri* (native conifer) heartwood, which is remarkably resilient to insect damage. The traditional roofing material for villas is cast iron. Windows are of the sash variety. Villas come in three styles. The **single bay villa** generally has an arched pediment with finial fretwork bracketing. The **double bay villa** is characterised by two bay windows at the front of the house. The **square villa** is the smallest and simplest of villa design giving the villa a box-like shape although the decorative features of the ornate veranda still remains.

weatherboard – wood cladding used on the outside of houses. Known as clapboard in the USA.

NORTH ISLAND

UPPER NORTH ISLAND

NORTHLAND

Largest city: Whangarei
Area sq km: 12,600. *Population of region:* 150,000 Whangarei: 47,000.
Climate: Average summer temperature 23.5C. Average winter temperature
15C.
Sunshine hours: 2016 per annum. Annual rainfall: 1500mm.
Airports: Kaitaia, Kerikeri, Whangarei.
Attractions and National Parks: Bay of Islands, Cape Reinga, Hokianga,
Ninety Mile Beach, Poor Knights Islands (one of the world's top diving
sites), Waitangi Treaty Grounds, Waipoua Forest, Goat Island Marine Re-
serve.

Geography and Climate

Northland runs from Cape Reinga at the very tip of the North Island in a
long thin curve all the way down to the border of Greater Auckland. It has
two magnificent harbours on the west coast, the Kaipara and the Hokianga.
Cape Reinga is where the Tasman Sea meets the Pacific Ocean in a swirling
angry mass and is for Maori a place of great spiritual significance as this
is where the departed souls leave from on their final journey, north to the
ancestral homeland, Hawaiki. On the east coast are white beaches and
sheltered bays, including the boaties paradise, the Bay of Islands. It's a
beautiful and diverse region with the largest remaining stands of *kauri*
forest left in New Zealand.

In a clockwise direction from Auckland the five geographic regions of
Northland are the Kaipara and the Kauri Coast along the Pacific western
coastline, The Far North starts at Kaitaia and includes Ninety Mile Beach
and Cape Reinga, some 350km north of Auckland. South of Ninety
Mile Beach and still in the Far North are the beaches and settlements of
Doubtless Bay and the Karikari Peninsula.

Just south of here is the Bay of Islands, 800km of coastline with 150
islands. The Whangarei region is south of the Bay of Islands and includes

North Island

——	State Highway
✈	Domestic Airport
✈	International Airport
----	Ferry Route

Cape Reinga

✈ Kaitaia ●

NORTHLAND

Whangarei ● ✈

Gt. Barrier Island

AUCKLAND

✈ **Auckland** ●

COROMANDEL PENISULA

Tasman Sea

✈ **Hamilton** ●

Tauranga ●

✈ Rotorua ●

BAY OF PLENTY

✈ Whakatane

East Cape

WAIKATO

GISBORNE

Taupo ✈

✈ Gisborne ●

✈ New Plymouth ●

HAWKE'S BAY

Hawke's Bay

TARANAKI

✈ Napier ●

● Hastings

✈ Wanganui ●

✈ Palmerston North ●

MANAWATU-WANGANUI

WELLINGTON

● Masterton

Picton ●

✈ **Wellington** ✈

the settlements of Matapouri and the Tutukaka coastline. Then there is the Kowhai Coast, on the east coast, closest to Auckland, which includes the marine reserve Goat Island and the settlements of Warkworth and the Matakana Valley, a boutique grape-growing region.

If all of Northland truly was the 'winterless north' as the tourist brochures like to boast then it would be a year round rather than a seasonal destination as it is now. In reality, the term only really applies above Kaitaia. The rest of Northland has high humidity in summer and frequent rain in winter and spring, especially on the west coast. But instead of annoying drizzle for days on end, the rain falls in great bursts, ferocious but short-lived. Parts of Northland can be reached within an hour from Auckland so it's not surprising that it's a favourite summer playground for those from New Zealand's largest city.

Cheerleaders for Northland point out that it's easier to get to than that other favourite holiday spot, the Coromandel Peninsula, with two points of access rather than one bottleneck. As well as good access, Northland is steeped in bi-cultural history and retains many of its old buildings. When it does rain there's enough going on to occupy even the most disgruntled sun-worshipper. And the beauty of Northland is that even in high summer there are still empty beaches and bays, provided you avoid Paihia in the Bay of Islands. And as you can see from the population statistics, for a region this size, Northland is sparsely populated.

History

Northland, Te Tai Tokerau in Maori, and known as the 'Birthplace of a Nation' was the earliest part of the country to be settled by both Maori and Pakeha. Maori influence and culture can be seen in many parts of Northland. In Maori legend Kupe, the great explorer was said to have sailed through the entrance to the Hokianga on the west coast and found it much to his liking, in contrast to a European group in the 19th century, intent on settling in Rawene. With no let up from three solid weeks of rain, they had an abrupt change of plan and packed up and headed off to Sydney.

It seems hard to imagine today that genteel Russell had a past so bawdy that it was known as 'the hell hole of the Pacific' in the early days of European settlement. The debauchery of the sealers and whalers who swaggered into port after months at sea encouraged the missionaries to see if the Lord could help them lead better lives.

The missionaries had rather more luck with Maori than they did with the sailors. So successful was the French Catholic Mission in Russell that Bishop Pompallier set up a religious printing press, which produced bibles in the Maori language.

It was the lawlessness amongst the visitors that prompted the local Maori chiefs to approach the British Crown in the first instance about imposing some kind of authority. This ultimately led to the historic signing at Waitangi in the Bay of Islands of the 1840 Treaty of Waitangi, Regarded as New Zealand's founding document, this was signed by Maori chiefs and representatives of the British Crown.

For more information on the Treaty, see the History section in Part 1 of this book. Almost as soon as the ink was dry, Hone Heke, the Ngapui chief found that the treaty was being breached and showed his contempt for British rule by chopping down the flagstaff at Russell a total of four times.

For the Maori that live in and around Waitangi this is an important centre of Maori culture. The Waitangi Day celebrations on February 6th at the treaty grounds are on occasion disrupted by a vocal minority who air their grievances in front of television crews, there to record any verbal upsets between protestors and politicians.

The story of Northland is a tale of two coastlines and the divisions are not merely geographic. The wildly beautiful and empty west coast was once teeming with fortune hunters and opportunists. On this coast once stood ancient native kauri forests (Agathis australis), which were cut down to, make ships' spars, houses and furniture.

After the loggers came the gum diggers. Kauris produce a sticky resin, not unlike maple syrup, which was a valuable raw material, used in linoleum and furniture varnishes. When the price for the gum increased this brought yet more prospectors. At one stage more than 2000 gum diggers were competing to extract the gum. At first it was harvested from the kauri stumps left by the loggers but when the supply dwindled, the hunt to find more gum became increasingly destructive until eventually even the ancient kauri swamps were dredged. Once the supply ran out all that was left was a barren and unproductive landscape.

Once the shipbuilding boom was over kauri was an important source of wood for the building and furniture trade. Kauri was fashioned into fine furniture as well as entire houses. Houses built of kauri wood have proved highly durable. A great many of these wooden clapboard style houses (called villas) are still standing and are considered by those that love old houses as highly desirable to live in. The secret of their longevity is the use of the heartwood, which is so hard that it can withstand attack from every other wood-boring insect, bar the native termites.

Although most of the native kauri trees had been felled by the early 20th century, logging for kauri was only banned in the area in the early 1950s when the remaining forest was saved and renamed as the Waipoua Sanctuary. Given the three-pronged attack on the kauri forests, it is remarkable that any kauri survived at all. While there's no real substitute for getting up close and personal with a kauri tree, to whet your appetite you can view the largest and grandest kauri tree of them all by going to www.hokiangatourism.org.nz, and clicking on the link: Tane Mahuta – (God of the forest). The largest of the species of native conifer known as kauri, this tree stands at 51 m high with a girth of 13m and is around 1200 years old, scarcely middle-aged for a kauri. The oldest known living kauri is Te Matua Ngahere (Father of the Forest), more than 2000 years old.

When the gum diggers and the loggers moved on, the legacy of these destructive industries were such that pockets of Northland never really recovered. The subsequent switch to agriculture and farming has had limited success as much of Northland is unsuitable for grazing and farming.

Because Northland's economy is still overly reliant on natural resources and agriculture, both slow growth industries, the region has never grown sufficiently to lift itself out of the economic doldrums. Northland has the highest regional unemployment rate in the country of around 6%, which is centred mainly around Kaitaia, Kaikohe and on the west coast.

The seasonal nature of the agricultural sector and the low wages is compounded by the almost non-existent public transport for workers in rural areas to be able to travel to their jobs. Young people have drifted away from Northland to the cities seeking a better life. But the tourists on board the luxury cruise ships that regularly call into the Bay of Islands over the summer would have no inkling that this was anything but an idyllic paradise.

Typical Properties for Sale

The **Kowhai Coast** around the village-like **Warkworth** offers the best of both worlds. Concert and theatre buffs are only an hour's drive from Auckland, the schools are good, yet it's more affordable than many of Auckland's better suburbs. And you'll get a lot more space. The **Matakana Valley**, just up the road is a boutique grape growing area where you can dine out among the vines.

Whangarei, two hours drive from Auckland has an attractive harbour and would be suitable for family living or a holiday house, especially in the countryside or out towards the dramatic coastline on the way to Whangarei Heads.

The Bay of Islands, the group of 150 small islands, of which only three mainland areas are developed is highly sought after and anything on or around the water will be expensive. Russell and Paihia though have barely more than a couple of thousand permanent residents. Kerikeri, though, seems to have it all: – a waterside location, a main street with cheerful sub-tropical plantings, an established café society yet one that retains some of fine historic buildings.

North of Kerikeri, it's beautiful but remote and suitable for holiday homes or a rural lifestyle, far away from the cares of city life. The fishing village of Mangonui is an attractive little place.

The west coast has recently attracted a number of alternative life-stylers including artists and writers. Available property is scarce and house buyers in this region should note that it is very rural and remote and that the nearest supermarket or medical centre may be up to 20km away by road.

Properties range from bare land to older style weatherboard houses, modern beach houses, and a few holiday apartments here and there as well as houses with orchards, hobby farms and horsy retreats.

The following prices are in New Zealand dollars except where indicated. Exchange rate data calculated January 2006.

Warkworth: In the Matakana area, close to vineyards , a 3 bedroom, 1 bathroom 1980s wooden house on 2 ha. with stables, shed and a stream. **Price:**$680,000 US$466,104 £267,022 A$628,768.

Ngunguru: With great potential as holiday accommodation this 3 bedroom brick house has estuary views, is close to the beach, shops and a sports complex. **Price:** $475,000.

Waipu: A hobby farm with family home on 2 ha. with 5 fully fenced paddocks. **Price:** $430,000.

Tutukaka: 5 ha. building plot with glimpse of the ocean. No building covenants, which gives the buyer the option of moving a house onto the site, or building a new one. **Price:** $230,000.

Near Kerikeri: 4 bedrooms, 3 bathrooms currently run as a bed and breakfast, this 1980s wooden house is on 7,085 sq m with sub-tropical fruit and citrus trees in the garden. **Price:** $599,000.

Matapouri: 4.5 ha of land with views of the Poor Knights Islands **Price:** $565,000.

Parua Bay: A 2 bedroom rustic cottage in a private coastal hideaway with distant water views 10km from Parua Bay. No neighbours for miles apart from possums and birdlife. Access via a 4.6 kilometre gravel road. **Price:** $220,000.

Mangonui: In the attractive and historic settlement of Mangonui an 1859 *kauri* cottage with a 3 bedroom, 2 storey architecturally designed house with its own deep-water mooring and water views. **Price:** $999,950.

Whangarei: Absolute waterfront 3 bedroom, 2 bathroom beach house at McLeod Bay on 1100 sq m. **Price:** $995,000

Russell: 180 degree views of the Bay of Islands from this 2 bedroom, 1 bathroom 1980s beach house with a garage for the car and a mooring for the boat. **Price:** $890,000.

If you plan to spend the summer, house hunting in the Bay of Islands you could be sharing it with 29,999 other visitors in January. But if you can delay it until February (surely the most miserable month in the Northern Hemisphere) the kids will be back at school and the prices will be better.

Agents for this area: www.harveys.co.nz, www.realestatenorthland.co.nz, www.raywhite.com, www.russellrealestate.co.nz, www.bayleys.co.nz.

AUCKLAND

Largest city: Auckland.
Area sq km: 5,600. *Population of region:* 1.3 million.
Climate: Average summer temperature 20C. Average winter temperature 13C. Sunshine hours: 245 days per annum. Annual rainfall: 1200mm.
Airports: Auckland International. Separate domestic terminal nearby.
Attractions and National Parks: Islands of the Hauraki Gulf including Tiritiri Matangi, a protected bird sanctuary. Waitakere and Hunua Ranges.

Geography and Climate

Auckland sits on a narrow isthmus between two harbours, the Manukau to the west and the Waitemata to the east. From Waiwera in the north to Drury, in the south, Greater Auckland stretches some sixty kilometres. To the west the city reaches as far as Henderson as well as the west coast beaches at Muriwai and Piha. Out east the spread of that urban sprawl is contained by the jewel-like Hauraki Gulf. Out in the Gulf, Waiheke Island is the eastern most point of Greater Auckland. Auckland's sprawl mirrors that of that other Pacific city, Los Angeles. Twice the size of greater London but with only 1.3 million people, it is one of the least densely populated cities in the world.

With safe swimming beaches in the eastern suburbs and the North Shore and good surfing on the west coast and 20 conservation parks within a 45-minute drive, it's not surprising that Auckland continues to attract new residents. They come to Auckland for the jobs and of course the lifestyle.

The Waitakere Ranges have an array of walking and mountain biking tracks, one of which includes the Pohutakawa Glade Walk leading to Karekare, where scenes from Jane Campion's award-winning feature film, *The Piano* were shot. Out in the Waitakeres are tree ferns, *kauri*, *rata*, and *pohutakawa* – unfamiliar names but once seen, these magnificent trees will remain etched in the memory. The forest is the place for bird life such as the iridescent green *tui* and the friendly fantails.

Dotted around in the suburbs are important natural sites including extinct volcanoes (there are at least 50) as well as a mangrove swamp along the foreshore in Remuera. Two of the largest volcanic cones are One Tree Hill (Maungakiekie) and Mt Eden (Maungawhau). Both were once the sites of Maori pa (fortified settlements) and the remains of house sites and food storage pits can still be seen. But it's mainly the views that draw the visitors. But there is one landmark that more than anything else is identified as uniquely Auckland and that is the third and most dramatic volcano of all, Rangitoto, the sleeping giant, sitting out in the Hauraki Gulf. Formed a mere 600 years ago, Rangitoto's distinctive conical shape means that the island is visible right along the coast from the North Shore down to the Eastern Beaches.

Often referred to as a mini Sydney, Auckland may have a harbour bridge, beaches and an attractive harbour but that's about all it has in common with its neighbour across the Tasman. Where Sydney has efficient public transport, Aucklanders are car dependent. And it's a scandal that a city of

Auckland's size has no decent airport access – the main route into town detours through suburbia, which can mean crawling through traffic at peak times. With no train or subway connection, passengers flying into Auckland International are forced to take an expensive taxi ride or wait for an airport bus just to get to the city centre.

The downtown area can disappoint those expecting a big city experience. Auckland doesn't have a world famous opera house or sophisticated shopping or any of the other attractions that international visitors have come to expect from cities. The Viaduct area, which has yachts moored nearby is pleasant enough and the ship-like Hilton hotel is a cleverly designed building. Along Quay Street where the ferries depart there are good views of Devonport across the harbour.

The leafiest parts in the centre are around the Auckland City Art Gallery and the university. A lovely park with a duck pond, a palm house and a winter garden surrounds the Auckland Museum. The best places to eat out are scattered around and not necessarily in the centre of town.

At night the downtown area empties out and can resemble a ghost town as most people have gone home to the suburbs. This can be disconcerting for international visitors. For a livelier experience, just head up to either Ponsonby or Karangahape Roads, the latter of which may be a bit scruffy but the charms of K' Road are that it has soul, whereas the Viaduct area, despite the restaurant called Soul, is pleasant in a bland way and lacks any real charm.

Aucklanders are regarded with suspicion by the rest of the country. Depending on who you talk to, they are brash, showy, shallow and materialistic. But as many Aucklanders know, much of that disdain masks downright envy. After all, Aucklanders seem to have it all. Their houses are worth more than any other real estate in the country, except for Queenstown's and many Aucklanders own property there too. Diners can eat out at a different restaurant every night of the year, and then there's the lifestyle. City types can throw off the suit jacket, jump into sailing gear and be off and away out into the Gulf within 30 minutes of leaving the office.

But this rather one-sided view of Auckland belies the true picture. It ignores the fact that Auckland is the world's largest Polynesian city where 11% of the population have Pacific ancestry, that 13% claim Maori ancestry and that 10% of its residents were originally from Asia. As a result Auckland is the only truly cosmopolitan city in New Zealand and that diversity is celebrated by all the different cultural attractions on offer.

Aucklanders have a reputation for not being as cultured as Wellingtonians but that's because there's so much more going on in Auckland. Instead of just an orchestra concert or a play to choose from, Aucklanders could be attending events as diverse as a Pacific Island fashion show or a display of Indian dance.

History

Maori have lived in Auckland for over 800 years but ever since *Ngati Whatua* made it their home, they faced considerable challenges from other tribes, eager to capitalise on its riches.

After the Treaty of Waitangi was signed in 1840 William Hobson, the new governor, wasted no time in relocating the capital from Opua in the Bay of Islands further south to Auckland. A Scottish doctor, who lived in Auckland just as it was elevated to its new status was one John Logan Campbell. Known as 'the father of Auckland', Logan Campbell was Auckland's first property speculator, who as well as owning a large tract of land, was able to wield political power by becoming its mayor.

Logan Campbell is fondly regarded, as instead of leaving all his land to his family, he gifted a large area of his estate to the city. The city's dog owners and joggers have been grateful to him ever since. Cornwall Park includes One Tree Hill and is a formally laid out park with exotic tree species from the Northern Hemisphere. Incorporating a home farm, grazing cattle and even a ha ha, all that's missing is the grand stately pile straight out of Jane Austen.

Depending on which survey you believe, Auckland is either the 69th most expensive city to live in, sandwiched between Lisbon (66) and Dubai (73) (Mercer) or 39th equal with Wellington, (The Economist's 2005 survey). The rise in value of the New Zealand dollar, rising fuel prices and house price inflation have all contributed to Auckland leaping up the ratings. In terms of quality of life, Auckland scored in the top 10, as Mercer ranks Auckland eighth equal with Sydney, Bern and Copenhagen.

Typical Properties for Sale

Although it now has the second highest median house prices in the country, (Queenstown has recently edged it out) at $395,000, central Auckland has some of the most sought-after real estate in New Zealand. Factors that influence the price of property in Auckland vary but being in the right school zone can add as much as 10% to the price of a house. Families will move into a zone just to ensure that they can get their children into either Auckland Grammar (boys) or Epsom Girls Grammar.

Grammar zone includes the 'old money' suburbs of Parnell and Remuera. The other highly sought after areas to live for those that can afford them are Herne Bay, St Mary's Bay as well as the Eastern suburbs beside the beach up to and including St Heliers. The most desirable parts of these areas are any that face north and the words 'northern slopes' and 'Rangi views' are shorthand for a view of Rangitoto and that the house faces the right direction for the sun. You'll see little change out of $1,000,000 for 4 bedroom family homes in these areas.

Property development is an Auckland disease – where grand old landmark houses have been moved from their original sites and relocated elsewhere. And in their place go grim boxy in-fill townhouses, entirely out of keeping with their surroundings. You'll find many examples of crimes against architecture in Auckland, where colours and materials have been chosen without any regard to either the natural environment or the surrounding buildings. Unlike many other of the world's cities there was no urban design panel in place in Auckland city until very recently so developers could put up pretty much any old monster they liked, with no aesthetic design considerations.

While it is hard to find a piece of bare land to build on anymore, especially near the centre, Auckland offers the potential house buyer one of the most diverse ranges of lifestyle of any city in the world. Take your pick from a modern apartment at the Viaduct Harbour, near the Team New Zealand yacht base, a cliff-top mansion on the North Shore, an inner city kauri villa, or a lifestyle block out west. In South East Auckland it's around 15-20% cheaper for houses that often have fine views.

The age and style of housing in Auckland depend very much on when the area was first settled. Because the North Shore was only linked to the city in 1959, most of the housing stock was built from the 1960s onwards. You'll find older houses in areas, which historically have had ferry services into the city, including Devonport, Northcote Point and Birkenhead Point. The most desirable areas along the North Shore are those that hug the coastline or have views over the inner harbour.

Gentrification of the previously run-down inner-city suburbs of Ponsonby and Grey Lynn has pushed those that can't afford to live close to the city far away to places such as Hillsborough or on the western side of State Highway 1 over on the North Shore. The outer suburbs are cheerless places that spread for miles. Most of them are impossible to get to unless you have a car.

'South Auckland' is shorthand for parts of Manukau City where there are pockets of urban deprivation, which have a reputation for being unsafe. The majority of residents of Manukau City (down near the airport) are law abiding and industrious. The great many positive initiatives tend to get ignored by the news media for the sake of a good story about gangs and violent crime.

The following prices are in New Zealand dollars except where indicated. Exchange rate data calculated January 2006.

Central Auckland, Newmarket: Enjoy views over the Waitemata from this north facing 2 bedroom, 2 bathroom apartment with garaging close to the central city. **Price:** $650,000 US$445,281 £ 255,110 A$600,716.

Eastern Suburbs, Glendowie: On 500 sq m facing north, this 3 bedroom house has open plan living and a dining room opening out to a spacious deck and garden. New kitchen, ensuite and rumpus room with double internal garage completes the picture. **Price:** $650,000.

South East, Cockle Bay: In South East Auckland, situated in a top primary school zone this substantial 5 bedroom family home on 809 sq m with landscaped grounds and lawn, perfect for entertaining. 3 living areas, 2 bathrooms, 1 cloakroom, a study and a balcony with glorious sea views. **Price:** $890,000.

North Shore, Devonport: There is nowhere else on the North Shore that matches Devonport for its seaside village atmosphere, the period houses and ferry service to Auckland. Expats are attracted to the area by the good schooling as well as the glorious beach on the Cheltenham side. Some say that the area is overpriced. Like most of the houses in Devonport this 2 bedroom *villa* is on a small site. It has 2 bedrooms, 1 bathroom, one living room, a dining kitchen, a deck, a patio and a single garage. **Price:** $568,000

West, Titirangi: Auckland's answer to Sydney's Blue Mountains. A cedar two storey house with 4 bedrooms, 3 bathrooms and 2 sitting rooms and an indoor spa in a private bush clad site on the fringe of the Waitekere Ranges. **Price:** $699,000.

Piha: A surfer's paradise, this beach house, on Auckland's wild west coast is situated on the next bay round from where *The Piano* was filmed. 1206 sq m of privacy, with native trees including mature kauri. An easy walk to the beach. **Price:** High $400,000s.

Helensville: If you want space then go west. Architecturally designed 3 bedroom house on 2.2ha. Timber flooring, log fire, 2 living rooms, designer kitchen and 2 tiled bathrooms. Double garage and outdoor living area. **Price:** $769,000.

Islands of the Hauraki Gulf, Waiheke Island: Unlike many of the other beaches around the world that share the same name, this Palm Beach has only a handful of houses. 200 metres away from the sand, and a plot of land with views over the bay. **Price:** $585,000.

South, Karaka: 4 bedroom brick family home, modern kitchen, double garage with storage, tack room and stable, hay barn, landscaped gardens, rural views on 4.2 ha. 45mins/1hr in rush hour to Auckland. **Price:** $990,000.

Agents for this area. www.barfoot.co.nz, www.prestigerealty.co.nz www.raywhite. com, www.harcourts.co.nz, www.bayleys.co.nz.

CENTRAL NORTH ISLAND

WAIKATO

Largest centre: Hamilton.
Area sq km: 7,363. *Population of region:* 381,800. Hamilton: 138,000.
Climate: Average summer temperature: Hamilton 23C, Taupo 22C. Average winter temperature: Hamilton 14 C, Taupo 12C.
Sunshine hours: Hamilton 2000 per annum, Taupo 1965 per annum.
Annual rainfall: Hamilton 1190mm, Taupo 1100mm.
Airport: Hamilton – regional connections as well as international to Australia and Pacific holiday destinations, Taupo – flights to Auckland and Wellington.
Attractions and National Parks: Waitomo Caves, Pirongia Forest Park, Lake Taupo.

Geography and Climate

The Waikato has a mild climate with high humidity in the summer and the occasional frost in winter. Driving south from Auckland, at the top of the Bombay Hills, is a magnificent view of the Waikato's rich pastoral landscape stretching out before you. To the east is the ridge of the Kaimai Ranges, dividing the Bay of Plenty from the Waikato and to the southwest the mountains of Pirongia Forest Park. The mighty Waikato River has its source to the south in the volcanic Lake Taupo and wends its way through to reach Cambridge, Hamilton and Huntly finally reaching the sea at Port Waikato, just south of Auckland.

The Waikato is home to all things dairy, and Fonterra New Zealand's largest dairy company has a base here. Just to the north of Hamilton is Woodlands, a kauri homestead in a grassy landscape, where the Anchor butter brand was founded in 1886. Even the local football team, Mooloo, is named in honour of the humble black and white Friesian cattle that made the fortune of many a Waikato farmer.

Although money doesn't grown on trees in the Waikato (sadly they were chopped down to make way for farms), it certainly grows in those fields, or paddocks as they call them in New Zealand. Cambridge and Matamata have long been associated with the bloodstock industry. Thoroughbred champions of the future take their first wobbly steps in a landscape sometimes referred to as a mini Kentucky.

Engineering service companies set up to service the dairy industry continue to be a strong earner for the region. It's not hard to see why Hamilton and the Waikato are thriving:- there's a reliable infrastructure, good schools, a university and three cities including Auckland all within a 90-minute drive.

History

The European settlers didn't take long to realise that the Waikato's productive soil held a great many riches. The only problem was that the land belonged to *Tainui*. The British Crown may have signed a treaty with Maori in 1840 but by 1860 the Government of New Zealand was made up of self-interested individuals who were not interested in negotiation in the same way as the Crown was.

Maori would not willingly part with their land, even though the Government tried to persuade them otherwise. The 1860s saw the start of the Waikato Land Wars where Tainui land was seized by force. In an attempt at elevating the status of Maori to the level of the British sovereign, a breakaway element called Kingitangi or the King Movement was formed. It was a last-ditch effort by Maori to find a way of controlling the European settlers insatiable demand for land. The base of the breakaway movement was in Te Kuiti, an area that became known as the King Country. For many years the King Country was a no-go area and it wasn't until the

1890s that the new settlers were allowed to set foot in there.

The present Maori queen, Te Arikinui, Dame Te Atairangikaahu is a descendant of the first Maori king and lives at the Turangawaewae Marae at Ngaruawahia, just north of Hamilton. It was in Ngaruawahia that the historic Raupatu Land Settlement was signed, where Government agreed to pay compensation to Tainui for land confiscated in the 1860s.

Typical Properties for Sale

The Waikato is a prosperous region with substantial houses in the country areas as well as to the south of Hamilton in Tamahere and near the airport. It's the ideal area to pursue a country life. Cambridge, within a 30 minute drive south of Hamilton is a pretty country town with good schools and provides a pleasant alternative to living in Hamilton for those looking to buy a house with some land attached.

Hamilton attracts relocating Auckland families priced out of the Auckland Grammar or Epsom Girls zones looking to find a more affordable lifestyle. Families relocating from the UK who are surprised at how expensive the Auckland market has become are attracted to the area for the same reason.

South Auckland is just over an hour's drive making commuting possible and Hamiltonians can take advantage of all that Auckland has to offer, without necessarily living there.

One of the most beautiful and unspoilt coastal areas within 45 minutes commute to Hamilton is Raglan, with its rugged and wild iron-sand beaches. Rather like Big Sur must have been 50 years ago, this beachside community caters for a wide range of ages and interests from retirees, families with holiday homes, alternative lifestylers and the surfing community. Manu Bay and Whale Bay, eight kilometres from Raglan have a reputation with surfers as having the world's greatest left hand surf break and Raglan attract surfers from all over the world, hosting international surfing championships.

There couldn't be much more of a contrast with a surfing lifestyle than a genteel and well preserved Edwardian spa town but one of the prettiest little places in the district is Te Aroha, (the place of love), at the foot of Mount Te Aroha near the Kaimai Ranges. Within a 45-minute drive of Hamilton, Te Aroha is a good alternative to Cambridge for those attracted to a country lifestyle. Property is more affordable than Hamilton and there are some beautifully restored villas. Te Aroha's central location provides easy access to the Coromandel and the Bay of Plenty for weekend trips.

Although at $265,000 the median house price is below the national average, prices in Hamilton have rocketed up in the past two years. A trickle-down effect from the Auckland boom and a vibrant economy has brought professionals south, looking for better value for money. In the best parts, along the river and around the lake, prices have crept up to rival Auckland's.

The biggest disappointment with Hamilton is that in the less desirable parts it still feels like a big suburb of Auckland and if a distinct identity is there, it's becoming increasingly hard to find, as so much of the countryside is being swallowed up by the relentless march of the bulldozer. Maps go out of date within a year as new subdivisions to the north east of Hamilton seem to spring up almost overnight.

Most of Hamilton was developed in the 1960s and 1970s so it's hard to find a house with much character. If you do want a wooden villa or a Californian bungalow you'll find them in the central city suburb of Claudelands and Hamilton East, along the river. There are attractive parks and Hamilton Gardens is a delight where there are river walks as well as themed gardens.

The best suburb for schooling is in Hillcrest, near the university. Unfortunately, unless you can afford to live by the river where there are substantial and attractive family homes with river frontage, the houses near the university are solidly built but ordinary looking, yet surprisingly expensive.

Hamilton does have a thriving arts scene, an excellent university in beautiful landscaped grounds and was the birthplace of Richard O'Brien, the creator of the Rocky Horror Show. Te Awamutu, a little country town south west of Hamilton was home to the musical Finn brothers of Split Enz and Crowded House fame.

Further south at Taupo, modest fishing lodges are on the market for under $600,000. Lake Taupo is almost as large as an inland sea and lakefront property represents good value compared with beachfront homes. And Taupo has that stunning mountain scenery as well.

The following prices are in New Zealand dollars except where indicated. Exchange rate data calculated January 2006.

Central Hamilton: Walking distance to town on the south side of the Waikato River, a 1920s 3 bedroom, 2 bathroom refurbished bungalow with polished floors, leadlight windows. Swimming pool, central heating and a double garage. **Price:** $490,000. US$334,981 £191,932, A$ 453,136.

Matamata: Or Hobbiton as it's known to the rest of the world. Not far from the location where the hobbit houses were built, a 1920s *Californian bungalow* on 1 ha. of grounds. 4 bedrooms, 2 bathrooms with some internal redecoration and upgrading required. Views to the Kaimai Ranges. Hamilton, Tauranga and Rotorua all less than an hour's drive away for commuters. **Price:** NZ $470,000.

Te Awamutu: This new subdivision offers both views and a larger than average plot of land. 1148 sq m site with views to Pirongia and the surrounding lush countryside. Within a 30-minute drive to Hamilton. **Price:** $127,000

Cambridge: A 4 bedroom, 2 bathroom family house with 2 living areas on 900 sq m. Could do with some internal redecoration. Near Lake Karapiro so an approximate 45 minute commute to Hamilton. **Price:** $400,000.

Hamilton: This solid but unexciting 3 bedroom, 1 bathroom brick house would make a great low maintenance rental investment as its centrally located. **Price:** $289,000.

Hamilton countryside: A lifestyle block on 4775 sq m with a 3 bedroom, 2 bathroom house with a study and double garage. Landscaped grounds and views to the river but with some modernisation needed inside. **Price:** $475,000.

Hamilton: On the river in a top school zone, this 4 bedroom, 3 bathroom plus ensuite executive townhouse on 547 sq m with double garage and decks looking out over the fast-flowing Waikato. Peaceful and private. **Price:** $615,000.

Raglan:. North facing humble beach bach with distant harbour views. 3 bedrooms plus a carport. 525 sq m. **Price:** $280,000.

Raglan: Estuary and mountain views from this 3 bedroom house on a 1282 sq m plot with subdivision potential. **Price:** $395,000.

Raglan: Ocean views of Whale Bay. 3 bedrooms, 1 bathroom. Perfect weekend retreat. **Price:** $975,000.

Taupo: Lakefront cottage with 2 bedrooms, 1 bathroom, 1 ensuite, single garage on 534 sq m. **Price:** $575,000.

Taupo: 8,171 sq m block of land with spectacular views of lake and mountains.
Price: $550,000.

Agents for this area: www.trademe.co.nz, www.lodgerealestate.co.nz.
www.harcourts.co.nz, www.taupofirstnat.co.nz.

THE GULLY SYSTEM

Hamilton's well-hidden secret has been its gully system – a series of streams that snake their way through the suburbs. Conservationists are encouraging homeowners to restore these nature reserves with native plants to bring back *tui*, the white throated and raucous New Zealand native bird species, which was all but wiped out in Hamilton because the surrounding area has been so extensively farmed.

EAST COAST

COROMANDEL PENINSULA

Largest town: Thames.
Area sq km: 23,530 *Population of region:* 39,000 Thames: 10,000
Climate: Average summer temperature 22C. Average winter temperature 13C.
Sunshine hours: 2200 per annum. Annual rainfall: 1400mm.
*Airport:*Whitianga – limited service flying scheduled scenic flights between Auckland and Great Barrier Island.
Attractions and National Parks: Cathedral Cove, Hot Water Beach, Karangahake Gorge, Coromandel Coastal Walkway.

Geography and Climate

The Coromandel Peninsula is technically part of the Waikato but because of its coastal position, distinct identity and popularity, it warrants its own section. The Coromandel is the finger of land that juts out into the Hauraki Gulf, to the east of Waiheke Island. On the western side is the Firth of Thames and on its eastern side, the Pacific Ocean. Dawn breaking over the Coromandel mountains is a truly breathtaking sight and one, which can be enjoyed by those lucky Aucklanders who live in the eastern suburbs.

Wags say that if you can see the Coromandel clearly then it's going to rain but if clouds obscure it then it's already raining. And rain it does, near the mountains, which explains why the area is so green.

The Thames Coast, which is on the western edge, is the most direct route up to Coromandel Town. The narrow and treacherous road (it's difficult not to look at the view), twists and turns its way along for 35km. Fringed by *pohutukawa* (Metrosideros excelsa), known as the New Zealand Christmas tree, their stunning red flowers are in full bloom in December.

The infrastructure in the Coromandel particularly the unsealed roads north of Coromandel Town helps keep the area free from tour coaches, but getting around can take time even though the distances may be short. Those that love the Coromandel willingly put up with the poor access via the one route in and out, by ensuring that they avoid Easter or Labour Weekend. The volume of traffic at holiday times is heavy but a notorious and unavoidable one-lane bridge can see holiday traffic waiting for more than an hour to cross. The bridge upgrade, planned some time in the future, is urgently needed.

One way to avoid this bottleneck is to avoid the road and take the passenger ferry service from Auckland. It's an hour each way by boat and you may even see dolphins.

Tourism, mining and forestry are the main industries here as well as mussel and oyster farming off the coast of Coromandel Town.

History

Long before the European settlers arrived a significant population of Maori lived on the peninsula, mainly in the sheltered areas along the east coast. This was where Maori hunted the moa, the largest flightless bird ever to roam these lands. In 1852 the aptly named Charles Ring found gold at Driving Creek, just north of Coromandel Town. As gold fever took hold, the town became the temporary home to more than 10,000 settlers. That first gold rush was followed by further discoveries at Thames, Coromandel and Karangahake. But it's not just gold in those hills, but semi-precious stones including amethyst and agate.

As well as gold it was kauri that attracted prospectors to the area. Kauri logging was big business for 60 years until all the kauri ran out. Where once the mighty kauri stood is now patched with tree ferns. Now and again there's the occasional forlorn-looking tree, which may have self-seeded. Even these stragglers give visitors a tantalising glimpse of how different the landscape must have once looked when it was thick with virgin forest. And as in Northland, after the loggers came the gum diggers.

Gold mining, unlike most of the other extractive industries did not cease in the 19th century but has been the major source of income, on and off over the years in the little town of Waihi. Silver as well as gold has been mined in Martha Mine which is finally due to be decommissioned in 2007, although other mining ventures are planned for the area after that.

At Hot Water Beach you can dig your own spa pool as water from a hot spring bubbles up under the sand. The Karangahake Gorge has a number of easy, flat walks where visitors can find out about the area's historical links to gold mining. The Coromandel Forest Park has long distance walks with basic accommodation for overnight visitors.

Typical Properties for Sale

Coromandel Town attracts writers, artists, conservationists as well as those escapees from the rat race. But it's not yet fashionable in the way of Byron Bay or Dartmouth in Devon. There's still a pioneering spirit up there and you're more likely to see a local driving a tractor than doing tai chi on the beach.

On the east coast you'll find a different crowd. The low-key resort of Whitianga is a mecca for holidaying Auckland and Waikato families, whereas nearby Pauanui is the place to bump into your neighbours from Auckland's tonier suburbs. Whangamata is geared to families and there's good surfing here along a beautiful beach.

The Coromandel suits those that work from home – either telecommuters or artists and writers. It's not ideal for relocating families as there's not much in the way of schooling or many facilities. And in winter it's very quiet. A town further inland such as Paeroa gives families more commuting options.

The prices on the western side of the Coromandel looking out on to the Firth of Thames are cheaper than the east coast but because there's only a few scattered settlements there's not much available for sale on this side. Buyers gravitate to the east coast for the beaches and the ocean views. Around Coromandel Town you'll find prices are somewhere between the two but even here it's no longer cheap. Buyers on the east coast need to bear in mind that the beauty is not in the housing but in the surroundings. An area like Waihi Beach mostly consists of 1960s and 1970s solidly built houses that are functional but mostly without charm.

People who have bought recently buy these properties both for the capital gain and with a view to removing the old house and building something more to their taste later on. Other families are content to leave as is, kitting the house out with basic furniture, creating a relaxed atmosphere far away from the stresses of city life.

Properties in the Coromandel range from modern beach houses, bare land to build on, a few holiday apartments and country homes on larger blocks of land.

The following prices are in New Zealand dollars except where indicated. Exchange rate data calculated January 2006.

Whitianga: At the coastal holiday resort of Whitianga, a 671 sq m gently sloping site ready for building with distant views to Mercury Bay. **Price:** $195,000 US$133,603 £76,482 A$180,271.

Tairua: With a river estuary and an ocean beach, this is a popular base for divers keen to dive the Shoe and Slipper Islands and the Alderman Islands. 891 sq m plot cleared for building. Elevated site with views across the harbour and the ocean. **Price:** NZ $395,000.

Pauanui: There's always a shortage of family-size holiday homes to rent over the January holidays in this popular beach resort, around two and a half hours drive from Auckland. This would make a good high-season rental investment. 3 bedrooms, 1 family bathroom and an ensuite in this modern wooden bungalow on a 605 squ m site. Just a walk across the reserve to the beach. **Price:** $699,000

Paeroa: This well-preserved little town, known for its antique and craft outlets is at the junction of two rivers. There's a golf course and good fishing available nearby. A large 2 storey brick 4 bedroom, 2 bathroom house with large living and dining room and a chef's kitchen, plus a double garage on 3.25ha. with post and rail fencing, native trees. Views of the Firth of Thames. An ideal family home.
Price: $599,000.

Whitianga: A 115 sq m 2 bedroom 1 bathroom apartment on the water overlooking the marina. Double garage. **Price:** $695,000.

Port Charles: You might need a four-wheel drive vehicle to get to this remote area near the top of the Coromandel Peninsula as the access road is gravel for part of the way. A 5787 sq m building plot with 360-degree views, which include the Coromandel mountains, Great Barrier Island and Port Charles. **Price:** $999,999.

Waihi Beach: Absolute beachfront, with ocean views. Two storey 4 bedroom house in need of updating, 2 living areas, 2kitchens and 2 bathrooms. **Price:** $1,500.000.

Agents for this area: www.rwwhitianga.co.nz, www.coromandelproperty.co.nz, www.rwwaihibeach.co.nz, www.rwngatea.co.nz,

HOLES IN THE GROUND

In December 2001 several houses collapsed into a disused mine shaft in the little town of Waihi, home to the Martha Mine. Drainage from the mineshafts below caused some support structures to rot. Waihi Beach, which is some kilometres away from the mining area was not affected. If a house is built near disused mine shafts then this information should be recorded on the LIM (Land Information Memorandum) reports held by the local council.

BAY OF PLENTY

Largest city: Tauranga
Area sq km. 12,247; *Population of region:* 257,600 Tauranga: 100,000
Climate: Average summer temperature. 23C Average winter temperature. 14.7C
Sunshine hours: 2260 per annum. Annual rainfall: 1198mm
Airports: Tauranga, Whakatane and Rotorua. Transtasman charter flights from Rotorua are due to start by Christmas 2006.
Attractions and National Parks: White Island (*Whakaari*), Mt Maunganui (*Mauao*) as well as outstanding beaches.

Geography and Climate

The Bay of Plenty was so named by Captain Cook in 1769 and the region has lived up to its bountiful reputation ever since. Today, it's an important area for fruit cultivation including kiwifruit, citrus and avocados.

The coastal area of the Bay of Plenty has a microclimate making it one of the sunniest areas of the country. The rest of the region has a warm, moist climate with few extremes of temperature, creating ideal growing conditions. Rotorua's lakeside location makes it slightly cooler than the coast.

Situated mid-way down the North Island on the east coast, the Bay of Plenty reaches south as far as the fascinating geothermal region of Rotorua. Joining the Coromandel at Athentree at the western end, the Bay of Plenty hugs the ocean past Whakatane and Opotiki towards the east. The Raukumara Range provides a rugged backdrop to these two coastal settlements.

With over 100km of sandy ocean beach and more sunshine hours than Biarritz, the area is a mecca for sun worshippers and lotus-eaters. Whether you want to swim in it, surf on it, fish in it, dive under it, or merely gaze at it, the azure blue Pacific Ocean that laps against the shores of The Bay of Plenty is truly mesmerising. It's no wonder then that the Bay of Plenty is the sun and surf capital of the country. And that reputation will only grow when surfers from around the country begin to use the Mount as a year round surfing destination, thanks to the first artificial surfing reef that opened in late 2005.

But for those who prefer a menu board to a surfboard, there's still plenty of opportunity to experience the great outdoors from the comfort of pavement cafes and restaurants. Mills Reef in Tauranga and Morton Estate at Katikati combine dining with wine tasting. Music fans will enjoy Tauranga's annual Easter jazz festival.

But it's not all hedonistic play – Tauranga works hard too. As well as a bustling centre for trade, Tauranga is the biggest commercial centre in the region. Timber, dairy products and the region's fruit are all shipped through the Port of Tauranga, the nation's busiest export hub. Domestic tourism is an important industry, which is fuelling the growth in the service sector.

History

The region has always held special significance for Maori. The monument at Maketu commemorates the landing place of the *Arawa* canoe, which according to Maori legend was one of the original canoes to sail from the ancestral homeland in Hawaiki.

In 1864 one of the most significant battles in The New Zealand Wars took place in the little settlement of Gate Pa. Government troops set up a blockade in the area as they believed local Maori were aiding the Maori king in the Waikato. Although Maori were heavily outnumbered they nevertheless survived the bombardment. The Mission Cemetery in Tauranga honours the dead of both sides who fell in battle.

The Bay of Plenty has two distinct economic and commercial regions, west and east. Tauranga and its ocean-side neighbour, Mt Maunganui, known affectionately as 'The Mount' are the hub of the Western Bay of Plenty while Whakatane with a population of just 18,000 is the main settlement of the Eastern Bay. While Tauranga is the commercial centre, as you head east it becomes much more rural, the towns are much smaller and thinly populated.

Tauranga's location at the entrance to a large natural harbour has been a key factor in the city's growth. In the 1950s when Tauranga and Whakatane were both sleepy beachside backwaters, the two were very much on a par. But when Tauranga was chosen over Whakatane as the new export port for the Bay of Plenty region, this fuelled an immediate growth in both jobs and population.

Tauranga is one of the fastest growing urban centres in New Zealand and if that trend continues, it will soon overtake Dunedin as the fifth largest urban area in the country. But Tauranga is no metropolis and not likely to become one, although over the Christmas and New Year summer break when the place fills up with holidaymakers, it can seem that half of Auckland has decamped to the seaside.

Once regarded as a place to retire to, Tauranga and Mount Maunganui are attracting a younger crowd, pushing the average age down to 38. The climate, lifestyle and work opportunities continues to attract incomers to the area, many of whom have ditched urban living in favour of a more balanced approach to work and life. And as well as attracting relocating New Zealanders the region has long been popular with those looking to move from other parts of the globe.

The Western Bay of Plenty's growth has put pressure on local infrastructure. Access is an issue especially between Mount Maunganui and Tauranga over the bridge that connects them. Mt Maunganui has an anti-social 'boy racer' culture where young testosterone-fuelled idiots race around in their high-performance cars disturbing residents' sleep.

POST EARLY FOR CHRISTMAS

The hardware store that doubles as a post shop in Bethlehem, Tauranga, enjoys a brisk trade at Christmas not just from local residents but from all over the world so that post can carry that coveted Bethlehem postmark.

Whakatane is unlikely to see anything like the same level of development as Tauranga. Although increasingly popular as an area for second homes, 300km is too far from Auckland for families to drive to at weekends. State Highway 2 which is basically an A road with passing places, is not only the main route to Tauranga but the Coromandel as well. There are regular bottlenecks at the northern end at Easter and at other holiday weekends.

Whakatane's isolation means that in winter it can be very quiet.

Although it's a pretty little place, there's not much to do when it's raining apart from family or community activities. When the sun comes out though you'll be enjoying all that wonderful coastline without the crowds.

Apart from the suburbs the alternatives in Rotorua are close to the lakes, especially for keen anglers.

Typical Properties for Sale

Many New Zealanders lump Tauranga, Mt Maunganui and Queenstown together as examples of the level of development they don't want to see in the rest of the country. But it's still premature to label this area a mini version of Queensland's Gold Coast. These may be high-density apartment blocks but they are no bigger than eight storeys. And thankfully, sensible public access legislation precludes beaches from ever passing into the hands of property developers.

Condominiums and apartments at Mount Maunganui may have all but replaced the scruffy kiwi beach baches but nothing man-made in this location can spoil the first sight of that magnificent mountain and that stunning ocean.

Location and views are the key factors in determining what price you'll pay for property here. A three-bedroom apartment or town house with ocean views is now around $1.5million. A two bedroom 60 square metre apartment with a harbour view with one bathroom and one parking space will cost over $650,000. A small two bedroom apartment with one car park, one bathroom and a balcony, within walking distance of the water but with no views starts at $400,000.

Apartment living at Mount Maunganui offers that perfect lock up and leave lifestyle for those that plan to divide their time between New Zealand and homes elsewhere. In blocks with on-site management, absentee landlords can hand their property over for full management so that it becomes part of a rental pool. Although the best prices and highest occupancy rates are to be had during the summer, it's still a popular area for weekend breaks in the off-season.

For relocating families looking for a four bedroom family home in a sought-after area of Tauranga close to good schooling, this will cost from $625,000 upwards on a smaller site. Three bedrooms in a similar area are around $575,000. Prices are cheaper the further east you go towards Whakatane for family homes but don't expect the price of second homes near water to be all that much cheaper.

While a house at the beach is the ultimate goal of many New Zealanders, the price of coastal property has risen so rapidly in the past few years that it puts it out of the reach of the majority of them. And even for overseas buyers, the thought of paying $850,000 for a plain and unlovely two-bedroom holiday cottage with basic facilities might make you think again.

The hidden gem of the area though has to be Tauranga's magnificent inner harbour, which curls around in hidden inlets and waterways from Tauranga right up as far as Athentree. Prices drop the further out from Tauranga but the lifestyle is tranquil and very liveable. On the river near the little town of Katikati, $990,000 buys a four bedroom three bathroom house on one acre with its own boat mooring.

A million dollars will buy you not just a home but also an income from the land. Depending on whom you talk to, kiwifruit compared to avocados is a more consistently reliable crop, although it's becoming more difficult to make a decent living as prices have dropped so much. Avocados are a high value industry and production barely seems to keep up with demand. But avocados can be difficult, according to industry insiders, as crop yield can vary significantly year on year. Anyone looking at buying any kind of horticultural business should do their sums very carefully and take the best advice they can. No matter how scientific horticulture has become, it's still a precarious way to make a living as no boffin has yet come up with a way to stop a freak storm wiping out an entire year's income.

The following prices are in New Zealand dollars except where indicated. Exchange rate data calculated January 2006.

Pukehina: A 3 bedroom wooden holiday house beside a tidal estuary with views **Price.** $560,000 US$383,682 £219,603 A$517,751.

Kauri Point: In a great fishing spot, between Katikati and Waihi Beach, a 1012 sq m building plot with harbour and farmland views. **Price:**$285,000.

Katikati: Rustic wooden country *cottage* on 6,432 sq m. 3 bedroom, 1 bathroom. Kitchen garden with fig trees. **Price:**$450,000.

Omanawa: Horse heaven. 1 ha. of flat pasture with 7 sheltered paddocks. A four bedroom nine year old house in mature gardens. Within 30 minutes drive of Tauranga. **Price:** $675,000.

Lake Rotoiti near Rotorua: The views are astounding but it's currently a humble little kiwi *bach* on 1019 sq m of potential. Ideal as a fishing retreat or build your own dream house.**Price:**$600,000.

Te Puna: Large family home in the country on just over 2000 sq m with swimming pool. **Price:**$695,000

Whakatane: A 4 bedroom wooden country cottage amongst mature trees on 1..1 ha, in the countryside. **Price:**$465,000

Ohope Beach: 3 bedroom, 1 bathroom wooden house on 809 sq m near the beach. **Price:** $439,000.

Agents for this area: www. harcourts.co.nz. (Katikati office), www.tepukerealestate. co.nz, www.norrish.co.nz

FLOODING AND SUBSIDENCE

Buyers in coastal areas in the Bay of Plenty should pay particular attention to the information in local searches and ask for an engineers report if necessary for matters relating to flooding and subsidence. In May 2005 a storm, which particularly affected the little settlement of Matata, saw some houses topple off cliffs. Many of the remaining properties were declared unsafe and were subsequently demolished. The parts of Tauranga that suffered similar problems will now have this information recorded on the LIM (Land Information Memorandum) reports held by the local council.

GISBORNE

Largest town: Gisborne.
Area sq km: 15,487. *Population of region:* 44,500 Gisborne: 32,000.
Climate: Average summer temperature 24C. Average winter temperature 14.5C. Sunshine hours: 2180 per annum. Annual rainfall: 1050 mm.
Airport: Gisborne
Attractions and National Parks: East Cape, Mount Hikurangi, Te Urewera National Park, Lake Waikaremoana,

Geography and Climate

The Gisborne region is blessed with mild winters and hot dry summers. In February temperatures can reach the 90s. It's drier than both Auckland and Northland and has a thriving horticultural industry, supplying produce for both local and international consumption. Gisborne has been one of the major grape-growing regions in New Zealand and is particularly noted for its chardonnay.

Gisborne's proximity to the International Date Line meant that as the first city in the world to see the light, it was the place to be during the Millennium celebrations. As news pictures were flashed around the globe, Gisborne led the way, silencing the doom merchants who had predicted the great global meltdown of the world's computer systems. It is in fact the sacred mountain, Mt Hikurangi, 1754 metres, the highest non-volcanic peak in the North Island that is the first place to see the sun.

This is one of the least populated regions in the North Island and because of its isolation, one of the least visited. Going to the region is like stepping back in time.

Even though there are vineyards (known as wineries) that grow chardonnay for the international market it's only really in Gisborne itself that there is much of a café society. If you drive along the Pacific Coast Highway, that links Opotiki to Gisborne along the coast up past Hicks Bay, the area reveals itself as wild, rugged and spiritual. It's as though Donegal on the west coast of Ireland had undergone a makeover and been relocated to the South Pacific.

The coastal route, a distance of 334km, is one of the roads least travelled, yet is one of the most spectacular drives in the country and is the ultimate 'get away from it all destination'. It's an unspoilt wilderness with beautiful bays and beaches, golden sands and surf beaches. Like Northland, Gisborne and the East Cape are areas that reflect a strong Maori influence and that culture is evident throughout the region. The local tribe is Ngati Porou who are a friendly and hospital people. Visitors should be aware that because they don't get that many tourists out there, shyness of locals could be wrongly interpreted as indifference.

On your travels you will pass many ornately carved marae (meeting house), painted Maori churches and hear conversations in the Maori language, *Te Reo*.

The region is home to the tiny settlement that featured in the film *Whale Rider*. There are low-key tourist trips to the area for small booked groups via the tourist office in Gisborne. It's best to check with the local tourist office regarding marae visits as there are a number of protocols to observe which they will advise you on.

Out along the beaches you will see local children riding horses bareback.. Surfers are attracted especially to Wainui Beach, one of the best surfing beaches in the whole country.

Further south is the magnificent Lake Waikaremoana and the Te Urewera National Park is truly one of the last green wilderness areas, with the largest stand of untouched native forest in the North Island. Outdoor activities in the park include horse trekking and white water rafting. The Lake Waikaremoana Track is one of New Zealand's Great Walks. Or how about trout fishing or water skiing on the local rivers..

Homebuyers looking for the great escape from city life will be attracted to the area for its excellent climate and scenery. It's not the kind of place you'd move to if you hankered after a big city lifestyle. While Gisborne does run to a cinema, you wouldn't move here if you craved theatres, galleries and shopping. But if you were looking for a holiday home the region would be a perfect place to escape to.

For a town of its size Gisborne does have a café and restaurant culture and many of the local eateries are near the beach or the harbour. As well as Midway Beach is the local beach the town has a number of parks and outdoor spaces. Within 30 minutes drive of the city centre is an arboretum with extensive woodland plantings and easy walking tracks.

History

Although Northland may lay claim to being the first area to be settled by both Maori and Pakeha, Gisborne and the East Cape were the first places where both actually set foot on dry land. Just as Maori had arrived in their *waka* (canoe) many years before, it was in 1769 that the surgeon's boy Nicholas Young first spotted land from the mast of the *Endeavour*. The peninsula was named Young Nick's Head in his honour but it was at Kaiti Beach near Gisborne where Captain James Cook first stood on New Zealand soil.

Typical Properties for Sale

While the Gisborne region feels remote and can seem as though life is still steeped in the past century, real estate prices are fixed firmly in the 21st century, especially as far as the apartment market is concerned. It's only in the past few years that developers have woken up to the area's potential and there has been any apartment market at all.

Given that the Gisborne and Eastland region has to be one of the cheapest places to buy property in an area that offers such a good climate and lifestyle, it's hard to see why you'd choose an apartment when the same money could buy a house on a large plot of land.

You only have to imagine how long a 509km drive from Auckland or a 534km drive from Wellington would take on a road network without fast motorway connections to see that the downside of the region is its isolation and the fact that it takes so long to get anywhere. For couples and small families, the faster and more convenient option would be to fly and then hire a car as Gisborne is linked by air to both Wellington and Auckland. And unlike many other remote places in the North Island, this one is dry and sunny all year round.

Like most regions of New Zealand there's a fair selection of different styles of property to choose from and the prices are still some of the best in New Zealand. The apartment market is confined to the city centre, bare land for building is still available near good beaches, and there are number of original villa houses which are still unspoilt.

The following prices are in New Zealand dollars except where indicated. Exchange rate data calculated January 2006.

Tolaga Bay: On a flat block of land of 6 ha. minutes from the Tolaga Bay wharf is a site for building your own home. **Price:** $125,000 US$85,664 £49,034 A$115,571.

Tokomaru Bay: Privacy and views: 3 bedrooms, 1 bathroom, a garage and a studio on an elevated 1841 sq m site surrounded by native bush. Views down to the jetty and across the bay. **Price:** $360,000.

Gisborne countryside: A 1930s 3 bedroom house with separate sitting plus dining room on 17 ha. of fully fenced grounds 35 minutes drive from Gisborne. Your own stand of native bush with trout fishing nearby. **Price:** $349,000

Gisborne: A classic 4 bedroom, 1 bathroom 1905 *villa* (a listed historic home where interior alterations are permitted) on 1012 sq m. **Price:** $295,000.

Gisborne: 3 bedroom, 1 bathroom 1930s house with leadlight windows and polished floors on 461 sq m. **Price: $285,000.**

Wainui Beach, Gisborne: A 617 sq m building plot across the road from the beach. A two-storey house would have sea views. **Price: $280,000.**

Gisborne: Apartment prices are not far off those in Tauranga and the Bay of Plenty, which is a lot closer to Auckland. Prices start at $400,000 for one bedroom and rise to a whopping $895,000 for 3 bedrooms and 3 bathrooms in a complex with river views. A 2 bedroom 2 bathroom apartment in the same complex. **Price: $625,000.**

Wainui Beach, Gisborne: 4 bedrooms, 3 bathrooms, study, chef's kitchen and a dining and family room which looks out to a courtyard, in an architecturally designed house on 1205 sq m near one of New Zealand's best surfing beaches. **Price: $860,000.**

Agents for this area: www.ljhooker.com, www.raywhite.com, www.thepropertycentre.co.nz, www.harcourts.co.nz.

HAWKE'S BAY

Largest town: Hastings
Sunshine hours: 2,190 per annum. Annual rainfall: 800mm
Airport: Hawke's Bay – Napier-Hastings.
Attractions and National Parks: Te Mata Peak, Cape Kidnappers, home to the largest and most accessible gannet colony in the world, Art Deco Napier, Lake Tutira Wildlife Refuge, Kaweka Conservation Park.

Geography and Climate

On the east coast, half way down the North Island is the fertile region of Hawke's Bay. The Mediterranean style climate makes it one of New Zealand's warmest and driest places in the country. The Ruahine and Kaweka Ranges are high, forested mountains that flatten out to the Heretaunga Plains where the cities of Napier and Hastings are located. Rivers wend their way from the mountains where they fan out to meet the Pacific Ocean. The cliff-tops of Cape Kidnappers cut a dramatic swathe across the coastal landscape.

Te Mata Peak is 400 metres above sea level and the Maori legend associated with it is that *Te Mata* was a sleeping giant and leader of the Waimarama tribes. A rival tribe from the Heretaunga Plains sent a fair maid to capture his heart. Te Mata proved his devotion by devouring the hills between coast and plain but died in the process. His unfinished work can be seen at a place known as The Gap. His body in repose forms Te Mata Peak.

The climate combined with the unique soil has made the Hawke's Bay area one of the most productive agricultural regions in the country. This was the first region to establish a high quality Farmers Market where artisan producers sell all manner of fresh and organic produce to the consumer. Impromptu picnics can be made up along the way as roadside stalls sell fruit, honey, cheese and chocolate.

As well as orchards and vineyards there are lavender gardens and olive groves that only enhance Hawkes Bay's reputation as New Zealand's premier region for wine and food tourism. There are over 40 wineries to visit.. Craggy Range and Sileni Estates are particularly noted for their wine and food.

There's plenty to do in the area for locals and visitors alike. Hawkes Bay hosts the Art Deco Weekend in Napier, the Horse of the Year, Harvest Hawkes Bay, and the International Mission Estate Concert. The best surf beaches in the region are along the coast from Cape Kidnappers at Ocean Beach and Waimarama Beach.

Matariki – the Maori New Year. *Matariki* is the Maori name for the seven stars or 'seven sisters', the Pleiades. Matariki appears in the eastern sky around the shortest day, towards the middle of June. It marks the start of the Maori New Year.

Matariki's progress across the sky was watched closely as if each star was clearly visible that meant that a bumper harvest was likely. Hastings is the place to be for Matariki where the week's celebrations are rounded off with a night of fireworks.

Tourism, agriculture and wine are the major industries in the region. Napier is a go-ahead little city, which ran the very successful 'Win a Life' promotion that received over 2700 entries from all over the world. The winning family from Britain started a trend with a further 50 families emigrating as a result of the campaign. In 2005 'Win a Dream Job' campaign was launched with the prize as six month's work at a winery.

History

Cape Kidnappers was called in honour of Captain Cook's Tahitian cabin boy on Cook's first voyage in 1769. Local Maori thought they were rescuing him when they tried to kidnap him but he managed to escape and swim back to the ship only after Cook's crew fired upon the canoes.

In 1931 Hawkes Bay was the site of New Zealand's worst earthquake disaster, measuring 7.9 on the Richter scale. The city of Napier and parts of Hastings were flattened. Land literally rose up from out of the sea, some 40 square kilometres of it, such was the strength of the quake. Out of this disaster, in which over 250 people were killed, rose a new city rebuilt in the classic architecture of the time – Spanish Mission, Stripped Classical and Art Deco.

Napier and Havelock North attract city dwellers looking to move somewhere smaller, where the pace of life isn't so frenetic, and where there's a real sense of community. The schools are good so that it's a great area for relocating families. Although the beach at Napier is stony rather than sandy, good beaches with great surf are within a 30-minute drive. Hastings is the main service area for all the surrounding farms, orchards and vineyards.

Typical Properties for Sale

Nearly all the wooden buildings pre 1930, were flattened during the earthquake. In Napier you'll find the antique and curio shops selling the Art Deco accessories needed to complete the look.

The following prices are in New Zealand dollars except where indicated. Exchange rate data calculated January 2006.

Havelock North: The country village of Havelock North is a prosperous and thriving little place with large family homes and an arts community. The area is known for good schools. In an established, leafy area, a 660 sq m flat building site. **Price:** $185,000 US$126,853 £72,603 A$171,225.

Rural Hawke's Bay: 20 minutes drive out of Hastings on a 2.88 ha. elevated site with rural views to the surrounding hills. Power and telephone to the site so that it's all ready to go. **Price:** NZ $190,000.

Waipukura:. In this country town, a 4 bedroom 2 bathroom 2 storey family home built in the 1920s, on a spacious 800 sq m site with new in-ground swimming pool,

2 fireplaces and a double garage. Within walking distance of a country primary school. **Price.** $400,000.

Napier: For those that love Art Deco architecture, a 3 bedroom, 1 bathroom renovated house in a street full of other houses of the period. **Price:** $320,000.

Napier Hill: Up on the hill overlooking the bay, a 3 bedroom, 2 bathroom 1980s house with huge entertaining decks. **Price.** $765,000.

Mahia Peninsula: Across the road from the beach a 3 bedroom, 1 bathroom old style Kiwi *bach*. The site is big enough to subdivide at 1275 sq m allowing not one but two houses. **Price.** $900,000.

Agents for this area: www.harveys.co.nz, www.harcourts.co.nz, www.thepropertycentre.co.nz.

THE LONGEST PLACE NAME IN THE WORLD

Sorry Wales but it's official, there's a much photographed signpost in Mangaorapa, central Hawkes Bay, longer even than the famous Welsh place name: *Llanfairpwllgyngyllgogerychwyrndrobwilliantysiliogogogoch*. The Maori name refers to a famous chief called the Land Eater who was said to have eaten up the land as he walked and the place refers to where *Tamatea Pokaiwhenua* played music to his lover: *Taumatawhakatangihangakoauauotamateaturipukakapikimaungahoronukupokaiwhenuakitanatahu*.

TASMAN COAST (WEST)

TARANAKI

Largest centre: New Plymouth
Area sq km: 7,273. *Population of region:* 102,900. New Plymouth: 49,100
Climate: Average summer temperature: 21.5C. Average winter temperature: 13.5 C.
Sunshine hours: 2,174 per annum. Annual rainfall: 1,436mm
Airport: New Plymouth – regional connections to Auckland and Wellington. *Attractions and National Parks:* Egmont National Park, Mt Taranaki, Whitecliffs Walkway.

Geography and Climate

Taranaki is on the west coast, approximately half way down the North Island. For a small region it packs in a great deal – mountain scenery, a rich pastoral landscape interior along with brilliant surfing beaches.

Mountains create their own microclimate and Mount Taranaki is no exception. In the foothills expect 7000 mm of rain per annum compared to around 1500 mm in coastal New Plymouth. Taranaki has the third highest rainfall and third highest number of wet days in the country. The west coast location does mean that it can blow the odd gale now and again, but to put it all into perspective, it receives over 2000 hours of sunshine per year. Rain combined with the rich volcanic soil creates lush green pasture and Taranaki, like the Waikato has grown rich on the dairying industry.

The perfectly symmetrical cone atop of Mt Taranaki (2518 metres)has ensured that the iconic mountain is one of the world's most photogenic. And it's not hard to see why it doubled for Mount Fuji in the Tom Cruise vehicle, *The Last Samurai*. And as the surfing Hollywood star found out, Taranaki is indeed one of the few places in the world where you can ski and surf in the same day.

In 1959 natural gas and oil reserves were discovered off the Taranaki coast. The largest natural gas field, Maui, which has contributed significantly to the area's economy, is not as extensive as once thought. Smaller gas reserves in the region will ensure that the economy stays buoyant. And Taranaki isn't solely reliant on oil and natural gas as the production of synthetic fuel, dairying as well as manufacturing are all important industries.

Taranaki has one of the lowest crime rates in New Zealand, although the tragic murder of a young German hitchhiker in 2005 temporarily sullied its reputation as a safe and friendly area. But equally, the strong community spirit and co-operation meant that police were able to apprehend the suspect within a matter of weeks. Community support has enabled the many parks and gardens in the region to flourish. One garden in particular, Pukeiti Rhododendron Trust is particularly lovely. 20 kilometres south of New Plymouth at the foot of Mount Taranaki, Pukeiti puts on a dazzling display of azaleas and rhododendrons, a 'must see' for every keen gardener.

New Plymouth is the major urban centre in the region and is particularly noted for its outstanding art gallery and museum, Puke Ariki. A city

A HOME IN

New Zealand

1930s bungalow, Auckland

Art Deco houses, Napier

Bach, Waihi Beach

Pub, Paeroa

'Willowbrook' B&B near Arrowtown

Apartments, Auckland

Edwardian villa, Te Aroha

in amongst a farming community, halfway between Wellington and Auckland is not the most obvious spot for a world-class contemporary art gallery. Although there is a long history of artistic patronage by wealthy individuals in Europe and America, the Govett-Brewster gallery started with just $100,000 from a bequest by long-time resident Monica Brewster. But Monica Brewster did more than merely hand over her money – she included a couple of conditions, stipulating that not only should New Plymouth have its own gallery but that it should be run by an individual of national standing in the arts. The gallery holds an important archive of New Plymouth's most famous son, the artist and kinetic sculptor Len Lye.

History

Taranaki has more than dairying in common with the Waikato. Taranaki's rich pastoral landscape was as much a prize to European settlers as the Waikato was and when local Maori couldn't be coerced into selling, the problems between settlers and Maori erupted in the first of the Land Wars of 1860. But because the Taranaki chiefs were one group that had neither signed the Treaty of Waitangi nor recognised British sovereignty, their actions were treated as rebellion. For ten years Maori engaged in guerrilla warfare.

Typical Properties for Sale

In the year to August 2005, house prices in Taranaki rose over 34% taking the median house price from $165,000 to $225,250 but still under the national median house price of $290,000. Although the population of Taranaki is decreasing, it's still a thriving little province with a stable economy that attracts gardeners, surfers, windsurfers and those with an interest in the visual arts.

The iron-sand surf beaches offer some of the best surfing and windsurfing in the country but these are not the sorts of places to take young families looking to paddle about in rock pools.

Those looking to relocate may be employed in dairying, retail, health, education, property, business or hospitality. For professionals the lower than average house prices means that they can have a good standard of living. And with New Plymouth's thriving arts scene, including playing host to the bi-annual WOMAD (World of Music and Dance) festival, this area has a lot to offer those looking to make New Zealand their home.

Holiday houses are cheaper on this windswept coast as they're unsuitable for young families and many locals prefer golden sands. But the views are still stunning and even though it's a four hour drive to either Auckland or Wellington this could be a great location for artists or writers. And even if you're not creative, one glorious sunset over the Tasman Sea could be enough to release that inner Wordsworth.

The following prices are in New Zealand dollars except where indicated. Exchange rate data calculated January 2006.

New Plymouth: Sympathetically restored 5-bedroom villa with 2 bathrooms, a large living and dining area with a large garden on a 4600 sq m site. **Price:** $499,000. US$342,582 £195,935 A$461,653.

Egmont Village: 4.5ha small-holding with farmhouse that needs updating inside. Established trees and a rose garden. **Price:** NZ $450,000.

Stratford: 1920s 2 storey family house with 4 bedrooms, formal sitting and separate dining room on 1012 sq m. **Price:** $299,000

Coastal Taranaki: A 3 bedroom beachfront bargain with views of coastline, the White Cliffs and Mount Taranaki. **Price:** $500,000.

New Plymouth surrounds: A home plus income (with potential as a bed and breakfast), 6 bedrooms, 2 bathrooms and 2 living rooms in this substantial 2 storey early 1900s villa. **Price:** $340,000.

New Plymouth surrounds: 3.7 ha. of lush gently undulating countryside with views to the mountain. **Price:** $220,000.

New Plymouth: 3 bedroom cottage recently redecorated on a flat site in a quiet street. Walking distance to schools and shops. **Price.** $212,000.

Agents for this area: www.rare.co.nz, www.century21.co.nz., www.harcourts. co.nz, tffirstnational.co.nz

LOWER NORTH ISLAND

MANAWATU AND WANGANUI

Largest centre: Palmerston North.
Area sq km: 22,215 *Population of region:* 226,000 Palmerston North: 72,681; Wanganui, 39,423.
Climate: Average summer temperature: 22.4C. Average winter temperature: 12.4C.
Sunshine hours: 1,723 per annum. Annual rainfall: 963mm
Airports: Wanganui – domestic. Palmerston North – Domestic and international connections to Australia and the Pacific.
Attractions and National Parks: Whanganui National Park, Manawatu Gorge, Tongariro National Park (World Heritage Site) including the active volcanoes Mt. Ruapehu, Mt. Tongariro and Mt Ngauruhoe, Whakapapa, Turoa and Tukino ski fields.

Geography and Climate

Manawatu-Wanganui reaches as far as the west coast of the North Island between New Plymouth to the north and Wellington to the south. Inland to the north it encompasses the area known as the Volcanic Plateau, a mountainous region with a variety of native plant life and some magnificent walking tracks. Here you'll find the Tongariro Northern Circuit Track (known as the Tongariro Crossing), one of New Zealand's great walks.

The Tongariro National Park, given World Heritage status for both natural and cultural values in the 1990s, with three snow-capped active volcanoes and ski fields nearby, sits right in the centre of the North Island. National Park is a four drive from Wellington or Auckland.

The hinterland of the Manawatu is steep and hilly and is an area known for sheep and dairy farming. The Whanganui River, New Zealand's longest navigable river begins its journey high up on Mt. Tongariro as a mere trickle. It flows for 290km (180 miles) flattening out as it reaches the flat alluvial plains, widening and disappearing into the Tasman Sea at Wanganui.

The river is the major centre for recreational activity in the region. With more than 200 rapids, it is nevertheless still graded as suitable for all levels of kayakers. Kayak and canoe are still the best way to experience the peace and tranquillity of the river, although thrill-seekers will enjoy the jet boat trips. The alternative and quieter option is a riverboat cruise.

Wanganui (the city) has retained its European spelling while Whanganui (the river) retains the Maori one. A referendum on whether to change the name of the town to match the river is due in March 2006. But Wanganui is going to have to do more than unify its spelling to alert New Zealanders that live outside the town of its existence. With no real swimming beaches to entice local summer holidaymakers, the region rarely makes it onto the itinerary of international visitors either, who are herded instead, along with all the other tourists, to Rotorua and Queenstown.

This may change though, as the Whanganui River could suddenly find itself reinstated as a must-see destination once Vincent Ward's million dollar epic film, *River Queen*, shot on location on the river is released worldwide.

The Manawatu Gorge is 15 kilometres north east of Palmerston North. It's a spectacular setting for a hike and can be walked in a few hours. The Manawatu region is traditional sheep and dairy farming territory, and as local farmers may tell you, it's the backbone of the economy. And here you'll find a breed of people generally unsentimental about animals and conservative in their politics. This is not the place to ask where the nearest Farmers' Market is located. Traditional farmers don't have a high opinion of ' city folk who play at farming.'

The majority of workers in the Manawatu-Wanganui region are not employed in the rural sector but in manufacturing, the retail trade and health and community services. In Palmerston North, education is a major employer.

Palmerston North, on the banks of the Manawatu River is the largest city in the Manawatu. Palmerston North came about because of its strategic importance as a major crossroads. This may be the reason why it's hard to find any real character or identity to the town. Seventy kilometres to the south east of Wanganui and 145 kilometres north of Wellington, the city of Palmerston North is home to Massey University, the second largest university in New Zealand.

Palmerston North resembles Hamilton to the extent that both were selected as sites for two new universities back in the 1960s. They are both inland, with similar housing, the majority of which lacks any real character. And like Hamilton, when the students are in residence, Palmerston North has a livelier feel than at other times of the year. Palmerston North, though, lack's Hamilton's ethnic diversity, and can seem to outsiders to be rather dull and provincial.

Wanganui was settled much earlier than Palmerston North and has well-preserved buildings with a mixture of villas, bungalows and stucco housing. It's a pretty little town and its location on the river gives it a pleasant ambience. Wanganui Collegiate is one of the top private schools in the country. Wanganui is 190 kilometres from Wellington. And like New Plymouth, Wanganui has a highly regarded gallery, the Sarjeant Gallery specialising in photography. The Whanganui Regional Museum is reputed to be New Zealand's finest provincial museum. And just because locals don't appreciate what they have in their own back yard, this shouldn't deter overseas buyers from relocating to the area. Wanganui-Manawatu and Taranaki are the two cheapest regions to buy property in the North Island.

Away from the two cities, the hinterland of the Manawatu may appeal to those seeking a rural holiday home or commuters to the two main cities, looking for a country lifestyle. Feilding, named as New Zealand's most beautiful little town stands out amongst the nondescript country settlements in the area.

History

Although the river is now used mainly for recreation, from 1886 to the early 20th century it was a major transport hub with commercial steamers connecting Wanganui all the way up Taumaraunui in the central North Island.

In the early 20th century the Whanganui River was billed as the 'Rhine of Maoriland', attracting as many as 12,000 tourists a year both locally and internationally. Steamboats and paddle steamers would ply the Whanganui River, a difficult and sometimes dangerous undertaking. The river was and still is the site of many Maori settlements.

Both Maori and Pakeha settled Wanganui early on. When the New Zealand Company in the 1840s ran out of land in the Wellington region, it was to Wanganui that the settlers went.

The mountains of National Park have no doubt brought great joy to those who have conquered them. But with joy also comes sadness. On Christmas Eve in 1952 the Wellington to Auckland train was derailed by a *lahar* or overflow from the crater lake on Mount Ruapehu. The train was swept off its tracks at Tangiwai, a tiny dot on the map just as it was crossing a bridge. This was New Zealand's worst rail disaster.

Typical Properties for Sale

In the year to August 2005, the median house price in Manawatu-Wanganui rose from $142,00 to $173,00, still well under the national median house price of $290,000. Although the region has had a drop in population of around 1% that's still less than Taranaki's which was 5% in the years from 1986 to 2001.

House buyers don't come to Manawatu and Wanganui for sea and sun. There are great views along the coast from coastal property but the beaches are unappealing to swimmers although they're great for those that like walking. The best outdoor recreation on offer has to be on and around the Whanganui River and in the Tongariro National Park.

Professionals relocating to the region for work will be pleased with the lower than average house prices, giving them the opportunity to buy more land or a bigger house than they would otherwise be able to afford in an area like Auckland or Wellington.

Holiday houses are better value along the Manawatu coast than they are further south in the Nelson region. Because it's under a two-hour drive from Wellington, the Manawatu could provide a second home option for those based in Wellington or as an affordable place to live for artists or writers. Those looking for a mountain hideout should head for the friendly little mountain town, Ohakune. Mountain lodges aren't just for winter sports – the mountain air is perfect for walking in summer and autumn.

The following prices are in New Zealand dollars except where indicated. Exchange rate data calculated January 2006.

Wanganui: River views from this 4 bedroom contemporary town house, with 3 bathrooms, 1 ensuite, double garage on a 547sq m site. **Price: $615,000.** US$422,220 £241,363 A$568,689.

Wanganui: Seafront with unrestricted sea views from Kapati Island to Taranaki. On a clear day you can see as far as the South Island. 4 bedrooms, 2 bathrooms, private beach access. **Price:** NZ $525,000.

Wanganui: A 2 bedroom, 1 bathroom rental investment. **Price: $112,000**

Wanganui surrounds: A 1ha. lifestyle block with 4 bedrooms, 1 bathroom, outside spa room, double garage and brick barbecue. Coastal and rural views. **Price: $395,000.**
Wanganui: 3 bedrooms, 2 bathrooms, balconies, rumpus, study and attic room in this 2 storey house. **Price: $350,000.**

Ohakune: 4 bedrooms, 1 bathroom ski lodge with dining kitchen, working coal range, tank water. Period wooden property made of heart native timber, *matai* floors and *rimu* joinery on 963 sq m. **Price:** $165,000.

Manawatu: A country retreat with bed and breakfast or other work from home possibilities. 6 bedrooms, 2 bathrooms, gas central heating, 2 living, 1 dining room, eat-in kitchen, garage, workshop, mature landscaped grounds with citrus, pip, and stone fruit trees as well as *kowhai* (favourite of nectar feeders such as tui). 3ha. divided into paddocks. **Price:** $450,000.

Coastal Manawatu: 4 bedroom 1 bathroom family beach bach on 800 sq m with rural views. Short stroll to beach. **Price.** $159,000.

Levin: In a country town within commuting distance to Palmerston North, is a 1900s villa with turret. 3 bedrooms, 1 bathroom on 1350 sq m. Needs restoration inside and upgrading. **Price:** $199,000.

Palmerston North: Great rental investment in this university town. 3 bedrooms, 1 bathroom, close to schools and shops. 500 sq m site. **Price:** $189,000.

Palmerston North: In one of the best suburbs, close to the university and in a good school zone, a 4 bedroom, (master with ensuite), 2 bathroom executive 2 storey home, office, rumpus room. English-style garden. Close to park and tennis courts. **Price:** $840,000.

Agents for this area: www.ljhooker.co.nz, www.realenz.net/harveys-palmerstonnorth,www.harcourts.co.nz, tffirstnational.co.nz.

WELLINGTON AND WAIRARAPA

Largest centre: Wellington.
Area sq km: 8,124 *Population of region:* 456,900
Climate: Average summer temperature: 20.3C Average winter temperature: 11.3 C
Sunshine hours: 2053 per annum. Annual rainfall: 1246mm.
Airports: Wellington. Main domestic hub between the North and South Island. Wellington's short runway only allows for short-haul international connections to Australia and the Pacific.
Attractions and National Parks: Kapiti Island Nature Reserve, Karori Wildlife Sanctuary, Waiohine Gorge, Castlepoint, Cape Palliser.

Geography and Climate

Wellington sits on the edge of a beautiful harbour, surrounded by verdant green hills at the southern tip of the North Island. Catch Wellington on a calm day and it is idyllic. But Wellington gets hammered on all sides when it starts to blow. When the gales sweep into the harbour from Cook Strait and the southerly winds blow all the way from Antarctica, it's definitely a case of 'Windy Welly.' There are 61 days per year when the wind gusts over 93 kph.

The design of Wellington's inner city high-rise buildings compound the effects of the wind as a sudden gust in a wind tunnel can, quite literally sweep you off your feet. To thrive in Wellington during bad weather, you'll need to learn the correct way to walk – at a steep angle. And despite that much-trumpeted Kiwi ingenuity, nobody has yet come up with a Wellington-proof umbrella.

New Zealand might be known as the adventure capital of the world but there's a certain white-knuckle ride the capital's cheerleaders forget to mention. Landing at Wellington airport is spectacular. Built on reclaimed land, the airport juts out into the harbour. Crosswinds, down draughts, Wellington has it all, but to the highly skilled pilots who fly this route, it's all in a day's work.

But if your first encounter with Wellington is a slightly wobbly one, the city more than makes up for that shaky start with its compact size and lovely harbour. Formed as a result of the flooding of a large valley and an earthquake, the city sits to one side of the harbour. Wooden houses cling to the steep hillsides and every spare site around the harbour seems to have a house on it. Pressure on space for a growing population meant that greater Wellington spread out into two narrow valleys, the Hutt Valley and Porirua some time ago.

Positioned over an earthquake fault line and with its steep streets, wooden houses and large harbour, Wellington has much in common with San Francisco, although without the damp fog. Catch Wellington on a fine sunny day with a brilliant blue sky and blazing sunshine and there's nowhere quite like it.

The dormitory suburbs outside the city area in the Hutt Valley and Porirua are in contrast to the lively centre, suburban and rather soulless. Lower Hutt, an area once favoured by international embassy staff is a good choice for those looking for houses with decent sized gardens. Lower Hutt's gem is the Dowse Art Gallery. Like the Govett-Brewster in New

Plymouth, the Dowse is the venue for cutting edge contemporary art. On the opposite side of the harbour from the central business are Day's Bay and Eastbourne. Day's Bay was the setting for Katherine Mansfield's finely crafted short story, *At the Bay*. It's a genteel little place and now very expensive to live in. Eastbourne, just around the corner is quiet and dignified and with its pebbly beach and retirees has a lot in common with its English namesake.

The Kapiti Coast, north of Wellington on the western side is becoming an increasingly popular area for commuters although from the northern parts it can take over an hour to get into the city at peak times. Here you will find good swimming beaches as well as little settlements along the way, the most built up of which is Paraparaumu.

Kapiti Island sits just off this coast and is run as a predator free bird sanctuary by the Department of Conservation. Visitors to this offshore haven need to pre-book and on weekends in summer months you'll need to book far ahead.

Cultural attractions though are Wellington's strong drawcard, including Te Papa, The National Museum of New Zealand. The capital is also the home of the NZSO (New Zealand Symphony Orchestra), and the National Archives, which displays the original Treaty of Waitangi.

Wellington, unlike Auckland has a lively downtown area, which is compact enough to be easily navigable on foot, and the city boasts the most comprehensive public transport in the country (yes, even commuter trains). And Wellington has good shopping with two standout stores in particular. Kirkcaldies and Staines (Kirks) is the best department store in the country with excellent customer service. And foodie heaven can be found just off Courtenay Place, in the shape of the gourmet food market, Moore Wilson.

The siting of this store just off the central downtown area means that even non-drivers can shop there too. There are, if you believe the hype, supposed to be more cafes and restaurants per capita than there are in New York and with all things considered, this is a very liveable city.

Wellingtonians are loyal supporters of the arts and theatre in particular. As well as being home to good theatre, Wellington hosts a bi-annual international arts festival.

But when Wellingtonians aren't playing they're getting down to serious work. The largest industries are business and property, then retail, health, community services and then government and defence. Wellington has always been seen as the administrative centre because of its status as the seat of government while Auckland has always been looked upon as the commercial centre.

The Wairarapa, to the north east of Wellington, at the foot of the Tararua Ranges in Maori means 'Glistening Waters.' The area is named after the 800 hectare Lake Wairarapa. The Wairarapa is physically separated from Wellington by the rugged Rimutaka hills. For many years it was ignored by those in the capital but in the past 10 years the Wairarapa has become the place for weekending escapees from the capital who can't seem get enough of either the pretty little country towns or the marvellous Pinot Noir and Sauvignon Blanc grown in the region. Because of its inland location, the Wairarapa has a more benign climate as it escapes the gales that batter Wellington. Martinborough has become the destination for wine tourism in the region. The Toast Martinborough festival held annually is an important event on the social calendar.

The Wairarapa coast has some stunning scenery including Cape Palliser, the southernmost tip of the North Island. It is home to a large breeding colony of fur seals. An hour's drive east from Masterton is Castlepoint where there is a beach suitable for bracing walks.

History

The *Ngati Tara* people first inhabited Wellington. Abel Tasman and Captain Cook both tried to enter the harbour on their respective visits but the winds were so bad on both occasions that they were unable to do so. It was not until 1840 that the eccentric Edward Gibbon Wakefield, through is New Zealand Company, purchased a tract of land in the area, which was originally named Brittania.

In 1865 Wellington because of its central location and harbour were chosen as the capital. The fierce winds of Wellington harbour have seen many a sailing ship founder along its coast. In 1968 the winds were too much even for a modern roll- on, roll-off ferry. The Wahine was dashed against the rocks just outside the harbour in 1968. Over 50 souls perished. Many of the survivors were rescued off Eastbourne beach.

Typical Properties for Sale

The market in Wellington, New Zealand's second largest city, is buoyed by its status as a capital and the fact that land in the city is scarce. It is therefore not all that surprising that median house prices are around $6,000 above the median average, at $296,500. Pressure on land to build on has meant that there has long been an apartment market in Wellington. The areas around Parliament (the Beehive) empty out on weekends as MPs and civil servants go home to their families.

Although Wellington has been better than Auckland at protecting its heritage, sadly, the oldest area of all, Thorndon, (birthplace of Katherine Mansfield), was sliced in two to accommodate a motorway, some years ago.

The country lifestyle on offer in the Wairarapa really does represent that perfect escape to the country but with seemingly fewer of the smellier drawbacks. There seems to be a real respect for heritage out there and old homesteads have been lovingly restored, often at considerable cost. You'll find these homes featured in magazines read by expatriate New Zealanders living in cramped flats and apartments in London, Sydney or New York, who, no doubt, dream of owning one on their return.

It's not out of the question to commute the hour and a half from the Wairarapa to Wellington, especially if you can work from home for part of the time. On the surface this is the archetypal New Zealand farming community, with its white sheep dotted around the hillsides, but conservative Carterton elected the first ever transgender mayor in the 1990s. Georgina Beyer resigned her post to become an MP in 1999.

The following prices are in New Zealand dollars except where indicated. Exchange rate data calculated January 2006.

Wellington: 3 bedroom villa in old established area with a separate cottage as office space. Open plan living with doors that open onto deck. **Price:** $630,000 US$432,315 £247,275 A$582,306.

Wellington: Superior apartment with 3 bedrooms plus en-suite to master, bathroom, gourmet kitchen and terrace that overlooks Oriental Bay. Covered car park. **Price:** $1,150,000.

Wellington: In a top school zone and established area, this substantial 2 storey family home on a site big enough for 2 houses with 4 bedrooms, 2 bathrooms, study, courtyard, secluded, views, double internal access garage. **Price:** $680,000.

Kapiti Coast: Allow an hour to Wellington at peak times from this recently refurbished 100-year-old 4 bedroom, 1 bathroom double bay villa with decks, triple garaging and a studio on a generous site. **Price:** $465,000.

Martinborough: A 3 bedroom weatherboard period homestead with self-contained guest accommodation. Meticulously presented and restored, the house comes with a tennis court, .5ha of established and well-tended gardens, plus another 1.6ha. fenced off into 6 paddocks. Farm sheds, a pond, a courtyard and mountain views. **Price: $650,000.**

Carterton: A 2 bedroom, 1 bathroom country cottage built in 1880 on 2023 sq m with a single garage and garden shed. **Price:** $210,000.

Greytown: 4 bedroom 1 bathroom villa in need of restoration on 1ha. 3 stables and mature trees. **Price.** $370,000.

Dannevirke: In a country district, named for its Danish settlers (the name means Dane's Work), a 4 bedroom 1 bathroom family farmhouse. 12.9 ha. of gentle contouring land with outbuildings. **Price:** $365,000.

Agents for this area: www.realenz.net/propertybrokers-martinborough,www.realenz.net/propertybrokers-greytown

SOUTH ISLAND

UPPER SOUTH ISLAND

MARLBOROUGH

Largest centre: Blenheim.
Area sq km: 12,494. *Population of region:* 42,300. Blenheim: 27,900.
Climate: Average summer temperature: 23C Average winter temperature:
13.3 C
Sunshine hours: 2400 per annum. Annual rainfall: 655mm.
Airport: Blenheim.
Attractions and National Parks: Marlborough Sounds including the Queen
Charlotte Track, 71 kilometres of native forest and The Molesworth Road.

Geography and Climate

Marlborough is the sunniest and driest area of New Zealand and sits at the
northeast tip of the South Island. The Marlborough Sounds: Kenepuru,
Pelorus and Queen Charlotte are a series of forested inlets and bays that
rise steeply from the deep green waters. With over 1500 km (930 miles)
of coastline, the Sounds contain salmon and mussel farms as well as
recreational reserves, over 55 in total. The Queen Charlotte Track is an
easy flat walk through native forest, a beautiful restful place where *tuis*
and *bellbirds* sing and friendly little *fantails* dart between the trees as you
walk by.

Marlborough is an area that was once dotted with woolly Romney sheep
but instead of running stock, many of these slopes have been converted
to grape production. Inland Marlborough is still sheep country, and this
is where Molesworth Station can be found, New Zealand's largest farm at
180,000 hectares. Over high summer, visitors to the region can drive the
Molesworth Road, (it's only open for a few weeks a year) and experience
the New Zealand high country for themselves.

Marlborough is the largest grape-growing and winemaking region in the
country. It's here that you'll find Cloudy Bay, the award-winning Sauvignon
Blanc wine as well as the actual bay where the name comes from.

History

Abel Tasman was the first European to take shelter in the Marlborough Sounds after many months at sea. He stopped at D'Urville Island in 1642. Over 100 years later, Captain Cook made detailed charts of the area. Some 50 years after Cook, French navigator Dumont D'Urville found the narrow strait now known as French Pass. *Te Awaiti* (now known as Picton) was originally a whaling station and in 1827 the first settlers arrived.

The Wairau Plain was the site of a conflict between the new settlers and Maori tribes in 1843. A disputed land deal by the New Zealand Company brought two *Ngati Toa* chiefs, one of whom was the powerful *Te Rauparaha*. An armed party led by Arthur Wakefield, the brother of the governor of New Zealand went to meet them. Ngati Toa met the party in peace but the settlers chose force over diplomacy, which had disastrous consequences as *Te Rangihaeta's* wife was shot.

Ngati Toa demanded *utu* or revenge and 22 of the Pakeha party including Wakefield were killed and the event became known as the Wairau Massacre. In Taumarina, 20km south of Picton, where the massacre took place, is a monument designed by Felix Wakefield, Arthur Wakefield's younger brother.

Typical Properties for Sale

Marlborough is in what's known as the Sunshine Belt, along with the Bay of Plenty and Nelson and in common with these regions, attracts lifestylers, retirees and international migrants. From 1986 to 2001, the population of Marlborough increased by 18.4%.

House price data bundles Marlborough and Nelson as one region, and one in which the market has been volatile over the past five years. A steady but modest increase in house prices was recorded from 2000-2002 but in 2003 median house prices rose a staggering 32.3%. And this was followed by a 25% increase in 2004. Prices have dropped slightly in the year to October 2005 and similar modest falls are expected to year-end. To put these figures into perspective, the median house price now stands at $262,500.

Attracted by the dry warm climate, new residents in Marlborough find that the easy going rural lifestyle enables them to buy a piece of land and become hobby grape or olive growers, or indulge in more relaxing pastimes such as gardening or enjoying vineyard lunches as well as taking advantage of the outdoor lifestyle on offer.

South Island

Legend:
- State Highway
- ⊕ Domestic Airport
- ✈ International Airport
- ---- Ferry Route

Tasman Sea

NELSON
⊕ Nelson
⊕ Blenheim

Cook Strait

MARLBOROUGH

⊕ Westport

Greymouth
⊕ Hokitika

WEST COAST

Christchurch ✈

Banks Peninsula

CANTERBURY

Timaru

Wanaka ⊕
Queenstown ⊕

OTAGO

SOUTHLAND

Dunedin ⊕

Invercargill ⊕

Foveaux Strait

Stewart Island
Oban

Pacific Ocean

In a major centre for wine production, it's not so surprising that the majority of employment vacancies in 2004 were in grape growing or wine making.

The following prices are in New Zealand dollars except where indicated. Exchange rate data calculated January 2006.

Blenheim: Organic olive grove/lifestyle block. 5.5ha. at Cloudy Bay, 10 minutes from Blenheim. Sale includes farm equipment. Flat land with a number of suitable sites for building your dream home. **Price:** $395,000. US$271,022 £155,032 A$364,706.

Blenheim: A category 2 Historic Places Trust listed building (270 sq m) 2 storey family house with 4 bedrooms, 2 bathrooms, modern kitchen, garage and additional covered parking. A 748 sq m site. **Price:** $500,000.

Havelock: Country retreat on 2.62 ha, this 3 bedroom, 1 bathroom house with chef's kitchen. Well-tended garden with olive trees and spring-fed stream. **Price:** $699,000.

Marlborough Sounds: Overlooking Kenepuru Sound, a 4 bedroom, 1 bathroom holiday home with a sleep-out on 1219 sq m bush clad site plus own mooring with access to beach. **Price:** $850,000.

Picton: In the picturesque port, known as the gateway to the South Island, Picton is the place to explore the Sounds. A 3 bedroom, 1 bathroom house built in the 1950s. House on 726 sq m. Open plan dining/kitchen and conservatory. **Price:** $250,000.

Agents for this area: www.harcourts.co.nz, www.realestateblenheim.co.nz, www.realenz.net/firstnational-picton

---

NELSON

Largest centre: Nelson
Area sq km: 10,207. *Population of region:* 87,000 Nelson: 42,900.
*Climate:*Average summer temperature: 22.3C Average winter temperature:12.2 C
Sunshine hours: 2400 per annum. Annual rainfall: 970mm.
Airport: Nelson.
Attractions and National Parks: Abel Tasman National Park, Nelson Lakes, Farewell Spit and Heaphy Track (a NZ Great Walk), Kahurangi National Park.

Geography and Climate

Nelson, to the west of Marlborough at the top of the South Island has a similar climate to the south of France, but without the *mistral*. And unlike neighbouring Marlborough, sunny Nelson doesn't dry out so much in the summer. Nelson is bounded by the Richmond Range to the east with Mt. Richmond (1756 metres) and the Arthur Range to the west. Its tallest peaks are Mt. Arthur (1795 metres) and The Twins (1809 metres).

The Waimea River and the Motueka River are two of the largest rivers in the region, starting high up in the Nelson Lakes area, flowing down lush green river valleys, before widening out on the flat plains and out to sea. Tasman Bay is a wide bay with tidal inlets dotted along the coast from Nelson to Motueka. There are golden sand beaches from Kaiteriteri westwards through the Abel Tasman National Park.

The three national parks in the region offer a variety of scenery and conditions. The Abel Tasman includes the Abel Tasman Coastal Track (a NZ Great Walk). The Kahurangi National Park is a wilderness and contains the Heaphy Track, which because of its westerly position can be a wet walk. The Nelson Lakes includes Lake Rotoiti and Lake Rotoroa and contains mountains high enough for skiing.

History

Maori first came to the region in the 16th century. The first tribe in the region was *Ngati Tumatakokiri* which remained the dominant tribe until the 18th century. In 1642 members of this tribe saw off Tasman and his crew from what was named Murderer's Bay, now known by the more appealing Golden Bay.

Fierce inter-tribal rivalry wiped out most of the Maori population and those that were left put up no resistance by the time the first European settlers arrived in the 1830s. This was as a result of would-be social engineer Edward Gibbon Wakefield and his New Zealand Company. Problems immediately arose over the New Zealand Company's right to the land, which had to be resolved before it could be distributed to the settlers.

Disaster befell the New Zealand Company in 1843 when 22 of Nelson's citizens were massacred at Wairau. A year later the company went bankrupt leaving the settlement with nothing.

The Nelson region has long had a reputation for attracting artists to the area. As well as painters there are potters, ceramicists, sculptors and glass blowers. In the 1970s the Motueka River Valley was home to a number of hippie communes, which co-existed within a mainly agricultural region. The alternative lifestylers living in the community provided a contrast with the orchardists and tobacco growers, like Manawatu farmers, not known for their liberal views.

Although the hippies have mainly all gone and got themselves 'proper' jobs, in their place have come winemakers and those involved in the tourist trade. The Nelson region today is a thriving and lively place with an interesting mix of people. One event in the region that sums up the successful harnessing of creativity and entrepreneurship is the World of Wearable Art Award started in 1987.

Now called the Montana World of Wearable Art Award, the show has got too big for Nelson and been snapped up by Wellington. Many Nelson locals were sad to see the event go, although there is still a WOW gallery in the city.

Despite the high profile of the artists in the region, it is agriculture, forestry and fishing and horticulture that are the mainstays of the economy.

Typical Properties for Sale

Nelson's mixture of great climate, laid back lifestyle and creativity has attracted many new incomers to the region. The city of Nelson is a compact little place with good restaurants and cafes, serving the local wine. The lively art scene means that there is always something going on and the place really does have character and charm. There are excellent schools in the region, including Nelson Girls and Nelson Boys Colleges to keep those families with school age children happy.

Locals like to look after their heritage and Nelson has some fine examples of period buildings that have been carefully restored. From 1986 to 2001, the population of Nelson increased by 22.7%.

As discussed in the section on Marlborough, the two regions are classed as one as far as house price statistics are concerned. The past five years have been characterised by slow growth followed by huge gains with prices dropping back to the year-end. The median house price now stands at $262,500.

Apartment living is still low-key in Nelson as most of its residents live in detached houses. A wide variety of lifestyles are on offer from early 20th century villas, lifestyle blocks out in the country and modern architecturally designed coastal property.

The following prices are in New Zealand dollars except where indicated. Exchange rate data calculated January 2006.

Nelson: 2 bedroom, 1 bathroom 1940s cottage on 455 sq m flat site with garden. Some upgrading required. **Price:** $220,000 US$150,878 £86,319 $203,345.

Nelson: On an elevated site overlooking glorious Nelson Bay, a 2 storey grand old character home (180 sq m) renovated throughout. 3 bedrooms, 2 bathrooms, modern kitchen, double garage on a 1176 sq m site. **Price:** $1,050,000.

Golden Bay: The steep and challenging drive over the tortuous Takaka Hill keeps Golden Bay as an exclusive retreat. 4 bedroom, 1 bathroom beach house. 2 minutes to beach on an easy care site. No sea views but this is reflected in the asking price. **Price:** $400,000.

Wakefield: A country life. 4 bedroom, 1 living, 1 bathroom home on 3 ha.. Swimming pool. French doors opening out to landscaped gardens and mature trees. Double garage. **Price:** $585,000

Coastal Mapua: Estuary and mountain views from this elevated bare site with power, water and phone to the boundaries. 3.42 ha. **Price:** $280,000.

Agents for this area: www.harcourts.co.nz, www.summit.co.nz

CENTRAL SOUTH ISLAND

CHRISTCHURCH & CANTERBURY

Largest city: Christchurch
Area sq km: 45,346. *Population of region:* 520,600. Christchurch: 334,107. Timaru:26,748.
Climate: Average summer temperature. 22.5C Average winter temperature. 11.3C
Sunshine hours: 2035 per annum. Annual rainfall: 635mm
Airports: Christchurch international and domestic terminals.
Attractions and National Parks: Aoraki Mt Cook National Park, Arthur's Pass National Park, Banks Peninsula, Hanmer Springs, Lake Tekapo, Lake Pukaki, whale watching at Kaikoura, Mt. Hutt ski fields, Lake Coleridge.

Geography and Climate

Canterbury has the largest land area in New Zealand and has the second largest population. It borders Marlborough to the north, and Westland to the boundary of the Southern Alps. The Waitaki River forms the southern boundary with Otago. These weather statistics, recorded in Christchurch do not apply to the alpine micro-climates of Arthur's Pass National Park and Aoraki Mt Cook and will vary away from the coast where it will be hotter in the summer and colder in the winter.

North Canterbury includes the coastal district of Kaikoura, which is the location for the highly successful whale watch tours. The deep waters around Kaikoura are a rich feeding ground for all manner of marine life, the biggest of which is the sperm whale. To the west of Kaikoura is the Hurunui in which lies the alpine and thermal village of Hanmer Springs. To the south east of Hanmer Springs is the exciting new wine region of Waipara Valley.

Mid Canterbury includes Waimakariri, just north of Christchurch along the coast and includes the country towns of Rangiora and Kaiapoi. It is known for its fishing, beaches, scenic countryside and fine produce. To the west of Christchurch, jutting out into the Pacific is Banks Peninsula, a pretty but sparsely populated area that includes Canterbury's oldest village, Akaroa. Banks Peninsula is, in marked contrast to the flatness of the Canterbury Plains, the only hilly area in the region. The waters off Banks Peninsula are the place to spot the rare Hector's dolphin.

A large part of Selwyn, extending from the Christchurch border to Arthur's Pass National Park includes high-country lakes and forest park. The surrounding areas are sparsely populated. Ashburton to the south is farming country and includes the popular ski field, Mt. Hutt and extends along the plains to reach the coast.

South Canterbury includes the region's second largest town, Timaru, in the Waimate district and out west is the Mackenzie, home to the glacier-fed blue lakes of Tekapo and Pukaki. And the Mackenzie country is home to New Zealand's tallest and most majestic of mountains, Aoraki Mt Cook (3755m).

North Islanders regard Christchurch as more English than even parts of England. There are the English names on most street corners; the River Avon where visitors can go for a leisurely punt and the building that stands out more than any other in this flattest of cities, the Anglican cathedral. Known rather unimaginatively as the Garden City, Christchurch homeowners take pride in their gardens and the public parks are full of annuals and colour. As Canterbury and the rest of the South Island have distinct seasons, this can come as a shock to Aucklanders not used to seeing bare trees in winter.

There are fine stone buildings in Christchurch, particularly around the university area. As well as living in a city that looks to its English past, Cantabrians, especially those from Christchurch are accused by other New Zealanders of holding on to colonial class-based values. The contrast with Aucklanders couldn't be more marked. In Christchurch where you went to school, matters; in Auckland it's a case of which suburb you live in.

Cantabrians though can get one over Aucklanders when it comes to the public exhibition of the visual arts. Christchurch has a new purpose built art gallery, while the visionless Auckland planners only seem to be able to cope with extending their old one. The Christchurch Art Gallery building is a metal and glass architectural statement and has considerably enhanced the city's reputation as a place to view the best of New Zealand art.

As well as art, Christchurch is known for its scientific links with Antarctica. As the nearest city to the great southern continent, Christchurch was the place where Scott and his ill-fated expedition departed from. Today it is home to the administration headquarters of the NZ, US and Italian Antarctic bases, a unique centre for international scientific co-operation. The International Antarctic Centre is a visitor attraction offering Antarctic education and entertainment, including a simulated 'Antarctic Storm' with a wind chill factor of minus 18.

History

Christchurch's English heritage dates back to 1850 when the Church of England chose it as a place for an ordered settlement and one where the farming land was run by the gentry. And those that were put in charge of the land made a great deal of money from the wool trade. Despite the attempts at social engineering further north by the New Zealand Company, the tone in the rest of the colony had been lowered somewhat. The Church of England was determined that would not happen in Christchurch and they set about building their churches where fine upstanding citizens could worship, instead of pubs where people could go for entertainment.

Banks Peninsula, to the west of Christchurch has an altogether different colonial past. Akaroa, meaning 'Long Harbour' in Maori was the site of the country's first French settlement. In 1838 Jean Langlois, a French whaling captain bought Bank's Peninsula from local Maori and then returned to

France. It took him two years to set up a trading company and by the time the 60 or so French settlers arrived in 1840, Britain had beaten France to it by signing the Treaty of Waitangi. Had they not done so then the history of the settlement of the South Island could have been very different and distinctly Gallic. The settlers were met by a British warship but were allowed to stay in Akaroa. In 1849 they were joined by a large group of British settlers and their land claim was sold to the New Zealand Company. A handful of streets in Akaroa still retain their French names.

Typical Properties for Sale

With a median house price of $259,000 Canterbury and Christchurch have a number of different styles of housing from farming homesteads to inner city apartments. Christchurch is ideal for relocating families with excellent schooling, and large family homes that still have some grounds, unlike their Auckland counterparts, which have succumbed to the blight of in-fill housing at an alarming rate. And with house prices at least 20% cheaper than Auckland's, Christchurch could be the ideal place to move to for those looking to combine the best of city life yet with access to an unspoilt landscape. Skiers will enjoy the ski field at Mt. Hutt, within a two-hour drive of Christchurch. Mount Hutt has the longest ski season in the Southern Hemisphere. And what's more, Christchurch has beaches and harbours all within easy driving distance.

For those looking for the country life, a base around the little country town of Geraldine could be a very good option. One of the nearest settlements to the wondrous Mackenzie Country, Geraldine is now attracting artists as well as remaining a rural town with a strong sense of community.

The following prices are in New Zealand dollars except where indicated. Exchange rate data calculated January 2006.

Hurunui district: 1930s family bungalow with 3 bedrooms, 2 bathrooms and double garage on 1ha. of well-tended grounds in a popular rural area. **Price.** $395,000. US$270,840 £154,977 AS365,269.

Banks Peninsula: 1 bedroom cottage with deck, spa and harbour views. Part of a resort style managed complex. **Price.** $292,000.

Christchurch: In a highly rated residential suburb and zoned for two sought after state schools, this 2 storey home of grand proportions (232 sq m), with 4 bedrooms, 1 bathroom, on 1194 sq m with lawn and garden area. Big enough for a pool or tennis court. **Price.** $895,000.

Ashburton district: *Lifestyle block* of 4163 sq m of gently undulating terrain ready for building. Mountain views. **Price.** $172,000

Mackenzie Country: Distant views to Lake Tekapo. A bit worse for wear but nonetheless authentic 2 bedroom, 1 bathroom holiday house in a landscape of outstanding natural beauty. Keep it or pull it down and build your own dream mountain lodge. **Price.** $250,000.

Agents for this area: www.realenz.net/alpinehouses, www.mcrost.co.nz, www.harcourts.co.nz, www.bayleys.co.nz

WEST COAST

WEST COAST

Largest centre: Greymouth
Area sq km: 23,336. *Population of region:* 30,600. Greymouth: 12,894.
Climate: Average summer temperature: 19.5C. Average winter temperature: 12 C.
Sunshine hours: 1850 per annum. Annual rainfall: 2575mm.
Airport: Hokitika.
Attractions and National Parks: Franz Josef and Fox Glaciers, Paparaoa National Park, Mt Aspiring, Coastal Okarito – home to the Kotuku or White Heron .

Geography and Climate

The West Coast (or Wet Coast, as it is sometimes known) is the long slender strip of coastal land bordering the Tasman Sea, bound by the Southern Alps to the east. The wettest area in the entire country, it's a wild and rugged place with rainforests, glaciers and a rocky and wind-swept coastline. Lonely Planet recently named the drive along the Coast as one of the world's most spectacular – although you'll need a car with efficient windscreen wipers in order to appreciate the view. He may not have been much of a poet but it was Captain Cook who named a certain spot on the West Coast Cape Foulwind after being stuck there offshore for a week.

Whether it's the icy wonders of the Franz Josef and Fox Glaciers or the geological formation of Punakaiki's pancake rocks, the West Coast abounds with unique natural features. The pancake rocks are but one feature of the Paparoa National Park, which contains forests, minerals and a number of different ecosystems.

The West Coast's rivers have important cultural significance to Maori, as this is where *pounamu* (greenstone or jade, which many war clubs were carved from) can be found.

At Okarito are the largest wetlands in New Zealand and it is a major feeding area for birds of which 70 different species have been recorded. The only breeding sanctuary for the rare kotuku, or White Heron is nearby at Whataroa.

History

The towns along the West Coast owe their existence to the gold mining that went on there in the 1800s. The little settlement of Reefton in the 1860s was the first place in the Southern Hemisphere that had a public electricity supply. After gold mining came coal mining and today dairy farming and the timber industry support the economy of the West Coast. The people of the region, 'Coasters' as they're known, are hardy, rugged but very hospitable. Coasters find that the geographical isolation from the rest of the country lets them get on with life. They don't really need to care what the rest of the country thinks of them,

Typical Properties for Sale

The West Coast is one of the four regions in the country to experience a decline in population. From 1986 to 2001, the population of the West Coast decreased by 8.2%.

The statistical sample is too small for specific house price data but it is fair to say that it is here you'll find some of the cheapest property in the country. But in 2005, the Coast saw a reversal in its fortunes with a revival of the coal mining industry. In January 2006 it was announced that the region was to have over 200 new jobs and the port of Greymouth was to be upgraded. 200 jobs might not sound much but for a previously depressed area – this could be just the kind of economic boost that it needs.

The Coast is not the place for city types looking for an easy life and it isn't going to suit families with school age children either. But anyone looking for splendid isolation at a reasonable price, or for those interested in the environment, then this could be the perfect place for a holiday retreat.

Don't buy property here if you're counting on a capital gain. Its unique lifestyle doesn't suit everyone but for those that do make a home here, they'll feel like they have the whole place to themselves.

The following prices are in New Zealand dollars except where indicated. Exchange rate data calculated January 2006.

Karamea: You could buy five properties on the Coast for the same price as one coastal property anywhere else. This 2 bedroom 1 bathroom holiday *bach* sitting in splendid isolation has distant views of river and sea. **Price:**$150,000 US$102,877 £58,830 A$138,661.

Granity: A 3 bedroom cottage on the beach in this tiny little settlement although it runs to a café and allegedly a cinema. **Price:** $195,000

Haast: It might rain frequently but it's a coastal piece of land with unobstructed views of the Tasman Sea. Direct access to the beach with water, power and phone to the boundary on this 959 sq m building plot. **Price:** $195,000.

Agents for this area: www.realenz.net/landmark; www.realenz.net/raywhitemotueka

---

LOWER SOUTH ISLAND

OTAGO

Largest centre: Dunedin.
Area sq km: 31,990. *Population of region:* 195,000. Dunedin: 107,088
Climate: Average summer temperature:18.9C. Average winter temperature:9.9C.
Sunshine hours: 1,590 per annum. Annual rainfall: 809mm
Airports: Dunedin, Queenstown and Wanaka.
Attractions and National Parks: Lake Wanaka, Lake Hawea, Lake Wakatipu, Mt Aspiring National Park, Ski fields at Treble Cone and Cardrona, Otago Peninsula, Royal Albatross Colony.

Geography and Climate

Weather statistics belie the reality of the huge variations in temperature and climate within the region. The above figures really only reflect the climate in Dunedin – not noted for its warmth or dryness. In central Otago summer temperatures can soar as high as the 30s and in winter when the snows fall, they can drop to below freezing in the high country.

Otago includes the lakes area of Queenstown and Wanaka where along with the majestic trio of mountains known as the Remarkables continues to draw visitors to the area from all over the world. The Remarkables offer some of Australasia's best skiing and snowboarding. Unlike much of the landscape of New Zealand there's a familiarity with this combination of lakes and mountains, reminding visitors of similar landscapes such as those found in the Swiss Alps or Italian Lakes area.

Sandwiched between Canterbury and Southland, Otago stretches along the coast as far as Oamaru, then spreads inland past Wanaka to its western boundary with the West Coast. Central Otago includes the picturesque settlements of St Bathans and Alexandria. The flat golden plains of the area known as the Maniototo with their backdrop of the mountains are a favourite subject matter of New Zealand landscape artist Graham Sidney. This is farming country, with dairying, deer and sheep as the principle farming activities.

History

Out in Central Otago you'll find the little settlements, all with Scottish names, such as Sowburn and Wedderburn. Links to the Scottish past are further evident in that, weather permitting the game of curling still takes place. Curling is a kind of bowling on ice. All over the Maniototo and indeed in many other parts of Central Otago, are the remnants of its gold rush past. Some of the old coaching inns and old stone buildings have been restored. But before gold-rush fever hit Otago, sheep farmers who were members of the Free Church of Scotland settled the area.

Otago's main city is Dunedin (the Gaelic name for Edinburgh) and whose settlers were obviously so homesick for Scotland they even put up a statue of Robert Burns.

Home to the University of Otago, Dunedin attracts students (known as 'scarfies' for their trademark neck wear) from all over the country. Known as a party town during term time, the relationship between landlord and student tenant hasn't always been an easy one. Tenants accuse landlords of providing expensive sub-standard accommodation, which they are forced to pay for during the summer holidays while landlords complain that there's no point in providing decent fixtures and fittings as they get trashed.

Those that live in Dunedin maintain that this situation was blown out of proportion by the news media and that the bad landlords have in the main been forced to provide better quality digs. If there is one part of the country though that is entirely unsuited to the wooden villa with their draughty single glazed windows, high ceilings and lack of central heating it is Dunedin. Yet the city is full of them. Dunedin does though have the largest and best-preserved collection of Victorian and Edwardian public buildings in the country.

Typical Properties for Sale

Prices rose between 1999 and 2000 with modest gains. In 2001 prices dropped back but in 2003 and 2004 substantial gains were made. House prices were due to fall by 9% to year-end in 2005. The median house price in Otago is still under the national average at $220,000.

Property buyers in Otago are as diverse as the region itself. Dunedin attracts many owner-occupiers, many of whom have been lured to the region from the North Island. A successful marketing campaign promised jaded Aucklanders cheaper house prices, no traffic jams and easy access to the ski-fields. As well as that there are many investors attracted to Dunedin by the captive student population. Because of the shortage of good property, landlords have done very well out of this market.

Locals prefer the quieter Wanaka area to Queenstown for their holiday homes although prices have shot up there recently too. Wanaka is like Queenstown was 20 years ago and its residents hope it doesn't get as developed. As the Southern Lakes area of Queenstown and Wanaka finally overtook Auckland in January 2006 as the place in the country with the highest median prices, if you want to buy into the area you'd better be quick.

Not surprisingly, the area attracts the well-heeled discreet and not so discreet international buyers. The actor Sam Neill not only lives in the area but also owns a boutique vineyard, Two Paddocks, which produces some very respectable Pinot Noir. Shania Twain is the latest international celebrity to attract media interest by taking the lease on an iconic sheep station. Her initial plans to build a house were rejected but were accepted when the project was scaled back.

Another international buyer whose Queenstown property purchase didn't go unnoticed in his home country of Australia was Bob Carr who was then State Premier of New South Wales. Many of those from New South Wales were angry at the hypocrisy that the person who imposed punitive taxes on property purchasers (and sellers) went and bought a house in a country that still imposes no stamp duty, even for second homes.

Trophy and coastal property is the one area where New Zealanders, particularly indigenous people, are understandably sensitive to the issue of foreign ownership. They see the Overseas Investment Commission, the body that oversees sales of coastal and trophy property over a certain size, as being too soft. But the reality is that much of New Zealand has been in foreign ownership for many years, it's just that the locals don't like to be reminded of it.

The following prices are in New Zealand dollars except where indicated. Exchange rate data calculated January 2006.

Queenstown: A waterfront 2 bedroom 1 bathroom apartment on the shores of Lake Wakatipu, open-plan living and under floor heating. **Price:** $499,000, US$342,582 £195,935, A$461,653.

Wanaka: 4 bedrooms, 2 bathroom, 1 ensuite executive house solidly built of local stone. Office, feature gas fireplace, open-plan kitchen. Elevated decks and views. Double garage. **Price:** $699,000

Queenstown: 3 bedroom, 2 bathroom new luxury apartment with double garage with lake and mountain views. 5 minutes to centre of town. **Price:** $699,000.

Dunedin: 1 bedroom 1 bathroom inner city apartment. 1 carpark. Ideal as an investment. **Price:** $198,000.

Dunedin: 3 bedroom, 1 bathroom character *villa* in South Dunedin with 1 garage on 250 sq m. **Price:** $185,000.

Agents for this area: www.southernlakes.co.nz, www.raywhite.com, www.ljhooker. co.nz, www.salescentre.co.nz

SOUTHLAND

Largest centre: Invercargill.
Area sq km: 34,000 *Population of region:* 93,600. Invercargill: 46,305.
Climate: Average summer temperature: 18.6 C Average winter temperature: 9.5C.
Sunshine hours: 1,600 per annum. Annual rainfall: 1,111mm.
Airport: Invercargill.
Attractions and National Parks: Rakiura National Park (Stewart Island), Catlins Coast.

Geography and Climate

Tucked away in the southernmost tip of the South Island, there's nothing between Southland and the great Southern Ocean. Southland stretches as far south as Stewart Island, across the wind-buffeted Foveaux Strait. It borders the Fiordland National Park to the west and Otago to the east.

Weather certainly isn't Southland's greatest attraction. With the lowest average summer and winter temperatures and the second highest number of rainy days, there are no real redeeming features about the climate. The bad news doesn't stop there if you look at the sunshine hours statistics. And there are the 17 days a year when the wind speed gusts over 93kph.

But this is one of the least populated regions in the country, it's lush and green and here you'll have the opportunity to encounter wildlife along the beautiful empty Catlins Coast or hike in a pristine forest wilderness. And Southland's rivers are a magnet for brown trout enthusiasts. Curio Bay has a petrified forest of kauri and other trees dating back to Jurassic times. Stewart Island is a bush-covered paradise teeming with bird and marine life. The island is one of the best places to see the nocturnal kiwi in its natural habitat. At night they come out to feed on the beaches.

Southland includes the main regional city Invercargill. The city once had a reputation for being drab and dull and even though it has a collection of fine old buildings it is flat and rather featureless. Invercargill is no longer the butt of jokes and the town has come a long way in the past 40 years:- When the Monty Python team were in town back then, one of the group ordered a three-egg omelette and was served an omelette with three fried eggs on top.

Southland's go ahead and publicity-hungry mayor Tim Shadbolt hit on an innovative plan to attract people to the region. Southland has experienced one of the greatest population declines in the country. In the years from 1986 to 2001 the area lost 12.7% of its population.

A tertiary education provider, the Southern Institute of Technology offered its students a fee free education and this attracted students from throughout the country to move to the area and finish their education in the southern most city. And in 2005 Invercargill was the proud host of the premiere of Roger Donaldson's feature film about motorcycle legend Burt Munro, The World's Fastest Indian.

History

The oldest town in New Zealand to be settled by Europeans is also one of its most isolated. 27 kilometres south of Invercargill, the port of Bluff was settled in 1824 as a sealing and whaling station. Invercargill was settled in the 1850s and its Scottish heritage is reflected today in the street names. Stewart Island was named after Willliam Stewart the first officer on a sealing vessel that arrived in 1808. In the 1830s Stewart Island was a thriving logging centre for the island's indigenous *rimu* forest.

Southlanders have a reputation for being reserved perhaps because many of its residents work out in the isolated farming country, but once you get to know them they can be very hospitable. By employee numbers the largest industry is not fishing or farming but manufacturing followed by the retail trade and the health sector.

Fishing is still though a very important industry as well as salmon and mussel farming. The most famous delicacy of all in Southland is the deepwater Bluff oyster. Superior to rock oysters these sweet tasting and juicy little bivalves are celebrated at an annual oyster festival.

Typical Properties for Sale

House price data for the region combines Southland with Otago, which includes the property hotspot of Queenstown. The statistics should therefore be treated with caution. Prices rose between 1999 and 2000 with modest gains. In 2001 prices dropped back but in 2003 and 2004 substantial gains were made. House prices were due to fall by 9% to year-end in 2005. The median house price in Southland (as opposed to Otago) is just $126,500, the cheapest real estate in the country.

Recently there has been a surge of interest in buying investment property in Southland. Students migrating southwards all need somewhere to live and investors have been attracted by the low house prices. Southland is only going to attract a certain type of person because of its geographical isolation – big city lights are a long distance away. Christchurch is 575 kilometres from Invercargill, an eight-hour journey by road.

The region may suit those looking for a fishing lodge, a get away from it all experience or those who want to live a rural lifestyle, far removed from the rat race.

The following prices are in New Zealand dollars except where indicated. Exchange rate data calculated January 2006.

Western Southland: A 3 bedroom, 1 bathroom, hunting lodge and farm on 293 ha. of rolling to medium steep land. Deer fenced. Nearest schools are 20km away and it takes six days for the post to arrive. **Price:** $1,995,000, US$1,368,338, £782,968, A$1,845,024.

Invercargill: Rental investment with tenant keen to stay. 2 bedrooms, 1 bathroom house with double garage. **Price:** $99,000.

Stewart Island: Very basic crib (or fishing retreat) which would be better pulled down. In an idyllic part of this very special island with bush access to swimming beach. Potential for sea views from new house. **Price:** $300,000.

Coastal Southland: 4000 sq m building plot with rural and water views on the way to Slope Point lighthouse. Easy access to the beach. **Price:** $100,000

Rural Southland: 3 bedroom, 1 bathroom family home in rural setting on 1012 sq m. Golf, fishing, hunting and skiing all close by. **Price:** $96,000.

Agents for this area: www.harcourtssouthland.co.nz, www.raywhite.com,

Part III

THE PURCHASING PROCESS

FINANCE

FINDING PROPERTIES FOR SALE

WHAT TYPE OF PROPERTY TO BUY

RENTING A HOME IN NEW ZEALAND

FEES, CONTRACTS & CONVEYANCING

FOREIGN EXCHANGE... HOW TO GET THE MOST FROM YOUR MONEY

Although a dream for many, buying a property in New Zealand can turn into a nightmare if vital parts of the buying process are neglected. Currencies Direct explain how one of the major causes of stress for overseas home buyers is overlooking the importance of the foreign exchange rate.

We would never dream of buying a house in the UK without knowing how much we were going to finally pay. So why when buying in New Zealand is this exactly what many property buyers do? Whether buying a property outright or in instalments, the purchase will no doubt involve changing your hard earned cash into a foreign currency. Unfortunately, no one can predict the exchange rate as many economic and political factors constantly affect the strength of the pound. Exchange rates are constantly moving and there is no guarantee that they will be in your favour when you need your money, so it is vital that you protect yourself against these movements. A lack of proper forward planning could potentially cost you thousands of pounds and reduce your spending power abroad.

The affect the exchange rate can have on the cost of your property can be seen if you look at what happened to the New Zealand dollar during 2005. Sterling against the dollar was as high as 2.7040 and as low as 2.4245. This means that if you were buying a property worth $300,000 it could have cost you as little as £110,946 or as much as £123,736, a difference of almost £13,000.

It is possible to avoid this pitfall by buying and fixing a rate for your currency ahead of time through a forward transaction. This is the Buy now, Pay later option and is ideal if you still have some time to wait before your money is due in New Zealand or if you are waiting for the proceeds from the sale of your UK property. Usually a small deposit will secure you a rate for anywhere up to 2 years in advance and by doing so you will have the security of having the currency you need at a guaranteed cost and knowing exactly how much your new home will cost.

Another option available to you if you have time on your side is a limit order. This is used when you want to achieve a rate that is currently not available. You set the rate that you want and the market is then monitored. As soon as that rate is achieved the currency is purchased for you. You can also set a 'lower' level or 'stop' to protect yourself should the rate drastically fall. This is ideal for when you don't have to make an immediate payment and you have a specific budget available.

If however you need to act swiftly and your capital is readily available then it is most likely that you will use a spot transaction. This is the Buy now, Pay now option where you get the most competitive rate on the day.

It is however fair to admit that many of us do not have the time or sufficient knowledge of these options to be in a position to confidently gauge when the foreign currency rates are at their most favourable, and this is where a foreign exchange specialist can help. As an alternative to your bank, foreign exchange specialists are able to offer you extremely competitive exchange rates, no commission charges and lower transfer fees. This can mean considerable savings on your transfer when compared to using a bank.

It is also very easy to use a foreign exchange specialist. The first thing you will need to do is register with them as a client. This is usually very straightforward and requires you to complete a registration form and provide two forms of identification, usually a copy of your passport and a recent utility bill. Once you are registered you are then able to trade. Your dealer will talk you through the different options that are available to you and help you to decide which one is right for you depending on your timing, circumstances and foreign currency needs. Once you have decided which option is best for you and agreed a rate you will then need to send your money. With clearance times at each end some companies can complete the transfer for you in as little as a week.

Even once you have bought your new home in New Zealand you need to make sure that you don't forget about foreign exchange. It is highly likely that you will need to make regular transfers from the UK whether for mortgage payments, maintenance expenditure or transferring pensions or salaries, and using a reputable foreign exchange specialist can make sure that you get more of your money each time, even on small amounts. This is because unlike your bank they will offer you competitive exchange rates on smaller amounts, no commission charges and often free transfers.

Currencies Direct is a leading commercial foreign exchange company; offering superior rates of exchange and a personalised service they meet the needs of thousands of private and corporate clients every year.

With offices in the UK, Spain, Australia, South Africa and India Currencies Direct is always on hand to help you. For more information about their services, please contact one of their dealers who will be happy to discuss your currency requirements with you.

UK Head Office:
☎ 0845 389 3000
E-mail: info@currenciesdirect.com
Web: www.currenciesdirect.com.

FINANCE

CHAPTER SUMMARY

- Banks. For such a small population, banking in New Zealand is a fiercely competitive business with a number of banks in the market.
  - Some banks target those intending to move to New Zealand by assisting them in opening accounts before they get there.
  - You cannot withdraw any money until you get to New Zealand and have presented yourself with your passport to a local bank officer.
  - Not all types of accounts are available to non-residents.
  - Credit card applicants who are non-residents generally need to hold some other investment account with the bank.
- **Transferring funds.** Predicting which way the exchange rate will go is best left to the professionals.
- **Mortgages.** In 2005 New Zealand lenders began offering 100% mortgages for the first time.
  - 30 year loans are not uncommon particularly in areas where property prices are high such as Auckland or Queenstown.
  - Many New Zealanders fix their mortgage rate to avoid the high floating rates.
- **Economy.** New Zealand is a nation of homeowners where money is tied up in property rather than in other forms of savings.
- **Unemployment.** New Zealand has the lowest rate of unemployment in the developed world, lower even than South Korea's.
- **Taxes.** There is no Stamp Duty payable on house purchases.
  - There is no Capital Gains tax.
  - Those that are resident for tax purposes in New Zealand

pay tax on all their income as there is no tax free personal
allowance.
O Only the self-employed pay an ACC levy
O **Insurance.** Third party car insurance is not compulsory
because of the no fault Accident Compensation scheme.
O It is the car and not the driver that is insured in New
Zealand.
O Insurance is not as expensive compared with the UK but
the cover may not be as generous either.

BANKING

The image that the New Zealand high street bank likes to convey is that
of the friendly local branch, full of cheery staff, willing to lend a sympa-
thetic ear when a customer comes in looking for a loan. But the reality is,
that offshore interests own most of the so-called New Zealand banks – the
Commonwealth Bank of Australia owns ASB, the ANZ now owns the
National Bank and the BNZ is owned by the National Bank of Australia.
Kiwibank and the TSB are about the only two banks that remain in local
hands.

Given the small size of the market, banking in New Zealand is a fiercely
competitive business. And while you might get a friendly reception from
your neighbourhood bank branch when you arrive in New Zealand,
the local branch is but one small cog in a very large enterprise and
personal banking has largely given way to impersonal banking. Now that
anonymous bank officials control the purse strings centrally, it scarcely
matters anymore, for personal customers at any rate, which branch holds
your account. All banks offer telephone and internet banking which will
enable you to operate your account, wherever you decide to live in New
Zealand.

Opening an Account from Abroad

Being part of a bigger, international banking network has its advantages,
particularly when you want to open an account from abroad. High street
banks have realised that migrants are a potentially lucrative sector of the
personal banking market, particularly if they are bringing capital into New
Zealand. Now there are whole departments set up specifically to assist the
banking needs of new migrants. The ASB, through the Commonwealth

Bank of Australia has an office in London, which allows those moving to New Zealand (as well as Australia) to open accounts before they leave.

But whether you open an account through an overseas office or via a high street bank's website, whilst you can deposit money, you cannot withdraw any until you get to New Zealand and your passport and other original documents have been verified in person by a bank official of the ASB.

While most of the high street banks will open accounts for non-residents, not all of them offer a full range of accounts. Check the banking websites for more details. The National Bank seems less interested than the other main banks in promoting banking services to non-residents, stating on its website that customers need to be resident for more than six months to open an account.

Bank Charges. Like banks everywhere, New Zealand banks charge you for holding on to your money; whether that is by imposing fees for processing cheques, using an ATM belonging to another bank or running your accounts. You can reduce your transaction charges by maintaining a minimum balance in your account. Don't overdraw your account without an authorised overdraft facility as you will incur hefty fees. There is no system of cheque guarantee cards either, and if you write a cheque without having sufficient funds in your account, it will not be honoured.

Resident and Non-resident Accounts

Banks need to know if you are either resident or non-resident for New Zealand tax purposes so that they can determine whether or not they are required to deduct Non-Resident Withholding Tax (NRWT) from the interest credited to your account. The rate of withholding tax depends on which country you are considered as tax resident. Banks require their customers to complete a Non-Resident Declaration to confirm their status. Note that the criteria for residency for tax purposes is unrelated to your immigration status.

Credit Cards

Non-residents can apply for a credit card but banks generally prefer the applicant to hold some other account, preferably an investment account with them. Credit card limits, particularly for new customers, are set at a much lower level than the dizzying amounts of credit on offer to long-term credit card customers in the UK. It can be no bad thing to have this automatic curb on spending. But if you were planning a shopping spree on holiday outside New Zealand, the local card won't have anything like the buying power that your UK one does.

Bank Contact Details

ASB: www.asb.co.nz.

ASB London Representative Office: Commonwealth Bank of Australia, Financial and Migrant Information Service, Senator House, 85 Queen Victoria Street, London EC4V 4HA;☎ 020-7710 3990; fax 020-7710 3990; e-mail londonmbs@cba.com.au; www.migrantbanking.co.uk.

ANZ: www.anz.co.nz.

BNZ: www.bnz.co.nz.

National Bank: www.nationalbank.co.nz.

Westpac: www.westpac.co.nz.

TSB Bank: (formerly the Taranaki Savings Bank) www.tsb.co.nz.

Kiwibank: www.kiwibank.co.uk.

Bankdirect: (the direct banking arm of ASB) www.bankdirect.co.nz.

Superbank: (direct banking promoted through supermarkets). www.superbank.co.nz.

The Economy

At the end of 2005, the Governor of the Reserve Bank of New Zealand, Dr Alan Bollard warned that New Zealand had a current account deficit of 8 per cent, one of the worst rates in the OECD. Not since 1986 has this deficit been so high. New Zealand, he implied, is a nation of profligate spenders. When the weekly pay cheque comes in, instead of depositing a proportion of that money into a 'rainy day' account or long-term savings plan, the Governor would have us believe that this nation of fun-lovers are off down to the shops for a plasma screen television, or booking their next holiday to Bora Bora. And now New Zealanders are officially spending 12 per cent more than they earn.

The truth is that there are a great many more New Zealanders borrowing to pay for unexciting but essential maintenance for their houses and are not all swanning off around the South Seas on holiday. Owning their own home is still a dream of the majority of New Zealanders, who would rather control their own financial destiny by buying property than pay a commission to a fund manager or share broker. There are many who still believe, rightly or wrongly, that property has out performed the share market in recent years. Problems start to occur though when the investment is tied up solely in the main home and there are no spare funds left to repair or maintain it.

It is hardly surprising that New Zealand is a nation of spenders, when you consider that the average annual salary is only £13,500, compared with the UK's £21,900. But it's not fair to blame the consumer when there are no tax efficient incentives to save, apart from buying a second property to rent out. Over three quarters of New Zealanders are employed by very small businesses, with ten employees or less, which do not provide any contribution to a superannuation or pension scheme. Even if an employee does pay into a private superannuation scheme, unlike the UK, there is no tax advantage in them doing so.

As well as admonishing consumers for their spending, the Governor recently had a go at the banks, which, he says, are far too ready to lend money which has helped fuel the boom in house prices. And as house prices have risen, New Zealanders have started to feel richer and there are some who have begun to unlock the capital in their major asset – borrowing off the house to buy cars, go on expensive holidays as well as pay to fix the roof.

Of course, this 'spend rather than save' mentality is by no means unique to New Zealand and is in part due to the change in attitudes of baby-boomers who seem determined to spend their kids inheritance while they're still fit enough to enjoy it. But New Zealand, unlike other OECD countries, has a very tight domestic economy which if put together with a very poor savings record, means that the outlook for the spendthrifts is not so good.

And as the Governor and many others believe, if the banks continue to lend at the rate they have been, sooner or later, as the interest rate rise starts to bite, some vulnerable householders, who are already deeply in debt, may no longer be able to service their mortgage. The banks have, predictably, hit back at the Governor's comments, saying that they are merely responding to customer demand. Any attempt at curbing borrowing or spending through government intervention will be a deeply unpopular move.

Over-regulation can have disastrous, unforeseen consequences and the banks, consumers and the business community would vigorously oppose what they see as meddling interference. The government has to be very careful in what it does, as with only the slimmest of majorities, Labour knows that the moment they show any hint of fiscal weakness , the opposition will be ready to pounce.

Although Alan Bollard is right to be concerned about the lack of savings in the economy, the negative picture he paints is rather inaccurate as overall there has been steady economic growth in New Zealand over the past five years. And the fact that New Zealand's unemployment rate is the lowest in the developed world at 3.4 per cent is remarkable. In September 2005 unemployment stood at its lowest level in 23 years.

There are some economists in the private sector who believe that the Governor is trying to micro-manage the economy in the short-term and lacks the vision needed to build a strong economy for the future. There has been debate in the media over the effectiveness of his policies. Critics have argued that that the interest rate rises have missed their target by failing to dent consumers' enthusiasm for spending and that businesses are suffering. Businesses that have to borrow to expand are forced to pay more for their money and the high dollar is denting the export sector. The flip side of all this is that with some of the highest interest rates in the OECD, New Zealand is a good country to invest savings. It will be interesting to see what happens to consumer spending when borrowers come to the end of their fixed-term mortgage deals.

Outlook. A surge in imports in November 2005 is likely to push the trade imbalance higher than economists had predicted, which could mean a trade deficit of as much as 10 per cent of gross domestic product. This could lead to a drop in the New Zealand dollar and some experts predict that the dollar could fall to 57USc by the end of 2006. If the predictions are right then there should be a flow on effect against the pound and the Australian dollar.

Interest Rate Rises

In 1999 the official cash rate (OCR) stood at 4.5%. It has been raised eight times since the start of 2004 but because the majority of New Zealanders have fixed rate rather than floating mortgages, the impact on borrowers took a while to take effect. In November 2005 the OCR stood at 7%. Banks were quick to follow suit and raise interest rates accordingly. Alan Bollard's Christmas present to the nation was to raise the official cash rate to 7.25%, in December 2005, making it the highest in the industrialised world.

To check the best interest rates on offer for borrowers and savers, go to:

www.interest.co.nz. In January 2006 their cheapest advertised floating mortgage rate was 8.7% with the Southern Cross Building Society, closely followed by Kiwibank at 9%. Note that Kiwibank is not available through intermediaries. The Heretaunga Building Society was offering the lowest rate on two year fixed mortgages at 7.75%, followed by Wizard and at 7.75%. The best rate on five year fixed mortgages was Bank Direct at 7.8%.

UK MORTGAGES

Buying a second home in New Zealand could see you taking out a second mortgage on your UK property as a convenient way of financing the purchase. The amount you will be able to borrow depends on your fulfilling the bank's usual lending criteria and the amount of equity you have available in your house.

NEW ZEALAND MORTGAGES

Despite Dr Bollard's dire predictions, while there are so many banks and financial institutions in the market, finding someone to offer you a mortgage won't be difficult.

But with some of the highest interest rates in the OECD, if you are immigrating to New Zealand and need a mortgage it would be best to do what most borrowers do and fix the rate. It is a sign of the times too that in 2005, New Zealanders saw the introduction of the 100 per cent mortgage, something that the Governor would probably like to do away with.

Any direct intervention in the banking and mortgage industry would only backfire and is in fact at odds with the official government policy as prior to the election Labour were keen to promote a scheme to enable first-time home buyers to get on to the property ladder. Those with 100 per cent mortgages are generally first-time homebuyers who may have been paying off a hefty student loan. These are precisely the kind of people New Zealand cannot afford to lose to Australia or the UK any more. If there was any hint that they would now be denied that opportunity to buy a house, they would be off overseas in a flash.

In 2005 New Zealanders were taking out loans for longer terms and in some areas such as Auckland or Queenstown 30-year loans are becoming commonplace. The Retirement Commission has spoken out against this trend, warning borrowers that paying off a loan over the shortest possible term, not the longest will help them save money in the end.

Types of Mortgage

These are just some of the more popular types of mortgages on offer in New Zealand:

Repayment Mortgage. The most straightforward of all the loans on offer. Initially the repayment pays off the interest but towards the end of the loan, the principal, (the original amount of the loan) is paid off. Borrowers see their mortgage debt decrease over time.

A Home Loan, Savings and Transaction Account. This type of loan offers a safety net, which ensures that the loan is paid off within the time that the borrower specifies. The best way to use such an account is to have any salary and other income credited into the account. It also allows borrowers to redraw any additional amounts they have paid in over and above the repayment schedule.

Revolving Credit. Although the theory behind this type of account is that it gives the borrower greater financial freedom, it is only suitable for the fiscally responsible who are not going to over exploit their credit facility.

Fixed Interest Rate. With a fixed rate you know the exact amounts that your repayments will be and it is worth fixing if you believe that there will be upward pressure on interest rates.

Variable Rate. The advantage of a variable rate is that borrowers are not penalised should they wish to pay back lump sums. Some borrowers choose to fix the bulk of their loan and put a smaller amount on a variable rate so that if they do have any extra cash they can make lump sum payments without being penalised.

Interest Only. This type of loan is only suitable for those that know they are going to be paying off the principal of the loan from time to time.

IMPORTING CURRENCY

Even though the money is coming via the UK, you will still need to convert it to New Zealand dollars to pay for the property in local currency and you could lose out when you exchange pounds for dollars if the dollar is still at a high level. When you eventually come to sell the property and have to convert dollars back into sterling you will once again be vulnerable to any change in the exchange rate.

There are a number of different ways to import currency and transfer funds and these are listed below. Bringing in large amounts of cash is not one of them. If you bring in more than NZ$10,000 in cash with you (around £6,000) you are required to declare it in a Border Cash Report to New Zealand Customs. Anyone with excessive amounts of cash on them will arouse their interest and could be subject to lengthy investigation. The assumption will always be that it is being used for criminal purposes. Given that security measures have been tightened considerably in all countries around the world since 9/11, it's not worth taking the risk just to avoid commission charges.

Electronic CHAPS Payment. The CHAPS system is an electronic inter-bank transfer, which the banks claim, arrives as cleared funds on the same day if it is sent from the UK.

Bankers Automated Clearing System (BACS). Transferring funds via BACS takes 3-4 working days. Internet transfers are usually sent this way so allow at least four days for funds to clear.

Cheque. Remitting funds to New Zealand via cheque is only recommended if none of the other alternatives are possible as cheques can take weeks to clear.

Remitting Large Sums. This can be done either by opening a foreign currency account with a New Zealand bank, keeping the bulk of the funds in either pounds or US or Australian dollars while waiting for the best rate of exchange, or you can use a specialist currency trading company such as the one listed below.

Five years ago some lucky migrants were getting as much as $3.30 for the pound. Those days are long gone and since then the dollar has remained strong against all the major currencies such as the pound and the US dollar. While there are underlying reasons for the current strength of the New Zealand dollar, trying to predict how low it will go is best left to professional currency traders. Financially savvy consumers could track the dollar for themselves and have the money in an overseas transaction account and elect to move their money when the rate hits a certain level.

A specialised company such as *Currencies Direct* (51 Moorgate, London

EC2R 6BH; ☎ 0845-389 3000; fax 020-7419 7753; www.currenciesdirect. com) can help in a number of ways, by offering better exchange rates than banks, without charging commission, and giving you the possibility of 'forward buying' – agreeing on the rate that you will pay at a fixed date in the future – or with a limit order – waiting until the rate you want is reached. For those who prefer to know exactly how much money they have available for their property purchase, forward buying is the best solution, since you no longer have to worry about the pound against the New Zealand dollar working to your detriment. Payments can be made in one lump sum or on a regular basis. It is usual when building new property to pay in instalments.

There is a further possibility, which is to use the services of a law firm in the UK to transfer the money. They can hold the money for you until the exact time that you need it; they will use the services of a currency dealer themselves.

OFFSHORE ACCOUNTS

You can operate your offshore bank account via the internet. Whether or not offshore banking is tax efficient will depend on where you are tax resident. EU expats are likely, under the European Savings Directive to be subject to an automatic withholding tax.

TRUSTS

The most relevant form of trust for home buyers in New Zealand is the most common form – the family trust. You do not have to have substantial assets to set up a family trust, although there are costs as well as administration charges involved in both the setting up and running of a trust.

The purpose of a trust is simple – a person or an organisation agrees to hold your assets, and because you give away your assets to the trust it is then treated for tax purposes as though it is not your money. But trusts cannot be set up solely as a way of minimising your tax liabilities – there must be other legitimate reasons for doing so, whether that is as a way of protecting your family home in case your business fails, to set up a fund to pay for your children's education, to ensure that a family asset or business remains in the family, or as a way of ensuring that children receive their inheritance.

The latter case is particularly relevant in the light of there being so many more blended families. Assets held in a family trust cannot be classified as relationship property and is therefore not subject to division in the unfortunate case of a separation or divorce. The trust must, though, have been set up long before the relationship started to founder, as otherwise a good matrimonial property lawyer could try to prove that the trust was set up purely to exclude the new partner.

By setting up a family trust you own fewer assets in your own name. But the advantage is that even though the trust owns the assets, you still have control over them, provided this is written up in the in the deeds. For example, if your house is sold to the trust, you will most likely still live in it, even though you do not own it.

How Trusts are Taxed

The tax advantages of setting up a trust applies particularly to top rate tax-payers who are taxed at 39 cents for every dollar they earn over $60,000. The income from a trust which is not distributed to beneficiaries is taxed at a lower rate, 33 cents in the dollar.

Trustees can choose to pass on income to beneficiaries who are over the age of sixteen. If the beneficiary has little or no other income then they will be taxed at 19.5 cents in the dollar. In other words, this represents a legitimate form of income splitting. One caveat to all this is that wages and salaries cannot be put through a trust in this way.

The minor beneficiary tax rule is where distributions to minors, (anyone under the age of sixteen), is regarded as trustees income and therefore will be taxed at the flat rate of 33%.

Asset Gifting. There are tax advantages of gifting away the assets that the trust owes you. In New Zealand you are allowed to gift up to $27,000 per year. For a couple the allowance is $54,000 per annum.

TAX IN NEW ZEALAND

The received wisdom is that New Zealand has high taxes but international comparisons prove otherwise. Although you don't have to earn all that much to be put into the top rate tax bracket, at least high income earners are not further penalised as they are in Australia where anyone earning over A$52,000 pays 42 cents in the dollar and anyone earning over A$62,500 pays 47 cents. And there appear to be fewer of the 'stealth' taxes than in the

UK. The Goods and Services Tax (GST) is 12.5%, and is less than VAT and unlike Australia, there nor are no compulsory payments for health insurance deducted from the pay packet either. However, levying GST on all goods unfairly penalises the poor. The excuse that it would too difficult to manage any exemptions is rather a thin one especially as the UK is able to exempt children's clothing and certain foods.

However, unlike the UK and Australia, wage earners are taxed on all their income. There is no personal allowance so that those on low incomes pay little or no tax. As you can see from the tax rates below, you don't have to earn all that much to qualify as a top rate tax payer.

2006 INCOME TAX RATES	
Up to $38,000:	19.5 cents in every dollar
$38,001 to $60,000:	33 cents in every dollar
$60,001 or above:	39 cents in every dollar.

Social Security Contributions. While you might not get a tax holiday on low earnings, employees pay no additional social security payment either. The self-employed must pay a levy to fund the no faults Accident Compensation scheme (ACC). Income from the management or operation of a business is considered in the calculation of the ACC levy. For those that work full-time (more than 30 hours per week) the minimum amount of earnings on which you pay ACC levies is $16, 640. The maximum amount of earnings on which you pay ACC levies is $88,728.

The ACC total levy for the year 1 April to 31 March 2005 for the minimum amount of earnings of $16,640 was $340.53. You can contact ACC directly: at the ACC Business Service Centre, PO Box 795, Wellington; ☎ 0508-4 26837; fax 0800-222 003; e-mail business@acc. co.nz; www.acc.co.nz.

Access to a retirement pension is automatic for New Zealand citizens and residents, unlike the British system, which relies on you having a full contribution record. However those with pensions obtained in other countries need to see the information below:

State Pension Provision for Those with Overseas Pensions. While anyone that has no pension provision and retires in New Zealand will be looked after by the state, this is not the case if you have worked overseas and have accrued money in either a private pension scheme or a compulsory state one. Under current law you could find that your pension entitlement is reduced or non-existent. What is more, the law makes no distinction between taxpayer-funded schemes such as the one in New Zealand and compulsory contributory schemes such as those in Britain, Ireland, Holland, Canada and the US.

While many members of the baby-boomer generation have no intention of relying on the state to provide them with an income in retirement, for those that have worked in New Zealand and paid taxes the current legislation seems very unfair. And the direct-deduction policy has meant that a number of countries, including the USA, and some countries in Europe are refusing to negotiate social security agreements with New Zealand over the issue. The Minister of Social Development has said that the issue is under review and would be re-examined after the October 2005 election.

Obtaining an IRD Number. All those eligible to pay tax in New Zealand are allocated an IRD number. You will need an IRD number for each child you are claiming family assistance for. You can apply for an IRD number in person at any Inland Revenue Department office or download the form over the internet and print it out. As documented proof of your identity, such as a certified copy of your birth certificate or passport has to be provided with the application form it cannot be emailed but must be sent to your local IRD office.

Calculation of Overseas Income. Anyone that receives income from overseas has to calculate the value of this income in New Zealand dollars. The IRD issues currency conversion tables, which enable you to calculate the exchange rate on the day you received your income.

Allowances Available through the Tax System. The Inland Revenue Department website has a fuller explanation of the various tax breaks available which are designed to ease the tax burden on families with dependent children. These include:

Family Assistance – which targets families with dependent children under 18. Note that there is a residency requirement to qualify. Family support is the main component of family assistance and is a payment made to low and middle-income families for each dependent child 18 and under.

Child Tax Credit – This is a payment for each dependent child 18 years or younger if the applicant does not receive any other government assistance.

Family Tax Credit – This targets low-income families who earn up to $18,368 per year. To qualify for this payment at least one parent must be working.

Parental Tax Credit – this is a payment paid eight weeks after your baby is born. Parents can apply within the first three months after the baby is born. This is paid either in weekly or fortnightly instalments or as a lump sum.

Paid Parental Leave – Parents are entitled to paid parental leave to care for either a newborn child or an adopted child under six for up to 13 weeks.

IRD CONTACT INFORMATION:
Calling within New Zealand: 0800-227 774
Calling from abroad: 64 -4-801 9973
Postal Address for Auckland and Northland: IRD, PO Box 1454, Hamilton
Rest of North Island: IRD, PO Box 39090, Wellington
South Island: PO Box 3752, Christchurch
www.ird.govt.nz.

MOVING TO NEW ZEALAND

UK Residents. Employees should ensure that they receive their P45 from their employer. Contact your local office of HM Revenue and Customs (formerly Inland Revenue) and notify them that you are leaving the UK. If you are leaving part way through a tax year, you may be due a refund so that it is important to fill out a tax return in order to sort this out.

You should obtain leaflet IR138 and this will advise you whether or not you need to fill out a P85 form. You become non-resident if you leave the UK permanently or for three years or more to work abroad full-time. There are a number of other criteria, which determines whether or not you will be resident for tax purposes in the UK. Over a period of four years your visits to the UK should not exceed an average of 91 days or more a tax year, not counting the day of arrival and departure. As it can be difficult to know whether or not you will stay in New Zealand before you've left the UK, you should discuss your tax affairs with an accountant or financial advisor first, particularly if you are self-employed or have income from other sources.

New Zealand has a double taxation agreement with the UK so that any tax paid in one country is offset by tax paid in another. But tax-free investments in the UK such as TESSA's, ISA's and offshore accounts are liable for tax in New Zealand and your personal allowance received in the UK is not recognised in New Zealand either. To check your tax liability contact the centre for non-residents:

The Centre for Non-Residents (CNR); St. John's House, Merton Road, Bootle, Merseyside L69 9BB; ☎ 0151-472 6196; fax 0151-472 6392; www.inlandrevenue.gov.uk/cnr.

US Citizens. US citizens and resident aliens are expected to file an annual tax return. They are liable for US taxes on worldwide income until they become permanent residents of another country. If you earn less than the threshold for paying tax you do not need to file a tax return. For 2005 the amount was $8200 for a single person. Other rates apply for married persons, pensioners and heads of households.

The USA has a double taxation agreement with New Zealand so that you should not end up paying tax twice. The criteria for residency are: either you have been a resident of New Zealand for a full tax year, which in the case of the USA is the same as the calendar year, or you must have been physically present in New Zealand for 330 days during a period of twelve months.

You can apply for a 'Foreign Earned Income Exclusion', which means that US citizens do not pay US taxes on the first $80,000 of money earned abroad. If you earn in excess of this limit taxes paid on income in New Zealand can be used to reduce your US tax liability.

The US Internal Revenue Service (IRS) has an extremely comprehensive and clearly written booklet called Tax Guide for US Citizens and Resident Aliens Abroad, Publication 54. It can be downloaded from the internet at www.irs.gov.

Package 1040-7 for Overseas Filers, which contains forms and instructions including Publication 54 can be obtained from U.S Embassies and consulates during the filing period (January to June). For answers to technical or account questions, you can write to: Internal Revenue Service, International Section, P.O. Box 920, Bensalem, PA 19020-8518 USA.

Overseas taxpayers can call the US for help at 215-516-2000. US citizens in New Zealand can contact:

United States Consulate General, Level 3 Citibank Centre, 23 Customs Street East, Private Bag 92022 Auckland; ☎ 09-303 2774.

Other Taxes

The good news is that currently there is no stamp duty for property purchases nor is there any capital gains tax. However, if the property is not a main residence, any gains made will be taxed as income.

Goods and Services Tax (GST). GST is not charged on the sale and purchase of residential property, unless the property is used by the vendor as part of a business. A GST exemption applies to the split use of a property which would apply if you were buying a commercial building with both commercial and residential tenants. While GST would be levied against the commercial part of the building, the residential part would be exempt.

If a purchaser buys a property that has been used for short term lettings which is classed as a going concern for GST purposes and then wants a change of use – to full residential where they are to live in the property, the purchaser must pay 12.5% of its value and then de-register for GST. This information will not generally be disclosed in the glossy advertising and that 12.5% you have to pay might mean the property is no longer such a bargain after all.

Local Taxes. Many Aucklanders believe they are overtaxed and can't understand why Auckland City and the Auckland Regional Council have to operate as separate entities. Auckland City levies rates on the property for rubbish collection, street maintenance and lighting and the ARC collects rates for transport, parks and the environment.

The system used to assess rates relies on a visual inspection of the property from the roadside and the local information held on the property by the council. For rating purposes a dilapidated three bedroom home with a garage will be assessed at roughly the same rate as a similar sized house but renovated. The total rates for a three bedroom home with a small single garage in Auckland's eastern suburbs for 2005/6 were $2076.01. Rates are due to skyrocket in the more affluent parts of Auckland in line with the rise in property values. Homebuyers should note that rates are payable on a property whether or not it is occupied. Rates can be paid on-line.

Pet owners should note that dogs must be registered with the local council and that an annual registration fee is payable. The dog registration fee in Auckland for 20056 was $62. All you get for your money is an identification tag that is used to match dog and owner in case your dog is found wandering. Fines are steep for anyone caught with an unregistered dog. Pleading ignorance about the law might work the first time that you're caught. But don't try it more than once as petty neighbours will have no hesitation in calling the council. The revenue collected is used to pursue dog owners with unregistered dogs and to police areas where dogs are banned, such as beaches during summer. Any unregistered dog is rounded up and carted off to dog jail. Dogs that aren't collected within seven days may be put up for adoption or on death row if they aren't suitable for re-housing.

All vehicles have to be licensed and the annual fee for a five door hatchback for 2005/2006 was $200.10. Payments can be made for six months in advance rather than the full year.

Wills

After purchasing a property in New Zealand, you will want to ensure that your will is up to date and that you leave your New Zealand property assets to your nominated heirs. It makes sense to make a will with your solicitor at the time of the property purchase who will advise you on whether your UK assets should be incorporated into the New Zealand will or whether they should be kept separate.

For those whose financial affairs are less complicated a free will writing service is available online via the New Zealand government owned Crown entity, the Public Trust. Providing you make the Public Trust your executor the service is free and can be updated at any time. Public Trust: www. publictrust.co.nz.

INSURANCE

When buying a house through a bank or a mortgage broker, they will be keen to sell you buildings, contents and car insurance at the same time, as this is where they are going to be earning commission. While it can be convenient to take out insurance at the same time that you buy your house, take time to read the small print as many policies provide only a basic cover and don't assume that you will get the same benefits as you would expect in the UK.

Drivers should note that it is the car and not the driver that you insure in New Zealand. Even if you are involved in a car accident caused by another party, you could find yourself paying for your own hire or lease car while you wait for yours to be repaired if you don't pay extra and take out a policy that provides this. If your car is off the road for several weeks, you could be paying out several thousand dollars in car hire, which may or may not be covered by the other party's insurer.

As one panel beater remarked recently, if he had to have a car for everyone involved in an accident he would need a whole fleet of them. And unless you happen to strike it lucky, courtesy cars are generally inferior to most late model high performance cars.

There is no compulsory third-party insurance required in New Zealand because of the no-fault accident compensation system. Where in Britain the prohibitive cost of third party insurance keeps the number of teenage drivers on the roads to a minimum, New Zealand teens can and do obtain their licenses at the frighteningly immature age of fifteen.

Despite the high-profile road safety campaigns, including one heart-wrenching personal account by a teenage boy who talks about how his mother was killed by a speeding driver, no government wants to be the one to put their hand up and introduce compulsory third party insurance because of the cost implications. The high rate of road accidents (many of which are caused by irresponsible young drivers) costs the country millions of dollars and causes life-long misery for the families and friends of the victims.

FINDING PROPERTIES FOR SALE

CHAPTER SUMMARY

- **Estate agents.** British buyers may find the hard-sell tactics in the larger cities more overt than they are used to.
  - Revealing your upper price limit will only encourage agents to show you properties in a higher price bracket that may or may not be negotiated downwards.
- **Prices.** Buying at auction is common practice in New Zealand.
  - Even houses marketed for sale by negotiation may not have prices.
- **Open Homes.** Properties are marketed via the 'open home' system.
  - House buyers can spend the weekend walking around houses on the market without an appointment.
- **Word of Mouth.** In areas where there is a strong sense of local community, would be buyers need to prove to locals that they will participate in community life.
- **Hard-sell Seminars.** Don't be taken in by the marketing hype.
  - Only poor quality property will be sold at such events.

CHOOSING WHERE TO LIVE

In Section II the snapshot of the types of houses on offer may have given you a better idea of where you might want to live. If you are moving to New Zealand with an employer then it's likely that the decision about where to live will be influenced by the travelling time to work. Given that three quarters of the population live in the North Island, with the majority of those based in the northern part of the country, statistically this is where you are most likely to end up.

Checklist for Buying in a Particular Location

○ **Affordability:** It is only natural to aspire to live in the best possible location when moving to another country. You wouldn't want to travel all that way just to end up living somewhere ordinary. But if you cannot afford the median house price it will take longer to find something suitable, especially in smaller areas where fewer properties come on to the market. It might just be that there are not enough available properties to choose from. One couple who emigrated from Israel found themselves stuck in the expensive Queenstown Southern Lakes area unable to afford a house because of rising prices. Despite the fact that they run a successful business in the area, people like them are finding that living even in paradise is becoming increasingly difficult.

○ **Travel times:** Part of the pleasure of moving to this beautiful country is that you can share it with family and friends when they come to visit. If you want your friends to come and see you or if you need to travel frequently for work, proximity to a regional airport is important.

○ **Schools:** For parents of school age children, being close to a good school is essential.

○ **Shopping:** The further away from the shops you are the more reliant you will be on your car. In rural areas it is the local petrol station that will function as general store, newsagent and source of the best gossip.

○ **Health:** In isolated rural areas there is a real shortage of general practitioners and dentists as young graduates tend to flock to cities or overseas so that they can pay off their student loans. Critical mass determines the level of health services with the greatest range of services in the bigger cities.

ESTATE AGENTS

The majority of real estate agents are perfectly ordinary and decent people, just trying to earn a living. But when good people earn no base salary and are paid purely by commission, it's not surprising that there are a few that will give prospective buyers the hard sell. Agents are self-employed, although they may represent a particular firm. There are no restrictions placed on numbers of agents or agencies operating in any one market. In an over-crowded market there are many agents who live from one sale to the next and earn very little.

As a result of this, if an agent hears an overseas accent, they will assume that you are, a) a cashed up buyer able to afford a very expensive property or b) that you are a recent arrival and don't know the system. If you are from the UK, an agent will assume that means London and the South East with its sky-high property prices and every American is of course from California. Once an agent has found out you have UK pounds, US or Australian dollars to spend you will receive many a phone call about fabulous (and expensive) properties for sale, unless you are suitably vague about where they can contact you. Australian and US buyers will have encountered similar sales techniques back home. Tell an agent that you come from Hull, where house prices bear no comparison to the South East and they will probably assume that you are some millionaire, trying to be discreet.

This only really applies to the areas where property is 'hot' such as Auckland, Queenstown, Tauranga and Mount Maunganui. In rural areas, country agents know that if they sell an overseas buyer a house in the district they will be seeing quite a bit of each other around the place. And if a country agent likes you, you will not only be privy to local gossip but could even get to find out where the best fishing spots are – provided you buy him or her a beer first.

Real estate agents have to be registered in New Zealand and to have passed a basic qualification. Would-be agents don't need academic qualifications to go on the training course of 40 hours, just fluency in English. Despite the minimum training requirement, agents are permitted to not only negotiate contracts on behalf of the vendor but can agree clauses in the Sale and Purchase Agreement which would normally be negotiated by a qualified solicitor in the UK. For more details on this, see the chapter *Fees, Contracts and Conveyancing*.

Real Estate Advertising. The regulations governing real estate advertising are not as strict as they are in the UK. As a result the real estate ads make entertaining reading especially when an agent makes creative use of the English language. And the companies that deal with expensive properties are some of the worst offenders. 'A prism of ocean views', 'serious sellers demand action', 'investors love a winner', and yes, that old stalwart, 'deceptively spacious.' But the best yet was in the details of a recently advertised house in Auckland: ' The Yacht Club is situated at the Eastern end and has become a breeding ground for the future sailors.'

Although hyperbole may be allowed, deliberately misleading potential buyers is not. One test case saw an agent promoting a so-called waterfront property, complete with an enticing photograph of the beach. The only trouble was that the photograph was taken from another house and the house for sale was neither waterfront nor had a view.

Agents do not provide the comprehensive flyers that are standard in the UK. detailing chattels, building materials, type of construction and most importantly – room dimensions. While you will get an overall size of the property in square metres, if you want to know the size of individual rooms, you'll need to measure these yourself. More expensive properties are marketed by very flattering photographs taken from the best angles.

Price. If there is one aspect of the house buying process that irks buyers from overseas more than anything else, it is the failure in New Zealand by some real estate companies to disclose an asking price, even if a house is not being sold by auction or tender. Only those people who are in the area will have any idea of 'market value', and even they can get it wrong. For overseas buyers anxious to know whether they can afford a property, the median value should show whether or not you are able to afford to buy in that suburb.

Agents will tell you that if they disclose an asking price and it is in fact too low, the price cannot be negotiated upwards and the vendor could be selling too cheaply. And because market conditions fluctuate so much in a 'hot' property market, they will tell you that they cannot accurately put a price on a property. The cynic might believe that putting a ceiling on the price of a property in fact puts an upper limit on the agent's commission.

While this works well for sellers in a sellers' market, when the market eventually swings back to favour the buyer, not disclosing an asking price can lead to a lot of time being wasted on both sides. And if agents in the UK, where house prices are higher, are able to put a price on, why can't agents in New Zealand do the same?

The way that agents avoid disclosing a price ranges from the pompous – 'expressions of interest invited' (that is, only those with serious money need apply) to the baffling FSBN – For Sale by Negotiation. Then there is 'buyer enquiry welcome from $200,000'. Where there is no price disclosed you will see the meaningless words: 'Price: By negotiation'. Some agents are more straightforward and at least give the buyer a price to start from: In the $900,000 range, mid/high $200,000 or buyers in a range upwards of $500,000.

Useful Addresses

Bayleys actively promote New Zealand as a desirable location for the residential market and for the farming community. As well as employing a buyer's agent in London, the company runs regular farming seminars around the UK and Ireland. Through an affiliate London estate agency, Bayleys operate a London display suite in the West End where their full colour glossy tabloid *Bayleys New Zealand Property Press*, is available. Bayleys also promote New Zealand real estate at the New Zealand Expo, the last of which was held in October 2005.

Bayleys UK: Buyer's Representative, ☎ 0845-601 9945; e-mail simon@ bayleysnz.co.uk; www.bayleys.co.nz.

Bayleys Display Suite: RH International, Nash House, St George Street, London W1S 2RQ; ☎ 020-7491 9791.

www.farmingnz.co.nz Look out for these regular farming seminars in your area.

Property Seminars

The Opportunities New Zealand Expo, which has been held regularly every six-months for the past few years in London and Manchester, is a bona-fide event and should not be confused with a hard-sell seminar (see below).

Primarily an employment event, the Expo is run to attract people with the right skills to consider migrating to New Zealand. But because over 60 companies from New Zealand attend, including real estate agents, this is your chance to have your questions about New Zealand answered in person, for less than the price of a cinema ticket. The first seminar in 2006 will be March and the second in October. For further information go to : www.smallworldmedia.co.nz.

HARD-SELL SEMINARS:

British buyers who had to endure the sales tactics of time-share touts in the 1980s may feel as though they are in a time-warp when they read this but New Zealand has yet to clamp down on property sales seminars. Although currently under review, these types of seminars, promoted in newspapers, are still unregulated. They promote property investment where investors are given very little disclosure or legal protection.

These seminars are often attended by buyers who are promised very high returns on rental investments where the figures are over-inflated. Investors are ripped off two ways:- firstly by paying over the odds for the property, and secondly by being forced to pay a high commission to the intermediary running the seminar. Enticements to attend can include the promise of a 'free' holiday to somewhere such as Australia's Gold Coast.

These sales pitches are often disguised as 'lectures' by so-called property 'experts' who will, no doubt have some impressive qualifications from a university that you have never heard of. The expert will just have happened to have written a book revealing the secrets of his property success, which you will be able to buy for a 'special price for a limited time only' at the seminar.

Usually though, these experts make their money by charging the 'mum and dad' investor or investors from South East Asia with limited English, a large fee for the privilege of attending the seminar. This was how some of the more dubious shoebox apartments in central Auckland were originally sold.

Property Viewing

The best way to ensure that one particular agent does not target you is to attend what are known as *Open Homes*. Incredulous as this may sound to the British buyer, houses can be inspected without an appointment by walk-ins, literally off the street. And no, you will not be subject to a bag search nor are there are security guards standing in every room either. US and Australian buyers will already be familiar with the Open Home system. Very expensive houses are not sold this way because of security and privacy concerns.

Advertised in the property press of the daily newspaper, Open Homes are held usually on weekends, Sunday being the most popular day. They attract a fair number of Open Home tourists, families on outings with no intention of buying but who like to take a look around the neighbours' houses when they are out. Open Home tourists are generally not afraid to express their opinion on everything from the décor and the photographs on the wall to what wines the vendors have in their cellar.

It's easy to spot an Open Home – just follow the line of cars and the advertising signs.

Attendees are expected to sign in and leave a telephone number and the diligent agent will follow this up with a phone call. Most agents ask you what you thought of the house but the good ones will ask if it wasn't what you were looking for, was there anything else they could help you with instead?

THE INTERNET

Savvy agents know that the internet is one of their best marketing tools, particularly for 'trophy' property. With the new technology, prospective buyers can have a virtual tour of the house and grounds. But potential buyers should be aware that buying over the internet, sight unseen is a huge risk. If a property seems cheap, compared with similar properties in the location or the location itself seems very reasonably priced, there is nearly always a reason for this.

One potential buyer from the UK fell in love with a rural property over the internet. The post and rail fencing and the long driveway with the cute little house looked perfect. But when she finally drove up the driveway the reason why the photograph had been taken at rather an odd angle suddenly became apparent.

Barely 50 feet from the house was an enormous power pylon which was but one of many unfurling across the landscape. The rural idyll turned out to be anything but. The countryside was flat and featureless, the nearest shop was a five kilometre drive and the house turned out not to be made of beautiful native timbers but was a modern version of an older house in what could only be described as slightly more solid than plywood.

Useful Websites

www.realenz.co.nz. Run by the Real Estate Institute of New Zealand, this is the definitive site for advertising New Zealand real estate. It is a multi-agency site and features properties right throughout New Zealand, with residential, commercial, lifestyle and waterfront listings.

www.tradme.co.nz. Trade Me is the New Zealand equivalent to eBay and is the country's most popular website. In 2005 Trade Me started up its property site. As well as private sellers this site attracts listings from real estate agents as well, although some of the official real estate sites have expressed disquiet about this new competitor.

www.harcourts.co.nz. Harcourts are a national chain.

www.ljhooker.co.nz. This Australian-owned firm is well-represented throughout New Zealand.

www.bayleys.co.nz. Bayleys have a reputation for being a company associated with more expensive property, although they claim that they deal in all price ranges.

Property Press: ACP Media Ltd, Cnr Fanshawe and Beaumont Streets,

Westhaven, PO Box 90106, AMSC, Auckland; www.propertypress.co.nz. These weekly glossy tabloid format listings are published in the more heavily populated parts of the country. Auckland has five separate publications covering the North Shore, Central Auckland, East Auckland, Central West and West Auckland. Wellington has its own edition, as does Manawatu and the Bay of Plenty. In the South Island there are only two editions, one for Otago and the other for the Lakes District (Queenstown and the surrounding area). *Property Press* publish the details of the weekly Open Homes.

www.therealestate.co.nz is ACP's site covering other regions of the North Island including Waiheke Island, Rotorua, Taupo and Taranaki. The postal address is the same as the *Property Press.*

www.nzherald.co.nz. The New Zealand Herald is the daily newspaper for the Auckland region. A weekly property pullout section with photographs is published every Saturday as well as the times and dates for Open Homes.

www.stuff.co.nz. This site, run by the publishers Fairfax, has handy links to all the other newspapers in New Zealand. There is a map showing you which newspaper covers which region. The newspapers are: *Waikato Times* (Hamilton and the Coromandel) *Manawatu Standard* (Palmerston North), *The Dominion Post* (Wellington and Wairarapa), *The Nelson Mail* (Nelson and Golden Bay), *The Marlborough Express* (Marlborough and the Sounds), *The Press* (Christchurch, Canterbury and the West Coast), *The Timaru Herald* (South Canterbury), *Otago Daily Times* (Queenstown and Southern Lakes), *The Southland Times* (Southland and Stewart Island). Links on the site will detail how you can access a hard copy of the paper.

www.propertystuff.co.nz. The on-line version of the property listings in the above newspapers. The site includes a handy e-mail alert, which will automatically send you notification of property that fit your criteria.

UK Property Magazines

Australia & New Zealand: Merricks Media Ltd, 3-4 Riverside Court, Lower Bristol Road, Bath, BA2 3DZ; ☎ 01225-786800; fax 01225-786801; www.australiamagazine.co.uk. This glossy bi-monthly magazine has features not just on property and where to live but covers all aspects of moving 'Down Under'.

Word of Mouth

In prime coastal areas such as the Coromandel Peninsula where there is a shortage of waterfront property, the word goes out within the local community that a family is selling their *bach*. They will tell their friends and if it is in a highly sought after location, the property will be sold privately, without ever reaching the market. The only way an outsider can hope to tap into this unadvertised market is to rent in the area first and show willingness to participate in the community.

The word of mouth effect is a powerful one especially if there are a number of permanent residents in the area who don't just use their house over the summer and then leave it empty the rest of the year. If word gets out that an overseas buyer is in an area looking for property, the assumption will be that they will be prepared to pay over the odds. While one or two may be tempted to cash up and sell to you, the community minded may want to see evidence that you will 'fit in'. Locals only get upset when international buyers choose to come to a friendly egalitarian country like New Zealand, then shut themselves away in a fortress and won't integrate.

WHAT TYPE OF PROPERTY TO BUY

CHAPTER SUMMARY

- **Buying land.** In rural areas where there is limited housing stock, you can buy a piece of land and either build on it or move a house on to the site.
- **Relocating a house.** A great house in the wrong part of town can be given a new lease of life by relocating it and it's probably one of the cheaper ways to invest in a holiday home.
  - Before relocating a house, check that there are no building covenants on the land that prevent you from doing so.
- In the smarter city suburbs many of the restored old wooden houses retain the façade but have been completely rebuilt inside.
- There is more emphasis on integrating the outdoor living area with the house than would be the case in the UK.
- A building inspector should test a house for moisture levels if it was built between 1990 and 2002 with monolithic cladding.
- Buy-to-let schemes do not exist in the same way as they do in the UK although many New Zealand investors borrow to buy investment property.
- You don't have to join a sustainable community but can commission an architect if you want an eco house.

How New Zealanders Live Now

New Zealanders that grew up in old wooden houses and bungalows tend to favour more modern places to live when they buy their own homes. Those Edwardian era houses are seen by some locals as outdated and uncomfortable. But any house, whatever its age, is going to deteriorate if it is badly maintained. And it is true that wooden houses require regular painting as well as more maintenance than those made out of brick or other solid materials.

Many New Zealanders refuse to acknowledge that they live in cold houses and are in denial that there is a winter. The older generation have a mentality that will have them put on another layer of clothing, rather than do anything about the heating system. One recent new arrival in Auckland compared the attitude towards central heating in New Zealand houses to that of Spain, where there seems to be a similar apathy and refusal to acknowledge that wintry conditions in houses are unpleasant.

The first thing that many buyers from overseas do when looking around New Zealand houses is to check where the radiators are and are surprised when they don't find them. While individual rooms may have some form of heating, it is only recently that pre-set heating appliances have become available. Being able to walk in to a warm house after a day out is still regarded as a luxury in New Zealand even though many British and US buyers may consider this as essential. As most people tend to buy a new house in spring or summer it's easy to forget about heating, especially when the vendor and agent tell you that it doesn't get cold.

Most new houses built by developers are designed for show rather than comfort with the emphasis on making the most of the summer months. North Islanders in particular aspire to new, open-plan houses with good 'indoor-outdoor' flow. The ideal position for the living, dining and kitchen area is at the back of the house, which is preferably north facing. The transition between living area and garden should be seamless, so that when the back doors are open it is difficult to define where the house ends and the outdoor entertaining area begins.

In winter, a poorly designed house is austere and uninviting. The much trumpeted 'indoor-outdoor' flow is just another way of saying that it gets draughty. While a new house is going to be better insulated than an older one, smart granite worktops, tiled bathrooms and no carpets will be unwelcoming in winter, unless you have a very good heating system.

Up until a few years ago, a request for double glazing would meet with a blank stare. New Zealanders are only now starting to realise how much money they could save on heating bills if they had a more energy-efficient house.

One drawback of the modern New Zealand open-plan house is that it doesn't cater for families with teenagers. If there's no way of closing off a television or music room — the rest of the family have to suffer with the loud music.

A considerable amount of effort and money goes into landscaping the outdoor entertaining area, as so much time is spent out there in the summer. New Zealanders with high value houses hire professional landscape designers to ensure that the outdoor entertaining area integrates with the house. Be wary of blowing the budget though. A heated pool, outdoor lighting, gas patio heaters and a brick oven will look fabulous but might mean you've overcapitalised on the property and may not get the money back when you come to sell.

In the past fifteen years in urban areas, back gardens have shrunk to such an extent that to find a house with a garden big enough to put in a pool is becoming increasingly difficult. The classic 'quarter acre section' that many New Zealand children grew up on has become a quarter of that size.

TYPES OF HOUSES

Villas

Built in Edwardian times, villas, made out of weatherboard were the first style of house to be mass-produced in New Zealand. The different style of villa include the classic *flat-fronted villa* and the *bay villa* (so called because of its bay window). Villas are characterised by their high ceilings, sash windows and craftsmanship. The best examples were made of native timbers especially *kauri* heart wood. The traditional roofing material was iron.

The typical villa has a wide arching central hallway with rooms off the hallway. The design flaw of the villa becomes apparent in winter. Although the high ceilings look magnificent, this makes them very hard to heat. The front door opens onto the street and there is no inner door to provide protection from the elements. In the main cities it is becoming increasingly hard to find villas that have not been extensively remodelled inside and 'improved.'

State Houses

The boom years in the early 1950s heralded a new era of prosperity. As the country thrived, new houses were needed for the workers who were helping to build a strong economy. Those who were dependent on welfare were not forgotten about either as New Zealand embarked on a building programme of public housing.

Known as State houses, these detached wooden bungalows were situated within generous grounds. Built by skilled tradesmen, state houses have a reputation for sound construction, with gardens big enough for a childrens' play area and a vegetable patch.

These properties are now highly sought after, either as starter homes or as investment properties and when a house is advertised as ex-state it will always attracts buyer interest. For those that still live in public housing, conditions are not as good as they once were. Councils in some areas are moving the original state house to the front of the grounds and building a second one behind it, much to the dismay of long-term residents.

Townhouses

The word *townhouse* refers to a detached house in an urban area, built within the past 20 years or so on a small site, usually with a courtyard garden to the rear. Overseas buyers coming to New Zealand for the wide open spaces are often dismayed to find that as many as three detached houses can be built one behind the other on one original site. These houses lack privacy and are overlooked by the neighbours. There will be a shared driveway and only the front town house will have a street frontage.

Auckland's North Shore coastline now has million dollar houses squeezed onto small sites, which might have distant sea views – once you look past all the other houses. If a house is at the top of a ridge the occupants may be able to see inside three or even four of the neighbours houses. Amazingly though, many New Zealanders value the view over the lack of privacy and are fans of new townhouses. They like the fact that they won't need to spend any money in the first few years and that the garden is low-maintenance.

Art Deco

These houses are not just popular with Art Deco fans but with buyers who want a solidly built house that requires less maintenance than a wooden villa. Dating from the late 1920s and early 1930s there are fine examples of Art Deco style throughout New Zealand but the best are in Napier. When the town was flattened by the 1931 earthquake, the city chose to rebuild in this style. Built of solid stucco, the only drawback is that the flat roofs can leak if the house is not well maintained.

Californian Bungalows

Californian bungalows built in the 1920s and 1930s range from grand family homes in the older established suburbs to smaller, more manageable three or four bedroom homes. For those looking for a house with character, the Californian bungalow is a better option than the villa as the ceilings are lower and it will be easier to heat. Like any house made of wood, these houses are high maintenance. But if you are prepared to put in the work, these are very attractive houses to look at as well as live in. They contain many period features such as hardwood flooring, leadlight windows and finely crafted doors.

Second Homes

It is the beachside location rather than the house itself that attracts New Zealanders to flock to the beach *bach* for their annual summer holiday. Many international buyers are perplexed as to why so many New Zealanders are willing to give up the comforts of home over the summer in exchange for a modest and architecturally uninspiring family bolthole. They cannot understand the attraction of the rather plain-Jane beachside settlements that have sprung up around the country that have little in the way of facilities apart from a dairy and a petrol station.

But for bach fans, part of the appeal is that they are a 'back to basics' experience. The point of the bach is to use it as a base to return to in the evenings after a day out fishing or going to the beach. And there is a great sense of community amongst second-homers who return year after year. The family beach bach bought for mum, dad and the kids in the 1950s will now be used by the extended family – that's if anyone can sort out a workable booking system.

Buy a low-maintenance house rather than a beautiful one – is the best advice for anyone contemplating a second home. A wooden bach might look cute but if you have to close it up for the winter you'll be spending all summer re-painting it. A 1970s brick and tile house is a much better option and the factory brick can be disguised with a coat of paint.

Other options for second homes include lakeside or mountain retreats. Or if you enjoy challenging restoration projects, how about renovating a big country house in an area like the Wairarapa, where you could create an ideal country lifestyle. Or better still, get the benefit of the previous owner's hard work and buy one already restored.

APARTMENT LIVING

Owning your own detached house with room for children to play was once the dream of many a New Zealander. While those that can afford the most expensive suburbs close to the city centre are still living the good life, many young people are starting to look for alternatives.

As apartment living on a large scale is a recent concept, the building regulations and the infrastructure have been slow to catch up. Noise problems from neighbours are cited as the most common complaint by apartment dwellers, yet councils are only now realising that some inner city buildings have inadequate soundproofing.

If you are going to give up a house and a garden in the suburbs, there needs to be plenty going on in town to compensate. Many new residents in Auckland City complain that more needs to be done to liven up the city centre. Council planners in New Zealand could learn a lot from their European counterparts where city centres are lively places for residents and visitors alike.

Modern Apartments

At the top end of the apartment market are the apartments built for owner-occupiers who have downsized from the suburban family home. These apartments generally have balconies, good views and are of a reasonable size. In Auckland you could be paying over $750,000 and may not necessarily even own the freehold for two bedrooms with a view, one car park, a storage locker and possibly on-site facilities such as a gym and pool.

At the opposite end of the scale are the apartments built for the investor, supposedly to house all the foreign university students coming to New Zealand to study. After a change of governance in 2005, Auckland City Council was forced to stipulate minimum apartment sizes as the tiny units being built for the foreign student market were so small that many of them could barely fit a bed in. Studio units now have to be at least 35 sq m, one bedroom apartments, 45 sq m, two bedrooms, 70 sq m and three bedroom units 90 sq m.

While it is easy to chastise previous developer-friendly council leaders for permitting the building of shoeboxes in the first place, it is the people of Auckland City who will have to live with the consequences, long after the developers have made their tidy profit.

In a market-driven economy it is the market – in this case, the students that this sub-standard accommodation was built for in the first place that have rejected the worst examples in favour of something more spacious. Who, after all, would choose to live in a multi-occupancy building in a so-called 'internal bedroom', (one without a window) in case there was ever a fire? Certainly none of the investors who bought these units. With a rise in interest rates and a reduction in the rent that they can charge, many investors who bought into the student accommodation market are now finding it hard going to turn a profit.

While it would be misleading to overstate the size of the problem – it really only affects a few streets away from the Viaduct area of downtown Auckland; given that so many fine historical buildings have been ripped down in the name of this 'progress', the people of Auckland deserve better.

Older Apartments

The blocks that were built pre-1990 in the cities are generally spacious and well built. The best blocks have the greatest number of owner-occupiers and are highly sought after.

The conversion of older buildings into apartment developments has been a feature in the main centres. These older style conversions may lack such features as balconies but the fact that many are made of stone or brick does mean that the exterior of the building is of solid construction.

Apartments with On-site Facilities

The more expensive blocks offer resort-style facilities with on-site security, a pool and tennis courts. An apartment in such a complex will be as expensive as a suburban house in a top area. If a building has a doorman, a marble entrance way and lifts, these all have to be paid for. While it is easy to be seduced into such a luxurious way of living, buyers have to factor in the hefty annual maintenance charges, or the body corporate fee as it is called. One recently advertised property selling for around $700,000 had annual body corporate fees of $12,500. While some regard it as good value for all that luxury, that is a sizeable amount to find every year and money that could be spent on paying off a mortgage.

BUYING LAND

In rural areas where there is limited housing stock, sometimes the best alternative to get the house you want is to buy the land and either build on it or move a relocated house on to the site. Relocated houses are discussed later on in this chapter. Buying a plot of land (called a section) for building on and then overseeing the construction of the building is one way to be certain that your are buying quality. But as Mike Cole says in the *Case Histories* section, it is important to choose both the right section and the best place to build on the site.

Before you buy you should have a geotechnical survey carried out which will cover such issues as drainage and soil stability. You should consult the LIM (Land Information Memorandum) to see what services have been provided as well as check the district plan for zoning and other requirements. Be aware too that banks aren't willing to lend as much on a section as they would on a completed house.

HOUSE AND LAND PACKAGES

Steps to Take When Buying a House and Land Package

- Ask to see what other developments the developer has built.
- Talk to an owner of one of their properties.
- Check that the builder belongs to a registered trade organisation.
- Ask if any of the developer's other properties have been subject to claims regarding weather tightness, (see Leaky Building Syndrome below).
- Ask what materials the house is to be built from. Only buy from that developer if the house is to be of solid construction.
- Ask for a higher level of insulation than is standard for the area and be prepared to pay more if necessary. It will save you money in the end on heating bills.
- Ask if a ventilation system can be put in to counteract the high levels of humidity and minimise the risk of damp.
- Check that the house comes with a guarantee.

LEAKY BUILDING SYNDROME

New Zealand's leaky homes crisis surfaced in 1998 when a group of residents in a trendy Auckland neighbourhood noticed that their houses, which were barely 18 months old, were beginning to rot. Built of weatherboard and stucco, The Ponsonby Gardens complex is a townhouse/terraced housing development of double-storied houses with upstairs balconies.

Buyers were attracted to the low-maintenance lock up and leave lifestyle, Ponsonby's café and restaurant scene and the ten minute drive to the central city. There was a mixture of owner-occupiers and rental investors, successful professionals at different stages of their careers.

Looking at Ponsonby Gardens from the outside, the houses showed none of the obvious signs that all might not be well underneath. And weatherboard, or clapboard as it is known in the USA, is a building material that has been used for over 100 years on houses that have never suffered more than the occasional dripping roof.

But the weatherboards in this development had not been put up by builders with anything like the same standards as the craftsmen that built the Victorian and Edwardian villas. A combination of a lack of ground clearance and cladding buried in concrete was just one of the contributory causes that led to leaking. More serious was the failure to ensure adequate control joints in the stucco plaster, which cracked, allowing water to seep in. Behind the plaster, instead of a waterproof membrane, was unsealed and untreated fibreboard. This board acted like a sponge that soaked all the water up.

In a region know for its high humidity levels, it did not take long for the houses to start to rot from the inside. A potentially hazardous toxic mould developed in some of the properties, producing respiratory problems for the unlucky homeowners.

Other reasons for the rotting given in this first test case for the Weathertight Homes Resolution Service were a failure of the waterproofing in the decks, flat roofing and inadequate flashings.

Many of the other larger developments in Auckland (built by the same developer, Taradale Properties) with the same problems, might have looked from the outside that they were built of solid materials. But for these types of buildings, a simple test can be carried out, which gives the prospective purchaser an indication as to whether or not a house is solid. Simply by knocking on an outside wall will confirm whether what looks like solid concrete, is in fact hollow monolithic cladding.

Monolithic cladding has been a popular product in the building trade for residential construction in recent years. For a developer with an eye on maximising profits, it was seen as a cheap product and one that was quick and easy to apply. A cladding of sheet material with an applied coating, to give the appearance of a seamless cladding, gives the building the appearance of one built in concrete, plaster or masonry. Referred to colloquially as 'chilly-bin' or 'plastic' houses, these types of dwellings have been most affected by leaky building syndrome.

In a landmark ruling in March 2005, the owners of Ponsonby Gardens were awarded $700,000 to fix their rotting homes. In a ruling that shocked some, the developer, Taradale Properties, a company liquidated in 2003, escaped blame. The site manager, the project manager, the architect, the waterproofing company and the Auckland City Council, who signed off on the building code compliance certificate were found liable. Those others ordered to pay were also able to wriggle out of any moral and fiscal responsibility by simply dissolving their limited liability companies. The local council was the only party that paid up. And in another twist, as the parties were found 'jointly and severely' liable, the Auckland City Council has had to bear the full cost. Ultimately it will be ratepayers who will fund any future repairs.

Many New Zealanders are seduced by looks over substance when buying houses and that is why many were unwitting victims of the leaky building crisis. It wasn't difficult for developers to find a market for their Mediterranean inspired housing. The dream of owning your own little slice of 'la dolce vita Down Under' soon became a reality as plaster-style houses in various hues of terracotta were built. And as fast as the houses were built they were snapped up by enthusiastic buyers.

With summer temperatures regularly matching those of the Mediterranean, those that bought into the lifestyle that these new 'low-maintenance' houses, might easily have felt they were in bucolic paradise. But one soaking in a sub-tropical Auckland downpour puts paid to any notion that the top half of the North Island has a climate like Southern Spain's. The rain, when it falls does so in great bursts, sometimes leading to localised flooding.

And while houses in Spain and Italy are generally built out of natural materials such as local stone, sometimes with walls a foot thick, earthquake regulations in New Zealand require that buildings have to be built out of materials that have some 'give' so that they can withstand the occasional jolt. But second-rate structures clad in plasticised fibrous plaster or stucco were not the answer, as many homeowners are finding out.

The Role Of Untreated Timber

In early 1990 the timber industry campaigned to promote the use of un-treated kiln-dried pine. The industry reminded regulators that houses in New Zealand were built with untreated timber before 1950. But what they failed to mention was that the timber in those days was better than fast-grown commercial timber could ever be. No timber available in New Zealand could match the durability of kauri heartwood, an outstandingly durable hard wood and a timber of such quality that no fast-grown sap-wood could ever match. And all those houses had eaves. Their proven durability is such that the Victorian and Edwardian *villas* and the 1930s *Californian bungalows* are still sought after, restored or not. And it is likely that many of them will still be standing, long after many poorly built late 20th century houses have passed their use-by-date.

The advantages of untreated timber were firstly that builders could have a dry timber that would not shrink as opposed to chemically treated timber which arrived on site, wet. And secondly, the forestry industry saw that cost savings could be made if the product they exported to Australia and Asia, untreated timber, could be used in New Zealand.

Where Did the Problem Start?

The leaky homes crisis might have become public knowledge in 2002 but New Zealand was not the first country to be affected. Canada and the USA warned of the problems of monolithic cladding and untreated timber back in the mid 1990s. A report on the Canadian crisis was in New Zealand as early as 1998. But Vancouver's leaky condos were attributed to poor con-struction and the recommendations in the report were ignored here.

Who knew what and when are just some of the issues currently being debated as the Building Industry Authority, councils, developers, architects and builders all seek to absolve themselves of the responsibility of paying to fix the problem. The true extent of the crisis was not known at the time of going to press. Between 10,000 to 20,000 homes could be faulty. There were 3000 claims lodged with the Weathertight Homes Resolution in June 2005 and at least the same number are going through the court system. But many thousands of people may as yet be unaware they have a problem. A house may look pristine on the outside but the mould may be hidden.

Stigma Affects Property Values. Anecdotal evidence from a study con-ducted from a small sample group in Auckland suggests that property val-ues have been affected by the stigma attached to leaky building syndrome. Even if a house has shown no signs of leaks, buyers avoid houses built be-tween 1990 and 2002 with: Mediterranean-style monolithic cladding (fi-brous plaster or stucco), a flat roof, no eaves, internal balconies, untreated kiln-dried timber, situated in an area with high winds. Such properties take longer to sell and may be marked down in price down by at least 10%.

Help for Prospective Homebuyers. Although the rule '*caveat emptor*' or buyer beware applies in New Zealand as much as it does in Britain, the onus on those sellers of Mediterranean style- monolithic clad homes will be to prove to future buyers that their homes have never leaked. Or, if they have leaked, that the house has been rebuilt to a much higher standard.

Moisture Detection

One enterprising company has developed a system that that can be used by consumers, which claims to measure the moisture content of timber. A system of probes aims to act like an early warning device to detect leaks before damage occurs. Building inspectors use a similar system so that if you are considering buying such a property, ensure that the company carrying out the inspection carries this equipment, so that a thorough check for leaks can be done.

RELOCATED HOUSES

At night, the sight of a convoy of large vehicles lumbering towards you down the highway, balancing what appears to be a house sliced in two can give many a car driver a fright. But don't worry, it will merely be one enterprising homeowner's solution to the 'right house wrong neighbourhood' dilemma. The buyer purchases an empty section, ensuring that there are no covenants on the title, and then hunts around for a suitable house to move onto the site.

Buying a piece of land and moving a house onto it was one way many New Zealanders found as a way of owning a little slice of paradise which didn't cost the earth. And it wasn't just the humble little bach that started life somewhere else, either. Many lovingly restored country landmarks may once have been one of the earliest houses built in Parnell or Remuera, but whose relocation has been so successful that they look part of the landscape.

Relocated houses are cut in half, moved on to the site and then repiled – the builder will place new wooden supports at regular intervals under the floor, mounted usually on new concrete footings. One way to tell if a house has been relocated is to check the exterior for original brick chimneys. In the grander houses, these have been rebuilt so successfully that it would be very difficult to tell whether the house had been there for ten years or a hundred.

Who Buys Them?

While many younger New Zealanders may find an inner-city apartment more in keeping with their urban lifestyle, relocated houses are still popular with canny investors or those looking for a holiday home who can no longer afford the modern-day equivalent of the traditional Kiwi *bach*. First or second homebuyers who run out of space find re-siting an older house a cheaper option than trading up and buying new.

Fans of older houses love the craftsmanship and detail that modern houses just don't have. And even though a badly maintained villa is going to cost a lot of money and effort to restore, for villa lovers, the chance to own an old building with exquisite original featuers makes the hard work seem worth it.

What Type of House is Suitable for Relocation? While house movers will tell you that almost any house is removable, a two storey-house with a concrete floor is going to be more costly to move than a older kauri villa complete with wrap around veranda. Some of these older houses are worth far less than the land they sit on so that developers remove them to make way for multi-unit developments. But rather than demolish them, these houses are recycled.

Where to Find Houses for Removal. There are companies that have houses on site that have already been removed and potential buyers can view these and go through them, in the same way that you would go shopping for a new sofa or a dining room table. www.qbay.co.nz started advertising houses for removal from Northland down to Otago. Check the main centres Yellow Pages listings for 'house lifting'. If a buyer wants a particular style of house the companies may know where one can be found. One Auckland company, Andrews Housemovers lists stock on www.andrews-housemovers.co.nz. Typical listings could include: a 240 sq m bungalow with nine rooms, exposed beams and polished French doors for $120,000 plus GST (Goods and Services Tax 12.5%) or a 130sq m three bedroom villa for $68,000 plus GST. The property section of newspapers is another useful resource for houses for removal.

Check with the Local Council First. Before you buy that section, ensure that you have checked with the town planning department in the area you plan to live as to what restrictions apply. As well as any building consents to place the house on its new site, a resource consent is required and this is discretionary. So while in practice this might mean that it is unlikely you will be able to relocate that holiday villa to the shores of Lake Wakatipu, you could find the perfect site not far away in the countryside.

Cost. While a relocated house can appear to be cheaper than building a new one, often the house will need extensive renovation. If a homeowner is prepared to do some or all of the renovations themselves then it could turn out to be a bargain. But removal costs are likely to increase with stricter legislation, which currently requires the removal company to obtain permits from the utilities companies and roading authority. Once on the new site the house will need to be fixed to its new foundations, re-piled and no doubt, re-wired.

TIMESHARE

If you thought timeshare had disappeared in the 1980s along with *Dynasty* style big hair and shoulder pads, according to the Consumers Organisation, the timeshare touts are back. Only this time it is not called timeshare but 'holiday ownership' or 'vacation clubs' but the reality with timeshare is that of course you never actually 'own' anything, just the right to use the property for a week or two for as long as you wish. And as the Consumers Organisation, point out, New Zealand has one of the highest levels of ownership of timeshare in the world. 26,000 timeshare owners might not sound like much but there are now 26 timeshare resorts dotted around a relatively small country.

The drawbacks of timeshare are the same in New Zealand as they would be anywhere else. It will never be 'home' as you may only spend two weeks a year in it. In fact, it is just like renting an apartment except that you don't have to go to the trouble of booking it and are guaranteed a holiday every year. While this might have seemed like a good idea when there was no such thing as booking last minute holidays online, it is difficult to see how timeshare sales agents are ever going to attract the younger monied set to buy into this concept.

Timeshare ownership has high set up costs as well as running costs to consider. Ten thousand dollars for a 50 year timeshare lease plus $400 running costs could mean that your week's holiday each year will cost $157 per night. And once you want to get out of your timeshare you may struggle to find a buyer.

Have a Free Holiday on Us!

A recent promotion for a 'premiere vacation club' offered the lucky recipient (only those that earn over $60,000 per annum) a free holiday in a summer hotspot, where the holiday company just happen to own a timeshare. All they ask is that you attend one of their presentations. As a further carrot to get you to the presentation the company promoted a free draw with various consumer goods as rewards.

Those that have attended such sessions report that the techniques used are standard high-pressure sales tactics. The risks of buying into a timeshare yet to be built are enormous. What sounds great on paper may not live up to your expectations.

The Consumers Organisation offers some great tips on the purchase of timeshare in New Zealand. Buy a second-hand timeshare, they suggest, it's much better value. They also recommend buying from a member of the New Zealand Holiday Ownership Council as this organisation has a code of practice which allows purchasers a five-day cooling-off period during which you can ask for your money back in full, whether the timeshare is new or second-hand.

Useful Addresses

New Zealand Holiday Ownership Council: PO Box 1648, Christchurch; ☎ 03 377 5888; fax 03 377 6116; www.nzhoc.org.nz; e-mail enquiries@ nzhoc.org.nz.

Commerce Commission: 44-52 The Terrace, PO Box 2351, Wellington; ☎ 04 924 3600; fax 924 3700; www.comcom.govt.nz

The Commerce Commission is the regulatory body for consumer affairs and has offices in Auckland and Christchurch (see the White Pages of the telephone directory or their website for further details). If the timeshare company that you are dealing with is not a member of the Holiday Ownership Council and you have doubts about them, then a quick call to the Commerce Commission for advice could save you considerable cost and heartache.

FARMS AND VINEYARDS

In 2005 www.farmingnz.co.nz ran regular farming seminars to British and Irish farmers. As well as presenting case studies on farmers who had success-fully made the move to New Zealand the seminars featured information on buying real estate. Anyone contemplating giving up the farming life in the UK or Ireland in exchange for one in New Zealand may be pleased at the relative lack of red tape compared with the EU. But with minimal regulation comes a corresponding lack of any safety net. With no farming subsidies available, farmers are not just at the mercy of the market for their living but the exchange rate as most of their income comes from exports.

While living on the land can be an immensely rewarding life, farmers cannot control the weather. In 2005 a group of crop farmers in the Poverty Bay area had their entire vegetable crop wiped out for the year in a freak storm. And hill country farmers regularly lose a large number of their lambs during late snowfalls. Owning a vineyard is a dream for many city folk but grapes should be regarded as a back up rather than a main source of income. These delicate fruits are fickle and labour-intenstive and are extremely susceptible to frost. In a major grape growing region like Marlborough, commercial growers are forced to spend thousands on hiring helicopters which hover over the grapes on frosty nights, blowing warm air on the vines to prevent frost damage.

Some developers have recently advertised properties within a grape growing area where the individual owners have the opportunity for a shared ownership scheme in a vineyard, presumably with certain rights on drinking the merchandise. For those that want the benefits of life among the vines without the responsibilities, this may be the perfect solution.

Overseas Investment Office. The Overseas Investment Office – part of Land Information New Zealand is the regulatory body that oversees the purchase of large blocks of 'sensitive' land – trophy landscape such as icon-ic sheep stations or large coastal blocks. This does not include productive farmland. As this is now assessed on a case-by-case, anyone interested in acquiring land, larger in size than any ordinary residential property should check with their solicitor and the Overseas Investment Office first at www.oio.linz.govt.nz.

Lifestyle Blocks or Small Holdings. Lifestyle blocks of three to four hec-tares are becoming increasingly popular with jaded city dwellers who will either plant grapes, graze alpacas or take up some other form of hobby farming. Farmers may be dismissive of 'townies' wanting to get back to nature but carving unproductive farmland into lifestyle blocks has made some farmers very comfortable in their retirement.

ECO HOUSING

For a nation selling itself to the rest as the world as 'clean and green', it is surprising that so few housing projects in New Zealand can really deliver on that clean and green promise. One notable exception is the Earthsong Eco-Neighbourhood in Waitakere, West Auckland. At present the Earthsong Eco-Neighbourhood has around 50 homes but in surroundings that include four acres of organic orchard and an area of native bush. The houses designed by an architect are made of rammed earth.

The principle behind Earthsong includes permaculture – or 'edible landscaping' as they call it. Solar heating and rainwater tanks are designed to save owners a considerable amount on their energy bills. There is an aspect to co-housing to the project – with some shared facilities such as office space and a library but the individual homes are fully self-contained. They are built in a cluster of terraced houses, rather than as freestanding detached houses. Owners of such properties must be prepared to contribute to the eco-community in a way that is outlined in their promotional literature.

Earthsong Eco-Neighbourhood, Swanson Road, Waitakere City, West Auckland; ☎ 09 832 5558; www.earthsong.co.nz; e-mail earthsong@xtra.co.nz.

Of course if you don't want to buy into the community aspect of living in such a development but are keen to build an environmentally friendly house, you can have an architect build one for you. One group of architects who have a number of their eco-houses listed on their website are *BBE Architects,* ☎ 0800 223 272; www.ecoprojects.co.nz; office@ecoprojects.co.nz

RENTING A HOME IN NEW ZEALAND

CHAPTER SUMMARY

- **Reasons to rent.** Find out what it's really like to live in a community before you buy a house there. Renting gives you the freedom to try out a new lifestyle before you buy into it.
  - Renting first may save you money in the long-term if you're not sure where you want to settle.
  - It is more cost effective to rent for six months than it is to buy and have to sell again if you change your mind.
  - You can walk away at the end of a tenancy without the worry of having to sell quickly.
- Rental prices and availability can fluctuate depending on the time of year.
- Don't assume that a serviced apartment will come with broadband internet access.
- Property listings are scarce in the first two weeks of January when estate agents are on their annual holidays at the beach.
- **The deposit.** Tenants can be asked to pay anything up to four weeks deposit.
  - The deposit is held by a government agency and not by the landlord.
- **Short-term Accommodation.** The biggest selection of short-term apartment accommodation can be found in Auckland, Wellington and Christchurch.
  - Short-term accommodation in smaller centres is found mainly in motels, motor lodges and bed and breakfast accommodation.
  - Holiday lets in holiday hot spots can be booked up as much as six months in advance for the January holidays.

○ **Home exchange.** A home exchange as an alternative to short term renting can be a great cost effective option for house hunters.

- ○ House swapping allows prospective homeowners the chance to meet the locals. Your hosts may arrange for a contact you can meet who can provide local advice and information.

- ○ A house swap could allow New Zealand visitors to the UK to stay longer, as the exchange rate from dollars to pounds makes hotels very expensive. A comfortable suburban home doesn't have to be in an exclusive neighbourhood, as long as it has good transport links.

WHY RENT?

Renting short-term in selected areas around the country gives prospective buyers an opportunity to try out a lifestyle before they buy into it. Many buyers coming to New Zealand hope to live differently from the way they did back home. But it is not uncommon to find that there is one family member who may be feeling apprehensive about such a big change. When you rent someone else's house they have to take care of any maintenance leaving you and the family time to explore your new surroundings and community.

If you've been yearning to live a different lifestyle, only by turning the dream into a reality will you ever find out if you're suited to it. And if, for any reason it doesn't suit you or your family's needs, you can move on, holding your head high and ready for the next challenge. One consolation is that at the end of the tenancy you can just walk away without the worry and expense of having to sell up and start the house search all over again. And when the time comes to make that all-important decision to buy, you'll have narrowed down your choices.

SHORT-TERM RENTALS

Because short-term fully furnished apartments in Auckland, Wellington and Christchurch are marketed to the corporate market, it can be hard to find anything larger than two bedrooms. While these apartments may be well appointed, with modern facilities and satellite television, the internet access could be old-fashioned dial-up rather than broadband or worse still, none at all.

Prices vary from city to city but in Auckland and Wellington, where you'll pay the most, deals can be negotiated at better rates for a longer term. Your money will stretch further in the South Island's largest city, Christchurch. For around 20% less, you'll have more space and even an extra bedroom.

Three bedroom apartments, although scarce, do exist but the options for family-style lodgings are generally motels or motor lodges. For families that want more privacy than a motel or a motor lodge, furnished houses are sometimes available in winter, when many New Zealanders head off in search of a second summer in the Northern Hemisphere. Some canny homeowners even let the family home out in the holiday month of January, when their occupants head off to their second home at the beach.

Holiday Lets

If you're looking to rent short-term in a holiday area, avoid January when rates are at their peak. While you'll find a good mixture of apartments and family-size accommodation in the Bay of Plenty, the Bay of Islands and Nelson, the best places get booked out at least six months ahead because Christmas and the main summer holiday break come at the same time, If you can leave it until February or even March, the days are still long and the weather can be its best. Not only will you have the pick of the accommodation but also you'll pay a lot less for it than at peak times.

The traditional bach or crib (if you're in Southland and Otago) may not offer much in the way of facilities but the location, close or right next to a beach is hard to beat.

Queenstown, the only real all-year round destination gets pretty busy on weekends during the ski season with domestic visitors and fills up with overseas tourists during the rest of the year. There are short-term fully furnished rentals available to suit most budgets. Prospective house hunters might get better rates if they're prepared to rent away from the main centre of town.

OTHER ACCOMODATION

Motels

In smaller towns the only fully furnished options may be motor lodges and motels, unless you can persuade a local estate agent trying to sell a house that an occupied house is better than one left empty. Motels catering for business travellers offer a better standard than those aimed at families.

The Qualmark system which rates a number of different types of accommodation has a reasonable rating system, although why a motel on a main road with drab furnishings but which happens to have a Jacuzzi-style plastic bath, should be awarded more stars than one with well-appointed rooms on a quiet street, is difficult to fathom.

Hotels

The hotel chains that do operate outside the main centres of Auckland, Wellington and Christchurch are to be found in the popular tourist resorts of Rotorua, Queenstown and the Bay of Islands. The scale tends to be low-key with smaller blocks rather than great towers. Look out for special deals out of season. In smaller towns the word 'hotel' is similar to the word 'pub' for British readers. In other words, a hotel in a small town may have a few rooms to let but make sure yours isn't over the bar. Things can get lively at weekends, especially in the winter months when a rugby game is on.

Upmarket Backpackers

If you thought your backpacking days were over, a quiet revolution has gone on over the past few years as the backpackers' market has become increasingly sophisticated. Baby boomers, who roughed it the first time they went around the world now demand modern facilities, just as much as their offspring do. A number of the more switched-on backpacking chains such as Base have been quick to capitalise on this growing demand. Of course it helps if you're backed by a major hotel chain, like the Accor group and can afford the capital investment.

While still catering for gap year students prepared to sleep in a dorm, they are responding to the needs of families and those individuals who wouldn't dream of sharing a bathroom with a stranger. Double rooms with ensuite facilities can be had at bargain rates, compared to hotels and even motels. Many travellers who could afford to stay elsewhere find the friendly, personal welcome and the chance to meet fellow travellers much more preferable than the faceless corporate hotel.

Farmstays and Bed and Breakfast Accommodation

Handy for the house hunter in rural areas, the farmstay can introduce those looking to move to the country to the reality of a rural life. Bed and Breakfast (Homestay) accommodation caters for all budgets. Prices depend on location but in rural areas in the off-season, discounted rates on luxury accommodation can be good value.

Useful Websites

www.tourism.net.nz. There's a great deal more on offer on this site than listings of where to find a bed for a night. You could be seriously distracted from your house-buying trip by the spas, fishing lodges and other attractions.

www.wotif.com. A last-minute accommodation specialist. Offers great deals if you're prepared to delay booking in advance. Good rates in the off-season.

www.jasons.co.nz. The Jasons site offers other useful travel related information as well as listings for all types of places to stay.

www.aaguides.co.nz. The site of the Automobile Association gives driving related advice, including maps and driving distances as well as the listings for budget to luxury lodgings.

www.holidayhomes.co.nz. A good selection of holiday homes on this site covering both islands.

www.nzholidayhomes.co.nz. This company says they do more than provide contact details and can assist clients with more personal advice on the area and amenities.

www.bookabach.co.nz The site to book the traditional New Zealand beach house.

www.truenz.co.nz/farmstays. Farmstays from Northland to Southland.

www.nzhomestay.co.nz. Bed and breakfast lodgings as well as farmstays.

www.accommodationnz.co.nz. Homestays and farmstays

Accommodation Guides

Jasons Travel Media Ltd publish *Motels, Apartments & Motor Lodges* as well as *Jasons SelectionsNZ* featuring b &bs, farmstays and lodges. The individual operators provide the information in these guides. They are available free from tourist information centres, featured accommodation operators and directly from *Jasons Travel Media Ltd: PO* Box 9390, Newmarket, Auckland 1031, ☎: 09-912-8400 fax:09-912-840.

The New Zealand Bed & Breakfast Guide: Pelican Publishing Company, ISBN:1589802926. Available to buy from bookshops.

LONG-TERM RENTALS

Properties for let for six months or more are generally unfurnished. You could struggle to find suitable furnished accommodation in the same location for a longer length of time. If you're based in an apartment block and

are prepared to move within the complex, there may be a similar apartment available when your short-term lease runs out.

Rental Furniture. If based in the main centres renting furniture and appliances is one option but it isn't cheap and the hire of the furniture package can be more expensive than the rent. Prices though, do drop the longer
the hire period.

How to Find Rental Properties

Wednesdays and Saturdays are the most popular days for real estate agents
to advertise their rental properties in the main daily regional newspapers.
Going via the newspaper first saves you the bother of ringing round all
the agents in the phone book, as most of them will only want to sell you a
house rather than rent you one.

Because the best rental property turns over quite quickly many estate
agents don't bother listing on-line. Larger agencies will fax or email you
a rental list but in small provincial towns they may not even have a list.
National real estate agency chains such as Harcourts, LJ Hooker and Ray
White list rental properties on their websites. Trade Me also lists rental
properties for all price brackets.

TENANCY AGREEMENTS

Periodic Tenancy

A periodic tenancy has no fixed date for the end of the tenancy and is suitable for tenants and landlords who want to rent for a short term. A tenant must give 21 days notice in writing and a landlord must give 90 days
notice. This kind of tenancy would be most suitable for house hunters or
anyone needing somewhere to live on a temporary basis while they wait for
the completion or settlement date on their new house.

Fixed Term Tenancy

Apart from those landlords looking to sell a property or those letting their
main home who might be going away for a few months, landlords renting
out unfurnished property prefer to let for a fixed term of six months or
more. The legal minimum for a fixed term is a month but landlords rent-

ing unfurnished properties argue that it's not worth letting a property for less than six months because of the wear and tear on the house caused by the frequent moving of furniture in and out of the house. In a fixed term tenancy, the agreement can only be ended on the date specified in the lease, unless by mutual consent, or by a ruling from the Tenancy Tribunal.

TENANCY LAWS AND YOU

Renting a property is a relatively hassle and risk-free business in New Zealand. Like Australia it is regulated by a hands-on government agency that mediates between tenant and landlord in a number of ways: If a deposit or bond against damages is requested by the landlord, any payment must be lodged with the Tenancy Services Centre within three weeks. Landlords cannot gain a financial advantage by investing and then earning interest from what is the tenant's money, nor can they claim that the tenant caused damage to a property, and then withhold a large chunk of the deposit for repairs.

Unlike a system where the balance of power weighs in the landlord's favour, the tenant is more likely to see their deposit returned to them intact. Tenancy Services acts as a low cost mediator in case of disputes between landlord and tenant. In addition to the mediation service, there is a help line, general tenancy information, copies of the Residential Tenancies Act and information on the Tenancy Tribunal – the final arbitrator for disputes between landlord and tenant.

Making an Application

The tenant makes an application to rent a property by completing a pre-tenancy application form. Tenants should bring with them a valid form of photo ID such as a passport or driver's licence. In order for the agent or landlord to carry out a credit check prospective tenants can be asked to provide details of their previous address and why they left it, their car registration and information on the make and model. If the car has been bought under a finance agreement any arrears will show up in the credit checks. Telephone contact details of two referees, one of whom must be able to provide a reference about credit worthiness is required. Anyone employed in New Zealand will be asked to confirm salary details or submit a bank statement showing proof of income.

Should the application be successful, a prospective tenant should find out how much money they will be expected to have with them when they sign the tenancy agreement. This could total as much as six weeks rent plus one week's letting fee plus 12.5% GST (Goods and Services Tax). For new arrivals that have only recently opened bank accounts and are waiting for chequebooks it can be a stretch to try to organise a relatively large amount of money at short notice. Some rental agents no longer accept personal cheques and will request a bank cheque or cash.

A written tenancy agreement will need to be completed and signed by the landlord and tenant before the start of the tenancy. Conditions can be written in that you both agree to. A landlord is entitled to limit the number of people who are allowed to live in the house or apartment.

At the start of the tenancy ensure that a property inspection report is carried out and that all the chattels are listed. Tenants are advised to take their own photographs of the interior of a property before they move as a visual back up to the inspection report should any disputes arise over the condition of the property at the end of the tenancy. The report lists the condition of each room in the property and is valid when signed off by both tenant and landlord. Both parties should keep a copy so that renters can be sure that they get their deposit back at the end of the tenancy. Ensure that the meters are read (including the water meter if there is one).

A CHECKLIST FOR TENANTS:

○ Connect the telephone and utilities. New account holders in New Zealand are generally asked to provide photo ID.
○ If the property has a water meter the bill will go to the landlord who will charge the tenant for metered water. Landlords pay for wastewater charges. If the water charge is taken out of general rates then the landlord pays for water usage.
○ Organise a mail redirection
○ Find out from the local council the day of rubbish and recycling collection.
○ Take out contents insurance and make sure this includes tenant liability.
○ Contact Tenancy Services after three weeks if they haven't confirmed that your bond has been lodged with them.

SUMMARY OF A TENANCY AGREEMENT

The Tenant's Responsibilities

- A tenant must pay the rent on time.
- Any damage caused by the tenant is their responsibility to organise repairs and pay for.
- Tenants must not make any alterations without the landlord's written consent.
- A tenant must make sure that the property is used mainly for residential purposes.
- The care and maintenance of a garden can sometimes cause problems.
- Landlords like to make it the tenant's responsibility to mow any lawn and ensure that the grass is cut regularly, unless stated otherwise in the lease. If a garden is extensively planted then the tenant cannot reasonably be expected to take care of it.
- Tenants must allow the landlord to enter the premises and consent must not be unreasonably withheld although they don't have to allow this if they haven't had 24 hours notice.
- Tenants are required to notify the landlord if repairs are needed. They are not permitted to withhold rent if they cannot get repairs done. In that event they should seek advice from Tenancy Services on 0800 83 62 62.
- Tenants are not permitted to change the locks without the landlord's permission.
- In the case of a periodic tenancy a tenant must give 21 days written notice that they are to vacate the premises.
- Tenants are required to leave the property in the same condition that they found it. It should be clean and tidy and all the rubbish must be removed. If the carpets were professionally cleaned before the start of the tenancy then the same must be done before you hand back the property. Many agents have got wise to tenants saving money and cleaning the carpets themselves and stipulate in the lease that tenants need to produce a receipt from a carpet cleaning company as proof that the work has been carried out to the required standard.

Landlord's Responsibilities

O A landlord cannot ask the tenant to pay more than two weeks rent in advance nor can they ask for more than four weeks rent as a bond against damages.

O A landlord cannot ask for key money unless the Tenancy Tribunal has agreed to this and they would only do this in special circumstances, for example if the landlord supplied a lawnmower with the property and asked for a small sum of money as deposit.

O A landlord must lodge the bond paid to them with the Tenancy Services Centre within 23 working days.

O A landlord cannot enter the premises without either giving notice or the tenant's consent.

O A landlord must give the tenant 24 hours notice for repairs and 48 hours notice for an inspection.

O As soon as any problems arise with a tenancy the landlord and tenant should try to negotiate between them to sort out any issues. If the two parties fail to reach agreement then contact Tenancy Services.

Termination of Contract. The landlord is entitled to apply to the Tenancy Tribunal if the rent is in arrears for more than 21 days.

Explanation of 'Address for Service'. An 'Address for Service' must be provided by landlord and tenant on the Tenancy Agreement.

For an 'Address for Service' to be legal it must be a physical street address as if an application is made to the Tenancy Tribunal legal documents cannot be sent to a post office box number.

If the address changes it is important to inform Tenancy Services. Tenants need to do this in order to ensure that the bond is returned to them as soon after the completion of the tenancy as possible.

Letting Fees

If you find a rental property through an agent, unlike in Australia it is the tenant rather than the landlord that pays the agent's letting fee which is one week's rent plus GST at 12.5%. If a property manager shows you a house or apartment there is no letting fee payable. Only a registered agent with the words MREINZ after their name is entitled to charge a letting fee. Private landlords have been known to take advantage of tenants from abroad by charging a fee and then pleading ignorance when they're pulled up for it. It's clearly stated in the Residential Tenancies Act 1986 that only registered agents acting in an official capacity, (that is letting someone else's house) can charge the fee.

Discrimination

The Human Rights Act 1993 stipulates that a landlord may not discriminate against a person because of their colour, race, ethnic or national origin, sex, marital status, age, religious or ethical belief, because they have children or because they are unemployed. A tenant who has grounds to believe they have been discriminated against can take the matter to the Tenancy Tribunal or to the Human Rights Commission.

> There is no legal requirement in New Zealand for either electrical or gas appliance safety checks although there is provision in the Residential Tenancies Act that landlords have a duty to comply with health and safety standards. It is the landlord's responsibility to ensure that for safety reasons a chimney is clean before the start of the tenancy.

HOME EXCHANGE

House swapping websites operate as introduction agencies for those looking to exchange communities and lifestyles with like-minded families. A home exchange can be a great cost effective option for house hunters. Trawling the internet sites of prospective house swaps showcased some very desirable properties in good areas throughout the country, from Northland down to the Southern Lakes. Judging by the photographs, the standard of housing advertised on these sites appears to be high and for many prospective house swappers, may even inspire a case of house envy.

But if you are worried that your home might not be as desirable as some of the homes on offer, the deal may even work in your favour. Even though that small flat in Edinburgh might not seem like fair exchange for a three bedroom beachside house in Auckland's sought-after eastern suburbs, the UK is a popular destination for New Zealanders who go not just for holidays but to spend time with family and friends. The New Zealand dollar doesn't go all that far in Britain and the price of hotel accommodation in tourist areas is prohibitive and many would probably love the opportunity to stay in a suburban home, rather than in a cramped hotel room if it is in an area with good transport links. And a comfortable base in a good location is more important than the number of bathrooms. House swapping allows prospective homeowners the opportunity to meet locals, something that might be denied them if they were merely renting a holiday home. A house swapper may set up an introduction with their friends who can be very useful for local advice and information.

Organisations that operate as introductory agencies for prospective house swappers include: *HomeLink International,* Homeexchange.com and Exchangesworldwide.com.

Aussie House Swap operates home exchanges between New Zealand and Australia. While house swapping isn't a new concept – organisations like *Home Base* and *Intervac* have been around for some time, the internet has given new life to the process, allowing potential exchangers to get to know each other through a series of email exchanges before they commit. And many of the properties advertised on the sites have a portfolio of photographs that allow you to go on a virtual house tour so that you can see exactly what you're getting, even down to the style and fit-out of the bathrooms.

Exchanges don't necessarily have to be done at the same time if the timing isn't right for both sides. Exchangers sign a contract which sets out the rights and obligations of both parties, and negotiate a fee to cover phone and the utility bills. Before you enter into any home swap agreement ensure that you contact your insurance company and ensure that your fellow swappers do the same. Many house swappers throw in a car for their visitors too and you will want to make sure that your New Zealand hosts have added you onto their licence as additional drivers. Make sure that they provide you with a detailed list of emergency contacts with information on local tradesmen and who to contact if any of the appliances go wrong during the swap. One final point to ensure before you swap is that the hosts have locked away valuables as their insurance policy may not include cover for accidental damage by third parties.

FEES, CONTRACTS AND CONVEYANCING

CHAPTER SUMMARY

- **Buying at auction.** Attend as many auctions as possible to become familiar with this popular way to sell property.
  - Employ an agent to bid on your behalf if you don't trust yourself not to get carried away in the heat of the moment.
  - Only if it is the house of your dreams and you are prepared to risk paying over the odds, should you consider making a pre-auction offer.
  - New Zealand has yet to outlaw vendor or 'dummy' bidding although reputable agencies do not allow this.
- **Valuation.** A valuation is sometimes the only way to gauge the correct price to bid.
- **Offers are legal and binding.** Only serious buyers should consider making an offer on a property as the written offer they sign is a legal and binding contract.
  - Before you sign anything have your solicitor check the contract for you first.
  - Direct the agent to the last page of the Sales and Purchase agreement which recommends both parties seek professional advice before signing.
- **Negotiated settlements – signing and counter signing.** Agents try to get both parties to reach a settlement on the day the offer is made.
- **Conditional contracts.** Conditions in a contract are a buyer's safety net.
  - Changing your mind is not a valid reason for backing out of a signed contract.

THE THREE WAYS TO BUY PROPERTY IN NEW ZEALAND

Buying property in New Zealand was until relatively recently, a straight-forward process, similar to the way that property is bought in Scotland – with no gazumping or the added stress of being forced to rely on the other links in the buying chain to complete their sales on the same day that you do. And from the outset the buyer would know if the house was in the right price range by the advertised asking price. The buyer would put in an offer and then the agent would negotiate between the vendor and the buyer until an agreement was reached. The only properties that went to auction were either mortgagee sales, unusual properties or those that were hard to sell.

Now, buying at auction is as common as negotiating a price. For international buyers who have never bought at auction it can seem an intimidating way to buy a house. But at least there is transparency at auction whereas with a house sold by tender it is a guessing game for interested buyers. But whether you buy at auction, tender or negotiate a price where there is no price tag; by paying for a valuation, the buyer can be sure that they are paying about the right price.

Capital Value (CV) and Land Value (LV). Local authorities use a system to determine the rating value of a property – referred to as the CV and the LV. These terms which you will sometimes see in property advertisements are a very basic valuation – carried out by a council officer who uses a combination of a visual assessment from the street as well as details held on the LIM of any improvements. The Council valuation takes into account what other houses in the area have been sold for, but does not take into account the chattels inside the house. Properties are re-evaluated every three years and you should only use the CV or LV as a yardstick. It does not replace the valuation as it is not as an accurate measure of a property's market value.

Buying at Auction

While discretion over financial affairs is an aspect of the British character, New Zealanders and Australians cannot be that coy if they are willing to conduct their house sale and purchase in such a public forum as an auction room. Some British people may recoil in horror at the very idea. To generate maximum interest in a sale, the agent may prefer to hold the auction on site at a weekend, to attract as many potential buyers as possible although most auctions take place during the week in the more discreet surroundings of the auction room.

An auction held on a weekend is a forum open to all comers, including those who have no interest in bidding – from curious neighbours, Sunday drivers on an outing and most importantly for potential overseas buyers, those looking to see how the auction process is conducted. Auctions in New Zealand are run in a relaxed fashion and once you are familiar with the auction process, you will be far more confident about bidding at auction if you have attended a few first.

Fans of the auction process say that it is the most transparent of selling techniques and reveals the true value of a property, underscoring the argument that a property is only worth what someone will pay for it. The counterargument is that it is a process designed to intimidate buyers. Many buyers would rather buy a property that has a set price and make an offer on that as they know that if their offer is accepted, that if all goes well and the house is structurally sound that they will not run the risk of paying for a builder's report and valuation that are useless if they are then outbid.

Agents love auctions as providing their marketing campaign has been effective, it gives them a set date to work towards to collect their commission. Some would say that selling by auction is a fair system as the market decides the value, not the vendor. Vendors with an unrealistic price expectation can find the process a humbling experience.

Both agents and auctioneers love the emotive atmosphere that potential buyers bring to the auction. It is in both their interests to ensure there is an element of excitement in the auction process. Auctioneers use well-established sales techniques to raise the emotions during the auction. Slick operators, they are adept at pitching one buyer against another and can easily spot a novice. But you can prepare yourself for such tactics. Don't get carried away by an over-enthusiastic auctioneer. You and not the auctioneer will be the one landed with paying over the odds for a property if you do.

If you find the whole process too nerve-wracking, you can always nominate a professional to bid on your behalf. If you set the upper limit before the auction starts then the agent bidding for you has to work within those defined boundaries.

Pre-auction Bids. You should register your interest as a potential bidder for a property to the vendor's agent prior to the auction but be very wary of revealing what you believe the property to be worth. Once an agent knows that you are interested do not be persuaded to put in a pre-auction bid unless you have your heart set on this property and are prepared to take a risk and pay over the odds. There is no guarantee that the vendor will accept your bid and may even be advised by the agent to wait until auction day.

All a pre-auction bid does is expose the potential buyer into disclosing how much they are prepared to bid. That information can be used against them by the vendor's agent to either set a price for the reserve, or if the reserve has already been set, it could mean that all the buyers who have registered their interest may be contacted and the auction will be pulled forward. If you made your best offer thinking this would secure the house you will be in for a shock as the auctioneer will open the bidding with that price. You will just have to hope that nobody else bids if you really have given your best offer. If another buyer bids against you then either you will end up paying more than you wanted to secure the property or you may on this occasion, have to walk away.

A Pre-Auction Checklist

- ○ Contact a registered valuer to get a valuation on the property to see if it is within your price range.
- ○ Arrange for a builder to carry out a building inspection.
- ○ Contact a solicitor to check the title and to attend to all the other legal matters that are involved in the purchase process. Ask the solicitor to take you through the auction documents so that you understand the sales conditions. These include the date and amount of deposit, the possession date and when the balance of the purchase price has to be paid.
- ○ If you have a pre-purchase approval of an amount from your mortgage lender then you should notify them that this is the property you are going to be bidding for. Sales by auction are unconditional and all the finance has to be in place before you bid.
- ○ Take a bank cheque for the deposit to the auction. Once your bid has been accepted you have therefore agreed to purchase the property and are required to sign the contract. If you change your mind you will still have to pay the deposit, usually 10% of the purchase price.

VENDOR OR DUMMY BIDDING

Vendor or dummy bidding has been outlawed in Australia and even though a number of the national estate agent chains are Australian owned, it seems odd that New Zealand has yet to outlaw this dubious practice. Rather than waiting for a change in the legislation, the more enlightened chains do not allow vendor bidding. As there is nothing transparent about vendor bidding, unless the auctioneer declares this, there should be no place for it in the auction process.

Subject to reserve. The seller in consultation with their agent sets the reserve price. Once this reserve has been reached the auctioneer announces that the property is officially on the market.

Passed in. When a property fails to reach its reserve price it is passed in. A period of intense negotiation follows where the highest bidder is given the first option to purchase the property at the seller's reserve price. If this process fails to secure the sale then the second highest bidder can then approach the seller's agent and the process is repeated.

Agents will do their utmost to broker a deal satisfactory to both parties and secure a sale on the day. If they fail, then the property will go back on the market. The reserve price will be put on it as the sale price and the property will then become 'subject to negotiation'.

Tender

The advantage for the seller of a tender is that it is conducted in private. The drawback is that the entire system is so discreet, especially with a closed tender, that the buyer has to go in blind, neither knowing the price expectation of the seller, nor what the other buyers are prepared to pay. The buyer fills out a written offer, which can include conditions and then has to wait until the day the tender closes. On the day that the tender closes the most acceptable offer is chosen by the vendor.

The seller may choose an unconditional offer even if it is not the highest price. If you are going to attach conditions to your offer then suggest the minimum number of days needed to tempt the vendor to choose you over another bidder. Because the buyer has to do much more research first as well as have their builder's report and valuation carried out before putting in a tender, this puts off all but the keenest buyers. Buyers that are prepared to take a risk bide their time to see whether or not the tender process has been successful and then make their offer if the house fails to sell this way and then goes on to the open market.

By Negotiation

The system most familiar to UK buyers, nevertheless the speed at which property transactions are conducted in New Zealand can come as a shock especially for anyone who has been stuck in a seemingly endless property chain. It really is vital then for prospective buyers to be very sure that the property they are going to put an offer in on is the one that they intend to buy.

All offers on New Zealand properties are made in writing and offers are legally binding once they have been signed by the buyer and counter signed by the vendor.

Therefore, it is the real estate agent that initiates the contractual process between buyer and seller, not the solicitors. Agents do have to undergo a training course and become a member of the Real Estate Institute of New Zealand in order to be legally permitted to do this. The document you will be asked to sign is called the *Agreement for Sale and Purchase of Real Estate*. The main points are summarised below.

You should of course go through this document with your lawyer but knowing what your obligations are before you sign allows you to organise what needs to be done in order to meet the deadlines imposed. And you should in any case alert your lawyer that you intend to make an offer on a property so that they have time to explain which conditions you should add to the contract and the exact wording to use.

The vendor's agent may try to put the pressure on you early on in the proceedings by setting an unrealistic time frame for you to complete all your paperwork. Before you put an offer in it is worth asking the local council how long they are currently taking to process the local searches or Land Information Memorandum (LIM). When an agent suggests five working days for all reports to be completed, make a counter offer of ten. If the agent then tells you that there are back-up offers then call their bluff and request to see them. This may do the trick and buy you the required time.

Summary of Main Points of the Sales and Purchase Agreement

Page 1 – The front page of the document contains the important information with the date of the agreement, the names and addresses of vendor and purchaser and the address of the property.

Estate. The choices are: fee simple (for a freehold property), leasehold, cross-lease (where a property has been subdivided from one site) or unit title (usually refers to an apartment).

Legal description. This is the information held by the council which shows the land area, and the reference number of the property on the district plan. This is the aspect of the contract that your lawyer will be paying close attention to ensure that what is being described is correct.

Purchase price. In a negotiated settlement the purchase price is the most common part of the contract that is countersigned by each party until they reach an agreement. The first step is that the buyer nominates a purchase price. This is not the final price that is to be paid as the vendor will countersign the agreement with his or her own price. In a model negotiated settlement the buyer will write the price $250,000 on the contract and put their signature against it. The vendor (who thinks that this isn't enough money) will cross out and sign against the buyer's figure and write $270,000 on the contract. The buyer will then cross out the new figure and sign it and meet the vendor half way with $260,000 and sign it. The vendor will agree the figure and sign their name next to the new figure of $260,000.

Deposit. Each agency works on a percentage figure of the purchase price as a deposit as the notes with the contract do not actually stipulate what percentage this has to be. The deposit can be as low as 5% of the purchase price.

Possession. Possession is the equivalent to the completion date in an English contract. Again, this is another part of the contract that may require negotiation especially if the seller hasn't yet found somewhere else.

Conditions. This is the key area of the contract that a buyer should be familiar with. The only time you should enter into an unconditional sale is if you buy a house through auction. You should satisfy yourself that you have checked out all the risks associated with buying the property before you sign, otherwise you risk losing your deposit.

Additional Clauses

The clauses you want to add to a conditional contract are:

- A clause that states that the purchase is subject to finance. Even if you have a mortgage offer from the bank, this clause allows time to complete the paperwork on this particular property.
- An additional clause stating that the property is subject to a valuation. Many prospective buyers do not believe that a valuation is necessary once they have put in their offer. The outlay of a few hundred dollars for a valuation could potentially save you thousands.
- A clause that states that the purchase is subject to a builder's report or a building inspection. The building inspector may recommend that you commission an engineer's report. These two professionals undertake similar work to the structural surveyor in the UK.
- One final clause you will want to add should include wording specifying that the purchase is subject to solicitor's approval. This general wording allows the solicitor to carry out the local searches and obtain the Land Information Memorandum (LIM) from council and ensure that there is nothing untoward with any aspect of the property. The LIM reveals what work has been carried out on the property and whether or not a building consent was granted for that work.

All of these clauses are extremely important for the purchaser to consider adding to their offer to purchase. Your solicitor will advise you of the exacting wording. Additional clauses may be included such as a clause relating to the checking that chattels such as dishwashers, and ovens are in full working order. If the property is highly desirable and there are a number of interested parties the purchaser has to try to minimise the number of clauses or else reduce the time allowed to get the reports back so that their contract appears enticing to the seller.

The clause that relates to OIA Consent refers to the Overseas Investment Authority and as stated in the chapter, What Type of Property to Buy, this only applies to the purchase of large areas of iconic or 'sensitive' property. The centre pages of the *Sales and Purchase Agreement* explains in detail what the terms used in the document mean. But the important information is on the first and last pages.

New Zealand agents that have no appreciation for the different ways that houses are bought around the world cannot be expected to give overseas buyers any special assistance in helping them understand the contract. A good agent will do this but if you encounter one who is complacent or who tries to rush you through the process, ask for an adjournment and call your lawyer.

Every buyer should read through the last page of the Agreement and if there is anything there that you don't understand and that needs further explanation then this is the point that you should assert your rights and request that you take the contract to your solicitor.

Signing and Countersigning

Contracts can be signed and countersigned a number of times until agreement is reached and agents will work long into the night, driving between the two parties to negotiate and try to secure a sale. While negotiation over purchase price is the most common reason for contracts to be countersigned by the vendor, another can be agreeing on a settlement date that suits both parties. If buyers require a long settlement date, because they have a house to sell first, they should check this out first with the vendor's agent to see if this is possible.

A vendor of an expensive property may trade a long settlement date in return for an increase in purchase price. While their investment is tied up waiting for you to settle they are prevented from investing their money and earning what can be considerable interest on it.

Pre Settlement Inspection. You are entitled to check that the property that you are buying is in the same condition as when you agreed to buy it. Do this as close to settlement date as possible and when the house has been vacated by the previous owners. You should inspect for any damage caused during moving, checking to see that all the chattels on the chattels list are in fact still there and have not been removed and that they are in working order. Make sure too that no rubbish has been left in the garage, or in attics or other storage areas. If there are any problems or discrepancies you should contact your solicitor immediately, who will then contact the vendor's and ask for any outstanding matters to be attended to urgently prior to settlement.

Title Search

It is your solicitor who will search the title for you to find out if there are interests such as rights of way and easements that can affect the future use of your property. You should also ask your solicitor to explain what in practical terms that can mean.

If the property you intend to buy is in an established area where all the adjoining sites have houses on them already, it is less likely that there will be any need for the local council to take up their rights with regard to the easement. Your solicitor can always find out if they are planning to upgrade any drains that pass underneath your property in the near future.

If your property adjoins an empty section then sooner or later it's bound to be developed. And you could be in for a nasty shock when you receive a letter from council stating that complete strangers have the right to dig up part of your garden to connect drains. Even though councils have a statutory requirement to ensure that all work has to be made good afterwards, you are the one that will have to put up with the disruption and inconvenience.

Freehold Title. A freehold title allows you the same rights as buying freehold in the UK. Of course if you want to undertake any development, you still have to comply with building codes and local council regulations.

Leasehold. The lessor owns the land on which the building is situated and the lessee pays the lessor ground rent. Leasehold can take different forms and you should seek legal opinion first before you make your offer. The most restrictive lease is a non-renewable fixed-term. Renewable leases which can be taken out for a designated number of years are subject to increases in ground rent. Ground rent is calculated as a percentage of land value. You should budget at least 5% of land value although the percentage will be clearly stated on the lease contract.

Freehold Cross Lease. When land is subdivided and when townhouses or terrace houses are built on a site, the owners of the townhouses each own a part of the freehold and are tenants-in- common. That means that one of the property owners cannot do anything with the land without the others permission. Each homeowner leases their houses from each other on identical terms such as 999 years.

Unit Title. When buying an apartment in a block your apartment may be either freehold or leasehold depending on whether the apartment owners own the land collectively or if this is owned by a third party. For example, the apartments in the Princes Wharf development on Auckland's waterfront are leasehold. If the block you are buying into is freehold then it will have a body corporate, an organisation set up to manage and maintain the development. Each apartment pays a fee each year to the body corporate for maintaining common areas. The more facilities on site, the higher the body corporate fees.

There will often be fairly draconian rules and regulations that restrict various activities at night time, including running washing machines and vacuum cleaners. There will be rules on whether pet ownership is permitted as well as rules regarding the drying of laundry.

Council Matters

Your solicitor should examine the Land Information Memorandum (LIM) held by the local council to check that everything is in order. But you can check out not just the LIM but also the property file by going to the local council and requesting to see this. Many councils now charge for this service. The property file may contain important information not on the LIM that relates to the building as well as resource consents and correspondence.

The LIM will contain information on features of the land and can alert homebuyers as to whether the house they are about to buy could be on land subject to: erosion, subsidence, alluvion (silt from flooding), flooding, and whether or not prior to the development for residential use there were contaminants or hazards stored on the site. The LIM will also detail any protected trees. A protected tree can require resource consent even for pruning. Trees do not have to be all that large or special to be protected. The removal of a tree without permission, either native or exotic, in an area where resource consent is required will result in a large fine.

Some councils provide LIMs via their websites, which can speed up the process considerably. The cost of a LIM varies between councils and whether or not you need it urgently. For a non-urgent LIM it is a statutory requirement that these are processed within ten working days.

Costs Associated with Buying a House

The good news for anyone buying into the New Zealand market is that there is no stamp duty to pay on purchase but even without stamp duty the costs of buying can soon mount up.

These are the kinds of fees you will pay in a metropolitan area for an average three bedroom house:

- *Solicitors charges* – allow $1000
- *For an urgent LIM* – allow $270
- *Building inspection* – allow $300
- *Valuation* – allow $300
- *Mortgage related costs* – $200
- *Engineer's report* (for steep sites) – $400

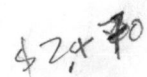

You should keep money aside for the other miscellaneous costs once you move such as upgrading the locks, putting in electrical sockets and plumbing in appliances.

Useful Websites

www.finda.co.nz Whether you need a lawyer or a registered valuer this site helps you sort through the listings of the professionals you will need to employ for your property transaction.

www.yellowpages.co.nz This site is specific to a particular location so that you can source professionals working in the area you intend to buy.

www.qv.co.nz Quotable Value are a company that provide both on-line valuations (which you have to pay for) and links to registered valuers. Currently the site is only available to those with Windows applications. Apple Mac users unfortunately have to rely on the post.

Part IV

WHAT HAPPENS NEXT

SERVICES

MAKING THE MOVE

BUILDING OR RENOVATING

MAKING MONEY FROM YOUR PROPERTY

SERVICES

CHAPTER SUMMARY

○ It can be very expensive to get mains services for telephone and electricity to isolated rural properties.

○ **Electricity.** Electricity is relatively cheap in New Zealand compared with the rest of the world, although it has gone up in price recently.

  ○ Consumers have a choice of electricity supplier.

○ **Plugs.** New Zealand plugs have three flat pins like Australia's. Appliances work in both countries with no adaptor needed.

○ **Heating.** Central heating does not really exist and New Zealand houses can be damp and cold.

  ○ A dehumidifier or a ventilation system is one way to ensure your house remains warm and dry in the winter.

○ **Gas.** Mains gas is only available in the North Island. In the South Island you'll need to use bottled gas.

○ **Water.** If you do not have access to a mains water supply, have the roof water tested by a laboratory to see if it is safe to drink.

  ○ Droughts are common in the eastern part of the country and you may need to buy in water.

Organising service connections to properties in towns and cities is simply a matter of proving your identity and that you can pay for the services required. The utility providers ask for standard information from applicants, including personal details as well as those that relate to the house. For renters this will be the name of your landlord and letting agent. New customers needing a landline connection are required to provide a copy of photo ID such as a passport.

In rural areas it is another matter. Not only is it very expensive to get connected to mains electricity and telephone services, there are other factors you may not have considered. For instance, in an isolated rural area there may be no mains sewer or water supply. These are services that most city dwellers take for granted but need regular maintenance which will have to be undertaken at your own expense.

ELECTRICITY

Electricity is generated in New Zealand from a combination of gas, coal, hydro, geothermal resources and increasingly, wind generation. Since deregulation in 1999, the private sector generates around 40% of the country's electricity. The government still retains control of the transmission company, Transpower. Since 1998 a parliamentary act ensured that companies responsible for distribution were to be owned separately from electricity generation and retail businesses.

As well as allowing the private sector to generate electricity, deregulation allowed electricity consumers to switch supplier. There are now around ten electricity retail companies, three of which, Meridian, Genesis and Mighty River power are state-owned.

New Zealand consumers, until recently, enjoyed some of the cheapest electricity prices in the world. In 2004 consumers were paying 15 NZ cents per Kilowatt-hour, while Australia charged 20 cents, the USA, 22 cents and the UK, 25 cents. But because of the decline in output from the Maui field, prices have started to increase.

Customers of Mercury Energy (Mighty River Power) can expect to pay 5% more for their electricity in 2006 and it is likely that there will be similar price rises across the board.

You can find out which electricity company offers the best deal in your area by logging on to the *Powerswitch* website: *www.consumer.org. nz/powerswitch*. Run by the Consumers Organisation it provides a good comparison of electricity prices in your area. In the areas that do not yet have a competitor for you to switch to, the site offers advice on how to save money with your current supplier.

Meters are supposed to be read at least three times a year although consumers are obliged to pay an estimated bill if the meter hasn't been read. Ring in with your own meter reading, if the company allows this. You can pay your bill through an automatic payment, by internet or telephone banking, with a credit card, by cheque, through pre-payment or in person at any New Zealand Post Shop. A discount incentive scheme may be available if you pay by direct debit.

Arranging a Contract over the Telephone. You don't need to stand in a lengthy queue just to get connected to an electricity supplier – it can all be arranged over the phone as most suppliers have a separate department for clients that are moving house. Check with your estate agent that the meters have been read and that the previous owners have paid up. As well as the address of the property you may need to supply the meter number.

Meters. Because meters are installed outside the property and the meter reader has to come on to the land to read it, you need to inform the electricity company if you own a dog.

Power Supply and Plugs. New Zealand's power supply is 230/240 volt, 50Hz and electrical sockets take a three-pin type of plug (not the same as the UK one). British appliances will work with an adaptor, North-American equipment requires a transformer as well as an adaptor but Australian appliances can just be plugged in.

Electrical Safety. As a precaution when buying an old house you should ask a qualified electrician to check that the wiring meets current standards. There is no mandatory safety inspection required even when renting out a house so it is up to you to ensure that the wiring is safe. It is very easy to overload circuits in old villas – all it takes is too many appliances run off the same circuit all being used at once. While the occasional fuse blow out is understandable in older houses, if it occurs on a regular basis then it's a sure sign that all is not well and time to call a registered electrician.

Bulbs. Both bayonet and screw fitting bulbs are in use in New Zealand homes, although bayonet fittings are more common in older houses.

Rural Properties. You have to have deep pockets to get a rural section connected in New Zealand, especially if the house is going to be further than 400 metres from an existing transformer. If it is within that distance and close to the road boundary then it may be just cabling that is required.

Although the costs of getting services to the gate have to be paid upfront by the owner of the land, before you purchase it, it can cost the farmer $25,000 per km for new power lines. Add on the cost of a transformer and high voltage extension at $5000. To make it economic to subdivide land the cost is going to have to be passed on. And it doesn't stop there. Although some savings can be made if all the services (power, telephone and water) can be run in the same trench, you could still be paying around $10,000.

Heating

Some New Zealanders live in a *Narnia*-like fantasy world when it comes to their climate, pretending that winter doesn't really exist there. Older people who were brought up tough, think nothing of putting on an extra sweater when it gets cold in winter, rather than acknowledge that the house itself is the problem. It is hardly surprising then that New Zealand homes are colder and damper than those in many other countries. There is increasing evidence that these damp and cold homes are contributory factors to the 800,000 cases of asthma and respiratory illness – one of the highest rates in the world. Poorly insulated houses contribute to the problem.

The concept of central heating, with radiators in every room does not exist in New Zealand yet, unfortunately. Very few houses have any system which can be pre-set. The more expensive type of portable oil fired radiators do operate on timer switches but this still won't give complete coverage of the whole house in the way that fixed radiators do.

Modern houses, with tiled floors and bathrooms are particularly cold in winter although some may have under-floor heating. The trend for open-plan living has made houses even colder as they become even harder to heat. A form of gas central heating is available but the system blows hot air and the house needs to be well ventilated. Individually controlled gas fires are an option but because gas fires aren't recommended in bedrooms you'll need back up heating to keep warm in winter.

There are a number of other steps that homeowners can take to make their homes warmer. These include putting in ceiling insulation as well as under floor insulation, which can be installed underneath wooden houses, providing there is a big enough crawl space under the house to allow access. Fortunately winter in New Zealand is short and it's only cold for four months of the year, unless you live in Otago and Southland.

Dehumidifiers. A dehumidifier is essential in winter, particularly in houses that don't get much sun. Many homeowners have theirs running permanently in the coldest part of the house (usually the south east corner). Make sure the dehumidifier you buy is one with a decent sized water container as it's a chore to empty it more than once a day.

Ventilation Systems. There are two types: (a) a heat recovery ventilation system uses a heat exchanger where air is pumped in from the outdoors and stale air is pumped outdoors, and (b) forced air ventilation blows dry air from the roof space around the house. How much such a system costs will depend on the size of the house but you should budget at least $2500. Ask the company to provide you with names of satisfied customers for you to contact.

GAS

The gas fields are concentrated off the central North Island coast. Mains gas is supplied to over 50 towns and cities in the North Island. The mains gas pipeline does not extend across the Cook Strait and South Islanders have to rely on electricity or bottled liquid petroleum gas (LPG) for their supplies. The price of mains gas works out favourably in comparison to the price of electricity although it's just recently gone up.

There are seven gas companies and at least two supply both electricity and gas. Consolidating your gas and electricity with one supplier may save you money and you will only have one bill. Meter reading and payment methods operate in a similar way to the electricity companies. The Consumers Organisation website www.consumer.org.nz allows you to compare the best deals for natural gas in your area.

Don't bother searching inside the house for anything as compact as a combination-boiler. The gas hot water cylinder is too big to go inside and will be attached to the outside of the house. The gas supply for the heating will feed into the house separately. Only registered technicians are permitted to carry out installation and maintenance of mains gas appliances.

There is no statutory requirement for regular gas safety checks to be carried out, but all gas appliances, especially un-flued portable gas heaters should be checked for wear and tear on a regular basis. The fumes that any un-flued gas appliance gives off may affect those people with respiratory problems so always ensure that the room is well ventilated.

Bottled Gas

Gas bottles sold mainly for cooking, barbecues, portable gas fires and patio heaters come in sizes of 4kg and 9kg. The 9kg bottle costs from $46.00 and these can be filled with liquid petroleum gas at service stations for around $22. Bottled gas can be used for heating, hot water and cooking but this needs to be organised with a supplier. The cost varies from region to region. The gas bottles will connect to the outside of the house and a registered gas technician will need to install this.

PORTABLE CABINET LPG HEATERS

Long been used as a way of heating a remote rural bach, portable LPG room heaters (with the gas cylinder integral to the appliance) have been banned from sale in Australia based on their previous poor safety history. New Zealand has yet to follow suit.

The *Energy Safety Service*, a division of the Ministry of Consumer Affairs at *www.ess.govt.nz/safety,* has a list of safety tips for their use, one of which is to carry out regular leak tests and to ventilate the room. They advise that an LPG service agent should service the appliance once a year. It isn't all that likely, though, that many bach owners are going to go to the trouble of calling out a service agent, (even if they could find one locally).

WATER

The mains water supply and wastewater is under the control of the local authority, which may have a separate company that runs this side of council business. In the larger cities water is metered and a separate bill will be sent out over and above the rates.

Turning off the Water. Ask the agent to show you where the stopcock is situated so that you know where to turn the water off in an emergency. You will never find it unless someone shows you: – usually in front of the house under a manhole cover in the pavement.

In rural Canterbury and Marlborough and other eastern parts of the country, drought conditions and water restrictions are a regular feature of late summer. If you live on a small holding or a lifestyle block with crops or stock, there will be times when you may need to buy in water. It will cost between $200 to $500.

New Zealand mains water is world class and only those on tank supplies should spend their money buying bottled water. Although there are some people who regard roof or rain water to be better for them, a recent Massey University study has proven otherwise. From the sample of 450, 30 percent contained enough bacteria to make the average person ill.

Unless you buy a house with a new water tank or have a new one installed (which will cost anything between $3000 to $4500) you should have the water quality tested by a Ministry of Health approved laboratory. Don't take the vendor's assurances that their roof water is safe to drink, just because it hasn't made them ill. Immunity can build up to unsafe drinking water.

Householders are advised to regularly inspect the tank for holes and to regularly clean out the tank as well as the gutters. The water should be tested regularly.

Waste Water or a Resource for Recycling?

Many rural properties will have a septic tank installed and you should have this checked as many older systems still in use were badly designed or incorrectly sited.

It is up to the property owner to ensure that the septic tank works properly and does not pollute the environment. One of the problems with septic tanks is that they do not suit the modern lifestyle, including modern appliances such as dishwashers and washing machines that pump large amounts of water into the system. Toxic household chemicals can also cause septic tanks to fail. One solution is to add an aerobic sand filter to the outlet of a conventional septic tank.

If you need to put in a replacement septic tank. or install a new one, seek advice from a plumbing and drainage inspector at your local council. An engineer who has experience in their design must design any new system. Soil conditions, the size of the section, the number of people in the household, and other factors such as ground water levels and whether or not the site is sloping will all determine whether or not your property is suitable. The cost of putting in a new septic tank, if the property is sited near natural water (a lake or a river) including tank and installation could be as much as $20,000.

The septic tank may have been a revolutionary invention in the nineteenth century, but when building from scratch, should homeowners be looking at a more up-to-date system and one with better 'green' credentials? Waitakere City Council (known as the eco-friendly council) has produced an excellent paper discussing in detail the merits of different forms of wastewater management, including information on recycling domestic water. Consult www.waitakere.govt.nz, which has a link to wastewater. There you will find information on environmentally friendly systems that can be combined, such as a composting toilet with a separate system for collecting and recycling grey water from washing.

Installing a Solar Hot Water System

Depending on the size of your house, installing a solar hot water system will cost between $3,500 to $8,500. This can halve your energy bills and the system will not only save you money in the long-term but also allow you to do your bit for the environment. The government subsidises the installation by providing interest free loans.

Fire Prevention in Rural Areas

Fire warnings are issued regularly over summer. In forested areas this may include a total fire ban. Fire prevention measures include storing firewood and flammable items away from the house and making sure that the property is cleared of any rubbish.

General fire prevention measures inside the house include fitting it with smoke alarms (testing them at the start and end of daylight saving), keeping a fire blanket in the kitchen and having the wiring in the house checked to ensure that it complies with current safety regulations.

TELEPHONE

Customers in Christchurch and Wellington now have an alternative provider to Telecom for the supply of line rental. Tellingly, when Telecom recently upped the price of line rental to domestic customers by nearly six percent to $42.20, customers in Christchurch and Wellington, who now have TelstraClear in their area, were only paying $34.80.

New subscribers need to provide a copy of their photo ID, such as a passport to arrange a new connection. The rest of the information can be given over the phone.

Directories and Yellow Pages. You can pick up spare copies of telephone directories at your local Post Shop if the property you buy has none in the house or else call Telecom on 123 for assistance on how to obtain them.

Mobiles. With only two key players in the mobile phone market, Telecom and Vodafone, these two companies, who operate a duopoly, have ensured that New Zealand consumers pay some of the highest charges for mobile phone use in the OECD. While prices have been going down nearly everywhere else in the world, Vodafone decided to raise its charges for calls over-

seas by 10c a minute. Between them Telecom and Vodafone are a billion dollar industry yet the New Zealand consumer is being treated with contempt.
For more information see *Communications* in *Living in New Zealand.*

SECURITY

Stealing from parked cars at tourist sights is the main petty crime problem
but homeowners shouldn't be complacent. There are still small towns in
the South Island where people rarely lock their doors but in the rest of the
country you will need efficient locks. Even window locks and bolts are not
going to stop the determined burglar but at least they will make their job
more difficult.

There is no point in installing an expensive alarm system if the front
door can be operated by one easily copied key. Make friends with your
neighbours and let them know when you are going to be away. Security
sensor lights around the outside of the house are a good idea. Because
wind or even a spider getting into the system can trigger an alarm, an
unmonitored alarm ringing in suburbia may not be investigated. Providing
your property is not too remote and difficult to get to a monitored alarm
system may be your best option.

You can leave windows open during summer without attracting burglars
if you use window locks. When going away, leave security lights on, and
use timer switches so that lights and radios can come on in the evening. As
well as cancelling the newspaper, ensure that you arrange for a neighbour
to collect your post as well as clear out all the junk mail. An overflowing
letterbox can be spotted from any passing car.

Home Insurance. Check the small print in your insurance contract to
see how long you are allowed to leave your property unoccupied. If you
do go away frequently then you should ensure that you have a monitored
alarm.

House Sitters

A house sitter could be the ideal solution to ensure that your house is occupied and cared for. A house sitting company will undertake reference
checks. Whether or not you pay the house sitter is up to company policy
but if you have pets or gardens to care for, then an offer to pay for the sitter's power bill will ensure that they will want to work for you again. As

many sitters are retirees, not all of them will want or be able to walk a large and boisterous dog so ask the company to provide you with a sitter who would enjoy canine company.

STAFF/CLEANERS

Buying a cleaning franchise is one of the ways that many new immigrants who came in under the old General Skills category were able to make a living. With New Zealand's low unemployment rate few people are interested in doing these kinds of jobs, unless they have a stake in their own business. This may be the only way you'll find a cleaner in wealthier areas. Expect to pay $60 per hour plus 12.5% GST.

Finding a Gardener. There are plenty of garden maintenance companies that will weed and tidy your garden as well as mow the lawn but not all employees of such companies know all that much about plant care. Ask your local garden centre if they can recommend a good local gardener who can assist with lawn care or propagation.

Hard landscaping and garden design is best left to specialist companies who will be able to advise you on what resource consents are needed to carry out the work.

Personal recommendations are the best way to find a suitable gardener or garden design company as that way you can see the gardener's work for yourself.

Caretaker. You may find it easier to employ a property maintenance company that will provide a cleaner and caretaker who will come in for a few hours each week. The prices of such services vary but expect to pay at least $60 per hour plus GST (12.5%). New Zealand is an egalitarian society and service is not really part of the culture. Whether staff will be prepared to work for rates as low as the minimum wage, ($9.50 per hr), when the average wage is over double that, depends entirely on where your property is situated. Even getting an unqualified student over the summer holidays through Student Job Search will cost you at least $12.00 per hour in the Auckland region.

MAKING THE MOVE

CHAPTER SUMMARY

- **Preparing for the move.** Start clearing out attics and garden sheds well in advance of the packers arriving.
- **Cars.** Whether you have to pay import duty on a used car you bring into the country depends on your visa.
- **Removals.** The firm you choose should be up-to-date with the latest bio-security requirements in New Zealand.
- **Pets.** Only dogs and cats are permitted to enter New Zealand.
  - Because of respiratory problems that can increase during air travel, there are restrictions placed on shipping snub-nosed dogs.
  - Get your pet used to their shipping container before they fly.

REMOVALS

What to Take with You to New Zealand

What to take with you to New Zealand will depend upon whether you are financing the move yourself or if an employer will be picking up the bill for the removal of your household effects. If you have to pay for the move yourself, the major cost could be the insurance (see the comment from the Taylor family, below.) You will, of course want to take antique furniture or other valuable items and personal effects but other worn-out items that need replacing anyway should be sold off or donated to charity and purchased in New Zealand.

If you have recently purchased an expensive television, it may be worthwhile taking it, even if the shipping company advises against it. Only if you are certain you want to live in an Edwardian era villa (many of which don't have built in storage), is it worthwhile taking wardrobes. By all means take heirloom pieces but New Zealanders don't tend to use them, preferring instead to have these built-in.

Clearing out unwanted items from the home should be tackled as far in advance as possible – especially attics and garden sheds. Put aside all the equipment that will need to be scrubbed and disinfected together, as this will ensure that they don't get forgotten.

Removal Firms

There are a number of large companies that specialise in international removals. Choosing a firm will be dependent on such factors as cost and delivery time. The shortest and most direct route will be the most expensive but you should be careful about opting for the alternative. The least amount of time your goods spend in a container, the better. Either the container will go on a circuitous route to get to New Zealand or it may be left sitting on the quayside, waiting to be loaded.

Then there is the consideration about what arrangements have been made for your temporary furnished accommodation in New Zealand. Most companies that move their newly recruited staff to New Zealand expect to have to pay to put a family up for a month, to allow for delivery of furniture, but may baulk at having to foot the bill for any longer.

As well as cost and speed of delivery you should choose a firm that is knowledgeable about your destination and is up to date on New Zealand's strict bio-security laws, which are among the world's toughest. New Zealand is free of foot and mouth disease and any such outbreak would be disastrous for an island economy heavily reliant on its agricultural exports.

Biosecurity New Zealand have to ensure that unwanted insect pests don't get into the country and rely on your co-operation to declare certain types of wooden furniture, particularly cane. Even if it was bought in the UK or the USA it may be harbouring insect larvae and you will need to note these items, as they will be, along with outdoor equipment below, the items most likely to be subject to inspection on arrival. There are strict rules regarding the need to disinfect items such as hiking boots, camping equipment, gardening tools, plant pots or any other items (including shoes) that may have been in contact with soil.

Whether you pack your own furniture and belongings depends on whether or not you have any fine furniture and antiques to ship as you may not be able to claim against insurance, if you pack these yourself and they break. Most firms have a special service for such items where they are bubble wrapped and then covered in corrugated cardboard. However, if your belongings only contain a few delicate or precious items, one way of cutting costs is to buy your own packing materials wholesale, doing all your own packing and then shipping everything in your own 20 foot or 40 foot container, provided by a specialist freight forwarder. You can save a few hundred pounds this way.

As anyone who has moved long distance before will know, it will be delicate items such as fine china or glassware that gets broken but because of the high excess charges it won't be worth claiming on the insurance. And you can bet that the chain store glassware will survive the trip but the Waterford crystal won't.

> The Taylor family who moved from Devon to New Zealand in 2002 had this to say:
> We read the information for immigrants given to us by the New Zealand immigration people (very useful pack with video) which advised against taking televisions. Only the really expensive ones from the UK seem to work in New Zealand. We were surprised that all the furniture from our four bedroom house managed to fit into a twenty foot container. We did take our fridge and freezer as they were brand new – even though some removal firms suggest you don't – in case they get damaged in transit. It can be tempting to take everything but only do that if it means that your goods still fit in the container. You don't want to find yourself having to pay extra for a container the next size up just because you decided to take a few extra worn out beds and mattresses.
>
> We took a risk on the insurance and decided that for the price it wasn't worth it. Of course, the ship could have gone down but we knew of another family who moved a valuable book collection and ended up paying £17,000 just for their insurance. We would advise anyone moving to go for an insulated container rather than a metal one as there is less condensation. The last thing you want to find when you unpack is that clothes and bedding have gone mouldy. We didn't pay extra for the insulated container – it was just that there was slightly less internal volume due to the extra layer of insulation.

Removal firms and freight forwarders that ship to New Zealand include:

Allied Pickfords: Heritage House, 345 Southbury Road, Enfield, Middlesex EN1 1UP; ☎ 0800-289 229; www.allied-pickfords.co.uk (UK). www.allied.com (USA).

Crown Worldwide Movers: 19 Stonefield Way, London, Middlesex HA4 0BJ ; ☎: 020-8839 8000; fax: 020-8839 8155; www.crownww.com.

Interconti Forwarding Ltd: P.O. Box 1 Landmark, Main Road, Salcombe, Devon TQ8 8LB; ☎ 01548-843191; fax 01548-843414; e-mail interconti@btconnect.com. Specialists in shipping cars to New Zealand for 46 years.

Robinsons International Moving Services: Nuffield Way, Abingdon, Oxfordshire OX14 1TN; ☎ 01235-552255 fax 01235-553753; e-mail international@robinsons-intl.com; www.robinsons-intl.com.

Importing a Car or Motorcycle

Whether you are exempt from paying duty on an imported used car depends upon a number of factors: if you are a first time resident and hold a permanent residency visa then you will not have to pay tax. There are conditions imposed, including providing proof that you have owned the car for at least twelve months, that it is for personal use and that the vehicle is not to be sold within two years. A Deed of Covenant, which you have to sign, stipulates that if you do sell the car within two years you agree to pay the tax owing on it.

Everyone else, including returning New Zealanders are liable to pay Goods & Services Tax (GST). GST must be paid regardless of how long you have owned the vehicle and however long you have been away from New Zealand. The importer must show proof of purchase preferably an original receipt and produce the overseas registration papers. Although there is a depreciation allowance granted for tax assessment – providing that the vehicle has been owned for a minimum of three months – the cost of shipping and marine insurance premiums is included in the GST calculation.

Owners of classic cars should be aware that all vehicles that have been registered outside New Zealand after December 1981 must have a Statement of Compliance from the manufacturer to confirm that it meets New Zealand standards. Information on standards can be found on the

Land Transport Safety Authority website at www.ltsa.govt.nz. Find out first, before you go to the expense of shipping that your car will be allowed out on New Zealand roads.

Used cars made in South East Asia are relatively cheap to buy in New Zealand and parts are readily available. It could be worth your while bringing in a late model, high performance European car as these are expensive to replace. Make sure that the make and model is available in New Zealand, otherwise spare parts, servicing and repairs could be a problem.

P.H.U. Blume of *Interconti Forwarding* advises that, 'there are savings to be made if you want to take a car with you if you choose to ship to Auckland and from a port like Southampton, where roll-on roll-off and conventional lift-on and lift-off services are available. Container services to other ports are at higher cost.'

Registering a Foreign Vehicle in New Zealand

The New Zealand equivalent of an MOT is a warrant of fitness or WOF. The WOF is carried out at testing stations or approved garages. As well as a WOF you will need to pay for registration, new licence plates and vehicle licensing. The cost of licensing depends on the size of the engine. The vehicle-licensing fee includes an Accident Compensation levy. Cars that are six years old or older require a new warrant of fitness every six months.

Useful Addresses

Interconti Forwarding Ltd: P.O. Box 1 Landmark, Main Road, Salcombe, Devon TQ8 8LB; ☎ 01548-843191; fax 01548-843414; e-mail interconti@btconnect.com. Specialists in shipping cars to New Zealand for 46 years.

Land Transport Safety Authority (LTSA): Transport Registry Centre, Private Bag, Palmerston North; ☎ 0800 108 809.

Automobile Association (AA): 99 Albert Street Auckland; ☎ 09-377 4460; 342-352 Lambton Quay, Wellington; ☎ 04-473 8738; 210 Hereford Street, Christchurch; ☎ 03-379 1280. The AA is a membership organisation and offers international members reciprocal services. The AA sells the Road Code book and provides free maps and accommodation guides to non-members. It has a breakdown and roadside assistance service. Many insurance companies now offer roadside and breakdown assistance as part of their car insurance package.

IMPORTING PETS

Pets are members of the family and it is only natural that you will want to bring your pets to New Zealand with you. With very few exceptions, only dogs and cats are allowed to be imported and there are restrictions on certain breeds of dog deemed dangerous which are banned by the New Zealand government as well as the airlines. Some airlines place restrictions on certain breeds of snub-nosed dog because of animal welfare concerns – these breeds are prone to increased respiratory problems when stressed. Dogs entering New Zealand must be nine months or older to travel and no more than 42 days pregnant.

While there is no official upper age limit for pets to travel, they do have to be given a clean bill of health from the vet first. An elderly dog or cat travelling from Australia may be none the worse for wear after a short three hour trip across the Tasman but it's a different matter if travelling from the UK. You should consider carefully whether or not it might be kinder to leave an elderly, nervous dog behind with friends or relatives rather than subject him to a long journey of up to 25 hours in a travelling crate. Although, as one economy passenger remarked, his dog probably had more legroom than he did.

The airlines say that it is a safe way for pets to travel, as according to estimates, a million pets a year are transported by air from which only 30 deaths or injuries occur. Most of these fatalities are preventable and due to over sedation. Vets do not recommend this because there is no way to judge how your pet will react to the potentially dangerous combination of sedatives and high altitude.

Although pets are checked and watered at the stopover en route to New Zealand, they are unsupervised during the flight. Pets should only be given a light meal before they fly and are not fed again until they reach their destination.

From Australia there is no quarantine and information on the testing and documentation necessary can be obtained from your vet. If travelling from the United Kingdom, Norway, Sweden, Singapore or Hawaii, an import permit is required from the Ministry of Agriculture and Fisheries (MAF). No quarantine is necessary but a series of tests, injections and procedures, including micro chipping are required for dogs, before the animal is allowed to be imported. Pets travelling from the USA have to undergo 30 days quarantine. You should check with your vet before the microchip is implanted that it can in fact be read by New Zealand scanners which have a standard of 134.2kHz.

Import and Export Permits

There are three different import permits issued by the Ministry of Agriculture and Fisheries (MAF), depending on which country you are coming from. If you are coming from a country where quarantine is required the import permit will not be issued until you have confirmation from a MAF approved quarantine facility that a booking has been received for your pet. As well as an import certificate you will need an export certificate issued by the ministry of agriculture in your own country.

The New Zealand government, as well as a number of airlines that transport dogs, have singled out four dog breeds that they will not fly nor allow into the country. They are the Togo Argentinos, the Fila Brazileiros, the American Pit Bull Terrier and Japanese Tosas. These include cross-breeds.

> Check with a pet transport company regarding the latest regulations concerning the transportation of snub-nosed dog breeds as a number of airlines refuse to carry breeds such as *Bulldogs*, *Pugs* and *Pekinese* for animal welfare reasons as they suffer from respiratory problems that increase with stress.

Because of New Zealand's status as an island nation and its desire to try to protect the country from any animal-borne diseases, you are not permitted to transport your pet as excess baggage. Many airlines now only accept pets to fly as unaccompanied cargo through a specialist shipper as airlines claim that too many amateur shippers fail to fill out the accompanying paperwork correctly.

How Much Will it Cost to Import a Pet? Your best friend is not going to travel cheaply, particularly if he is a medium to large dog. If travelling from the UK allow £150 for vet costs and £1200 for the travel. The import permit will set you back NZ$130, then there is the cost of shipping. If coming from a country that requires your dog to be quarantined for a month, this will cost around NZ$1500.

Preparing your Pet for the Journey. You can minimise the stress on your dog by getting him used to his travelling container some weeks before he is due to travel. Ask your pet shipper to loan you a regulation container. Start training your dog to get used to his container by putting his favourite toy in there. You may have to coax him in there using food treats and ensure that you never close the door on him. The goal is to have your pet become so familiar with his container he will want to sleep in there.

Animals on long haul flights will be placed in the animal hold, at the front of the plane, which is pressurised and heated during the journey. Animals are usually last to be loaded and first to be off-loaded. Make a specific request to your pet shipper that your pet is hand loaded and off-loaded. If you have a choice of refuelling stops for your pet, choose the one, which has the better climate. Shipping from North America, the connection from Los Angeles or San Francisco should be direct. Pets may not fly from parts of North America during the summer months because of extreme temperatures. The same conditions may apply during periods of extreme cold.

Useful Addresses and Websites:
www.maf.govt.nz. Website for the government department in charge of the importation of live animals into New Zealand.

International Air Transport Association www.iata.org. Website with links to airlines that transport pets. The British Airways site is particularly informative regarding pet shipments and airline approved containers.

Defra, Animal Welfare Division: 1A Page Street, London SW1 4PQ; ☎: 0870-241 1710, fax: 020-7904 6961; www.defra.gov.uk. Although primarily the site for the Pet Travel Scheme (PETS) there are excellent tips on preparing your pet for a long journey.

Independent Pet and Animal Transportation Association Inc: www.ipata.com. A membership organisation not affiliated to the airlines with a directory of members as well as advice on shipping pets.

Pet Shippers from the UK.

Airpets Oceanic: Stanwell Moor, Middlesex; ☎ 01753-685571 and 0800-01 85571; fax 01753 681655; www.airpets.com. Based at Heathrow they can arrange pick-up, delivery and quarantine and vet services.

Skymaster Air Cargo Ltd: Room 15, Building 305, Cargo Centre, Manchester Airport M90 5PY; ☎ 0161-436 2190 fax 0161 499 9312; e-mail pat@skymaster.co.uk and airpawspets@yahoo.co.uk. Skymaster, based at Manchester Airport, can arrange collection, flight bookings, as well as kennelling and veterinary procedures and supply of IATA-approved pet carriers.

From the USA.

JetPets: 9111 Falmouth Ave, Playa del Rey, CA 90293-8617; ☎ 310-823-8901; fax 310-305-8297; www.JetPets.com for all pet transportation from the Los Angeles area.

At the time of writing, the first cases of bird flu in Europe had been confirmed and certain preventative measures were being put in place by governments around the world. It is too early to know what effect bird flu will have on the shipment of animals by air across the world. Contact Defra or your pet shipper for further information.

BUILDING OR RENOVATING

CHAPTER SUMMARY

- It is the property owner's responsibility to apply for building and resource consents and to ensure that a code of compliance is issued on completion.
  - Incorporating sustainable building design into your house plans will save you money in reduced power bills as well as being better for the environment.
- **Pools.** All new pools including spa pools are required by law to be fenced.
- **Gardens.** There are at least three different climate zones in New Zealand and climate as well as soil type will determine what you can plant.
  - Public gardens are a good place to find ideas for your garden.
  - Some local councils require resource consents for tree trimming as well as removal and the rules are strictly enforced, particularly for native trees.
  - Your garden centre will advise you on what to plant as a number of plant species have become invasive.

THE HIDDEN COSTS OF RENOVATION

Restoring a previously neglected house can be extremely rewarding and a good restoration should increase value. An old house that combines well-restored original features with modern additions such as a good quality kitchen and bathrooms is ideal. This will not only make the house very comfortable to live in but will find favour with buyers, should you ever need to sell.

Many buyers mistakenly believe that all it will take to get an old house up to scratch is a coat of paint and a set of new curtains or blinds. Getting the sums wrong can mean that would-be renovators then have to live in a less than perfect house for longer than they expected to.

Sometimes renovators adopt the ad-hoc approach to restoration – doing the essential work as soon as they move in and then having the rest done over the course of a few years. Doing it this way may mean you go over budget without realising it. If you want to spend $80,000 on a kitchen in a house you bought for $300,000, then go ahead – but only as long as you are doing so for reasons of comfort, aesthetics and your own enjoyment.

There is no doubt that the kitchen will be the most expensive room to renovate. New designer kitchens can range from $15,000 to $60,000 plus for a state-of-the-art kitchen. Cheap and trendy stores like IKEA don't exist in New Zealand.

Renovating the existing kitchen with a new bench top, drawers and doors will cost you at least $5000. Choose granite for the bench top and the budget rises accordingly. The problem with renovating is that the renovated parts tend to show up the rest of the house. There is no point in going to the trouble of renovating a kitchen if the floors are worn cork tiles. Choose ceramic tiles and that will cost you from $125 per square metre. Timber flooring costs from $250 per square metre.

The second most expensive room to renovate after the kitchen will be the bathroom. New Zealanders that travel abroad have developed a taste for expensive European bath and tap-ware. To retile a bathroom and replace standard fittings will cost from $6000. To move plumbing will add to this cost.

If you are handy with a paintbrush or good at tiling, and plan to undertake your own decorating, New Zealand is awash with DIY stores. New Zealanders are known for their enthusiasm for doing-it-yourself but as Helen Davies points out in the Case Histories, paint is expensive. Some stores, (try Bunnings or Mitre 10) run courses in DIY so that you can up-skill to tackle certain jobs. As the going rate for any contractor in Auckland and Wellington starts from $45 per hour, you could save yourself money in the process.

As anyone who has ever bought a house from a DIY electrician or plumber will know, there are some jobs that amateurs should never be allowed to touch. As well as placing restrictions on some plumbing, electrical and gas work; from 2009, certain building work will be restricted to licensed builders. Only those who have the qualifications and ability to carry out the work will be permitted to become licensed. Some restricted building work may be carried out by amateurs who are supervised by a licensed building practitioner.

BUILDING AND RESOURCE CONSENTS

Whether it is for alteration, building from new or removing or relocating existing buildings it is the property owner's responsibility to get a building consent. The Building Act 2004 states that some of the work that needs consent includes:

- **Alterations.** This includes moving a load-bearing wall.
- **Demolition or Relocation.** Relocating or demolishing an existing building.
- **Decks above 1.5 metres.** Anything under this height is not deemed a safety risk and does not require consent.
- **Retaining Walls.** Any retaining wall higher than 1.5m above ground level or any retaining wall that retains a driveway, even if it is under this height.
- **Fences.** A substantial fence made out of concrete or a fence over two metres high.
- **Change of building use.** This might include converting a garage into an extra room.
- **Swimming Pools and Spa Pools.** Even putting in a spa pool requires resource consent, (see section on pools below).

Certain jobs will require you to get what is known as Resource Consent. In Auckland City for example, you need resource consent just to trim even a small exotic tree (native trees having greater protection). According to Consumer Build, some councils check building consent applications to see if a resource consent is required as well. At the end of the building job it is the homeowner's responsibility to ensure that the building consent has been carried out to the specifications required and to apply for a code compliance certificate.

CHOOSING THE RIGHT TEAM

Any tradesperson that you select for a renovation or building job should be properly qualified and belong to a professional trade organisation. Ask to see their work and to talk to their previous customers. An honest tradesperson should show no hesitation in letting you inspect work or talk to other customers. Ask too if the work comes with any guarantee. Key personnel in the team – the architect, project manager and lead builder need to have an empathy and understanding with what you are trying to achieve. The project manager should assist you with a contingency plan in case you can't afford to get all the work done in one go.

Be wary of the cheapest quote – that is no guarantee that the job will be done to your exacting standards. Whoever you choose has to have the right insurance, including public liability. An unregistered tradesperson may not carry their own insurance, resulting in their being no compensation available to you should anything go wrong.

Builders can belong to one of two trade organisations – the Certified Builders Association or the Registered Master Builders Federation. Both organisations require their members to have a recognised building qualification and to have worked in the building industry for some years. They both operate a code of conduct and provide guarantees of workmanship.

If the job is substantial and requires a complete re-design then you will want to employ an architect. The architect's design has the potential to add value to your house and choosing the right one for your project is not just a matter of selecting a registered architectural practitioner. Some months before you plan to start your project, collect newspaper cuttings of new houses that you admire. The property section in the weekend edition of the *New Zealand Herald* and the *Property Press* often feature the names and details of architects and builders in their editorial. The specialist publications: *Urbis, Architecture New Zealand* and *Progressive Building*, (all published by AGM Publishing) feature the best of recent New Zealand architectural design. Glossy monthly magazines, available at newsagents include *NZ House and Garden* and *NZ Home and Entertaining*, the latter of which features an annual Home of the Year Award.

If you are undertaking a restoration of an old building make sure that the architect you employ doesn't just want to rip out the whole interior and start again. So many old houses have been re-developed to the extent that all that remains from the original is the front of the house. Ripping out rooms and replacing them with an open plan design destroys any character the building once had.

Building an Eco-friendly House. The Building Research Association of New Zealand (BRANZ) operate a Green Home Scheme which offers those building a house (as well as existing homeowners) a method of assessing how new homes rate on key environmental issues. Good design can make a home more energy efficient and more comfortable to live in.

The principles behind eco-housing mean that the materials chosen are less toxic than conventional building materials, that they use passive solar energy where possible and incorporate systems to recycle wastewater.

Useful Contacts and Websites

AGM Publishing: publishers of *Urbis*, *Architecture New Zealand* and *Progressive Building*.
Easy Guide to Eco-Building – Design Build and Live with the Environment: BRANZ, www.branz.co.nz.
Certified Builders Association (CBANZ): www.certified.co.nz.
Electrical Workers Registration Board (EWRB): PO Box 10-156, Wellington; ☎: 04- 472 3636; fax: 04 473 2395; www.med.govt.nz/ewrb.
NZ Home and Entertaining: www.acpmedia.co.nz.
NZ House and Garden: www.fairfaxnz.co.nz.
New Zealand Plumbers, Gasfitters and Drainlayers Board: PO Box 10-655, Wellington; ☎ 04-494 2970; fax 04-494 2975; www.pgdb.co.nz.
Registered Master Builders Federation (RMBF): www.masterbuilder.org.nz

POOLS

At the height of summer, where better to relax than around the pool in your own garden? As well as enhancing the look and value of your property, having a pool is a convenient way of entertaining friends and family.

Sadly, though, around five New Zealand children a year die in domestic swimming pools and these fatalities have prompted a re-think regarding the regulations on pool fencing.

By law all domestic swimming pools and spa pools must be fenced off. As well as complying with the legislation in The Fencing of Swimming Pools Act, the fencing has to comply with the New Zealand Building Code. Information on the building code can be found on the Department of Building and Housing's website at www.dbh.govt.nz.

New Regulations Cover Existing Pools. It has been spa pool owners and people who are more concerned with aesthetics than safety who have grumbled the most about the new regulations. An unfenced pool could provide too much of a temptation to the neighbours' children, not to mention pets and wildlife and it is the pool owner's responsibility to ensure their pool is safe.

If you are buying an existing property with a spa pool that only has a lockable cover, check with the local council over its legality. Since 2002 lockable spa pool covers were no longer considered to be an adequate safety barrier, An exemption in the regulations allows that, if the pool was inspected and approved before the new laws came in, it may be legally compliant.

If the house you are buying or have bought has an existing pool, this should be inspected carefully by a building inspector. A badly maintained pool with cracks or other signs of poor maintenance could be more of a liability than an asset.

The guidelines on pool fencing in brief are:
- **Height.** The pool fence must be at least 1.2m high from the ground.
- **Gaps.** As well as not being climbable, there are regulations regarding gaps between the vertical bars as well as under the fence.
- **Boundary Fencing.** It is not a good idea to include a boundary fence as part of a pool fence. You cannot really control whether or not a neighbour has planted trellis or put a structure next to the fence to allow children to climb over. If this does happen, your fence would no longer comply with the regulations.
- **Lockable Gate.** Gates must be the sort that close and latch automatically.
- **Pool fencing around the immediate pool area.** The fencing cannot extend to lawn areas, children's play areas or the whole garden. Only certain equipment relating to the pool is allowed in the immediate area.

Building a New Pool. Two other regulatory hurdles need to be passed before your dream of 50 laps before breakfast can become a reality. You will need a building consent for putting in either a spa or a pool. You should include drawings that show where you intend to put the fencing as well as a plan of the immediate pool area. Your local council may also require that you need a resource consent.

GARDENS

If you adore everything to do with gardens and gardening, New Zealand is the place to indulge your passion. If you've lived in a climate of freezing winters and hot, sultry summers, you will marvel at the range of plants the New Zealand gardener is able to grow. In the upper part of the North Island and in pockets of Nelson and Golden Bay, you are only limited by your imagination in what you can plant in the garden.

Visit Public Gardens for Inspiration. Before you plant your own little modest patch of green, visit a local public garden. That way you'll see unfamiliar new plants and how they might best feature in your garden. In every town and city up and down the country you can find public displays of plants and flowers.

Auckland has its Regional Botanical Gardens south of the city centre in Manukau City, but the Domain in the city centre and Myers Park both have fine displays of herbaceous borders and magnificent trees. The Domain has a Winter Garden and a fernery. Hamilton Gardens, as well as incorporating a fine display of roses has a series of themed landscaped garden rooms from around the world that should inspire any amateur gardener.

Further south, Wellington Botanical Gardens makes the most of its hilly site, and in Christchurch, as well as the roses and English style planting, these gardens incorporate a variety of native plant species. And in the Dunedin public gardens, azaleas are a feature.

If you are in New Zealand during spring (October-November) it's worth detouring to New Plymouth just to visit Pukeiti. At the foot of Mount Taranaki, this garden has one of the world's most beautiful backdrops in which to see rhododendron and azaleas, incorporated into a native bush setting.

New Zealand gardening style has finally stepped out of the shadow of its colonial past and has forged a new identity. And it isn't just gardeners in New Zealand that think so. The New Zealand entry in 2004 at the Chelsea Flower Show won a coveted gold medal and proved to many New Zealand gardeners that with imaginative planting you don't have to sacrifice colour to have a native garden.

Billed as the Southern Hemisphere's version of the Chelsea event, the annual Ellerslie Flower Show, (held at Auckland's Regional Botanical Gardens in November) is the gardening event of the year. Unlike at Chelsea, the show gardens at Ellerslie have been designed with the home gardener in mind.

You can buy a simple testing kit from the local garden centre to find out what kind of soil you have. In addition to testing the soil, work out which areas you need to plant and how much sun, wind and exposure your site will get. By then you'll have a better idea of the kind of look you want to create. Either draw a plan of the garden or employ a professional garden designer to do this.

Many urban gardens have been influenced by garden makeover programmes with their instant fix approach to gardens fashioned in the latest trendy styles. Currently sub-tropical 'easy-care' gardening is 'in' while labour-intensive cottage gardens are 'out.' Gardens landscaped by professional garden companies tend to be full of similar plants – that look the same week after week throughout the year. Auckland is not tropical Queensland – despite what some garden designer may believe and it does have marked seasons. Rather than obliterating the seasonal variation the best gardeners find ways of integrating both sub-tropical, native as well as deciduous plants.

Sub-tropical gardens can be labour-intensive as they require frequent watering. Given that New Zealand has long and generally warm summers, many gardeners install an automatic watering system. This allows gardeners to go away for their summer holidays, knowing that the garden won't shrivel up in their absence. The alternative is to plan a drought resistant garden or to use plenty of mulch. Mulch is a New Zealand gardener's best friend – retaining moisture as well as suppressing weeds. Container gardens can be a chore to water too. Even if you only have a small courtyard, fewer, larger containers, rather than many small pots will be kinder to the plants as their roots won't bake or dry out as much in the hot sun.

One downside of gardening in New Zealand is that it is a year round activity in the warmer parts of the country. While Northern Hemisphere gardeners get a chance to pack away the gardening gloves and retreat to the sofa with next year's seed catalogues, in New Zealand you'll be too busy mowing the lawn and weeding.

The Kitchen Garden

You don't need much room to create a kitchen garden – even tomatoes can be grown in a pot but if you do have some space, imagine the satisfaction you'll get from picking your own produce. Whether you want a grapefruit for breakfast, or lemons for the evening gin and tonics, all you'll have to do is walk across the back lawn to get them. In the sub-tropical kitchen garden, how about growing figs, limes or avocados?

Problem Plant Species. That combination of abundant rain and warm sunshine, which makes gardens so lush, has had a few unfortunate side effects. The early settlers who brought species like gorse with them (to remind them of Scotland) were not to know that this plant would one day become one of New Zealand most difficult plant pests to eradicate.

Rebecca, recently arrived from the UK, relates this story:

I asked at an Auckland garden centre for a Jasmine plant, only to have the checkout operator make an announcement for someone to come to the desk. A rather hairy long-shorted, socks and shoes type stormed down the aisle. When I enquired about Jasmine he became quite animated and told me off for asking for such a noxious weed, which is banned in this region.

Jasmine fans shouldn't be too dismayed as there is a less invasive alternative to the pink variety, which smothers the forest once it gets into the wild. One country's flower is another's pest plant and millions of dollars are spent each year on getting rid of pest plants and the list is increasing all the time. To do your bit for the environment requires a re-think on what to grow in your garden. You only need to go out into the wilderness to see what damage some introduced plant species have had on parts of the eco-system.

To assist you in what to plant and what to remove, contact your local council who will give you further information on which introduced plants threaten native communities. Each gardening region of the country – northern, central and southern, has its own particular problem plant species. The invasive plant pests that are a problem throughout the country include: Climbing asparagus (Asparagus scandens), Japanese honeysuckle (Lonicera japonica), Banana passionfruit (Passiflora mollissima & P. mixta), Chinese Ladder Fern (Nephrolepis cordifolia), Periwinkle (Vinca major), Cotoneaster (Cotoneaster glaucohphyllus, C. franchetti), Pampas (Cortaderia selloana, C. jubata), German ivy (Senecio mikaniodides), Chinese privet (Ligustrum sinense),

Garden centres have to be up to date with the regulations as they are banned from selling or propagating pest plants. The list of banned species is regularly reviewed. At the time of writing, the Auckland Regional Council (ARC) were reviewing certain introduced palm species including the Phoenix palm, which causes injuries to gardeners because of its large spikes. The Department of Conservation is another source of information at www.doc.govt.nz.

Conservation is but one of the reasons that in the past twenty years there has been a resurgence in interest in planting native gardens. But because the habitats of native plants are localised it is best to check with a native plant nursery first as to what variety of native species will best suit your soil and location. There are a number of New Zealand native plants like the Renga Renga lily that make excellent ground cover. This is a much better alternative to the clump-forming and ubiquitous Agapanthus – the latest invasive species to be included on the ARC Pest Management hit list.

If you live in a coastal region with the right soil conditions, the sight of the Pohutekawa (known as the New Zealand Christmas tree) in flower is enough to make a returning ex-pat's eyes mist over. The small to medium size Kowhai tree is a brilliant yellow and like the Pohutekawa is beloved of nectar-feeders such as the white throated Tui. Native species are versatile and look great combined with sub-tropical plants such as cycads or even desert plants like succulents, all of which grow well in the Northern region. Further south, native plant species look wonderful within a setting of Rhododendron or Azaleas.

Insects and Other Pests in the Garden. Mosquitoes are prevalent nearly everywhere in New Zealand but gardeners still have a fighting chance as the common species found there are only really active at dawn and dusk. While there are plants that help to keep insects away, it's better to ensure that they don't take up residence in the first place. Birdbaths or even an inch of rainwater in a watering can may be all that it takes to provide the ideal breeding ground for mosquitoes to thrive. Plant saucers are another favourite spot. Washing out all such containers with disinfectant will mini- mise their presence as will keeping away greenery from the outside of the house. Herbs and plants such as basil, rosemary, lavender and lemon ver- bena are said to keep the insects away.

New Zealand's creepy crawlies are relatively benign and there are no snakes. You might suffer a few painful bites but there is nothing out there that can kill you – unless you suffer from severe allergies. Possums are a nuisance in suburban gardens. That noise on the roof at night, which sounds as though someone is breaking in, will just be a possum or two taking a shortcut to get to your fruit trees. Cute they might be but with over 90 million brush-tail possums, these native Australians are wreaking havoc on the habitats of a number of highly endangered native bird species.

Books and Magazines for New Zealand Gardeners

A Guide to the Identification of New Zealand Common Weeds in Colour, E.A,
   Pritchard.
Complete New Zealand Gardener, Geoff Bryant and Eion Scarrow; a prac-
   tical guide (with good photographs) to all aspects of gardening in New
   Zealand from assessing your site and climate to information on plants as
   well as techniques for caring for the garden.
Landscape: Gardens by New Zealand's Top Designers, Rosemary Thody. Cre-
   ative inspiration for your garden.
Organic Gardening for New Zealand Gardeners, Random House.
Plant Me Instead, NZ Dept of Conservation. A helpful guide to solve the
   problem of what to plant instead of potentially invasive species.
100 Best New Zealand Native Plants for Gardens, Fiona Eadie.
Subtropical Plants for New Zealand Gardens, Jacqueline Sparrow & Gil
   Hanly.
Yates Garden Guide, Anon. Full of practical tips.

Protected Trees

Some councils have strict controls over trees of a certain spread and height.
You may require Resource Consent even to trim them. These trees are
listed in the District Plan. Your solicitor should bring the details of any
protected trees on your property to your attention during the purchasing
process. The rules governing native trees are even stricter. Trying to sur-
reptitiously lop off a branch of a *pohutakawa* when you think no one is
looking may backfire on you.

> One East Auckland resident put in a Resource Consent application to trim a Liquid
> Amber tree and fed up after four months when she hadn't heard anything, rang
> Auckland City Council and finally got a verbal okay to trim the tree. When the tree
> surgeon had done his job a nosy neighbour rang the council alleging breach of a
> Resource Consent. A council officer came round immediately and presented the
> owner with a stern warning denying that the verbal consent had never been given.
> It was useless arguing the case and there was no apology over the time taken to
> respond to the resource consent application.

MAKING MONEY FROM YOUR PROPERTY

CHAPTER SUMMARY

○ Bed and Breakfast income should be regarded as a supplement to rather than a main income.

○ **Running a Home Business.** New Zealand is a nation of small businesses where 86% of people are employed in firms employing five or less.

   ○ One of the challenges to running a business from home is not to become socially isolated and to remain connected with other business people doing something similar.

   ○ There is government advice available for those wanting to start up new businesses.

○ You'll need to advertise your holiday home or bach on a website to reach your target market.

○ **Selling On.** Give your house a makeover before you put it on the market.

   ○ Agents' commission is high in New Zealand.

   ○ Agents may be forced to lower their fees in the future because of increasing competition from internet marketing.

B & B

Offering bed and breakfast is one way to supplement your income although property owners who live in popular tourist or lifestyle destinations do this not just to make money but as a way of meeting people. Many owners of bed and breakfast accommodation say that it is a labour-intensive job as there is the laundry change and cleaning to attend to, taking the bookings and the fact that you don't get a lie-in even on a Sunday morning.

To be listed in a guidebook such as The Bed and Breakfast Book, would-be hosts should first read the schedule of standards listed at the back of the publication. These include compliance information on safety, including the requirement to provide fire and smoke alarms. Dining and guest rooms as well as communal areas and the kitchen all have to be kept spotless. But the hard work does have its rewards, one of which includes repeat custom.

If you are considering offering bed and breakfast you should check with your local council first to check that your property complies with the local by-laws. These include having the right level of insurance. If you have a swimming pool or spa for guest use the fencing off of these areas must comply with the regulations. How much you can charge will depend entirely on which market you are catering for and where your house is situated. Prices start at around $50 per head.

B & B is offered by a mixture of overseas residents, empty nesters as well as the active retired. If you specialise in a particular regional cuisine or cook with organic produce it's a good idea to include this in your advertising.

RUNNING A BUSINESS FROM YOUR PROPERTY

You can run a business from home providing that your visa allows you to do so. Because the nature of work has changed in this digital age, you could of course set up a home office even if you are ordinarily resident for tax purposes in another country but needing to keep in touch with your business interests off-shore while at your New Zealand holiday home.

Sometimes even getting electricity and the internet can be a challenge – even if you are in the IT business, as Andy relates

One advantage of working from home is that location can be less important as the daily commute is history. However, other factors replace travel time and I'm running a business that really depends on two things being there; electricity and the internet. When we first decided to move out to the Waitakeres about seven years ago, we accepted that some of the things we previously took for granted in town might be less available or non-existent. We didn't quite realise the full implications of the fact that our power is more likely to drop out, especially during the winter storms and that Telecom wasn't remotely interested in providing us with a modern or reliable telecommunications infrastructure. Initially, struggling along with dial-up internet access was tolerable but as broadband became the norm for everyone else it started to be increasingly difficult to do things that others are now taking for granted (and therefore to collaborate). I need to send and receive large documents and move data around. I rely on e-mail and I want to use the internet to keep my telephone bill down.

> *It's now six years since we moved here and Telecom still refuse to even contemplate helping. They don't even want to talk about it. Fortunately, being in the IT business gives me some knowledge and we now have broadband, connecting us to the world via a very long radio link across the Manukau Harbour. It's not earth shatteringly fast but it's better than dial-up. The power still goes off, twice this week, one occasion blew up the broadband link. Two of our three phone lines just gave up the ghost, one for about three days, but that's unusual. And, in case your wondering, yes, the mobile does work. If you stand at the front of the garden, on a raised bit of lawn and lean slightly east, it works just fine. Mostly.*

Useful Contacts

Joining the local branch of a membership organisation such as the American Chamber of Commerce (www.amcham.nz) gives new residents the opportunity to link in and build up a network of business contacts. Whether you join for the presentations and guest seminars, or the networking events or even the golf tournaments, such an organisation provides a valuable link between your own culture and that of your new country.

'New Zealand is an economy of small businesses. 86% of registered businesses employ less than five people. The key challenge is isolation – not having people around to bounce ideas off.' (source Business in the Community website). Business in the Community is a registered charity and provides free business mentors to small businesses – an invaluable resource for business people starting up in a new country. They can be contacted at www.businessmentor.org.nz.

Whether you live in Christchurch, Wellington or Hamilton, there will be a local Chamber of Commerce for you to join. The Auckland Chamber of Commerce (www.b-vital.com) offers training and mentoring, seminars and discount schemes on insurance, petrol, vehicles and financial services.

Given that New Zealand is a nation of small business owners, there is a great deal of good (free) advice offered to anyone running a business. The National Library of New Zealand's Te Puna Web Directory has links to all the regional economic development agencies, the Chambers of Commerce, as well as the Small Business Enterprise Centres of New Zealand (community based organisations located in rural areas).

Those involved in the creative industries should go to www.creativehq. co.nz (an initiative for those in the Wellington region) and read the inspiring stories. Creative HQ helps Wellington based creative entrepreneurs with infrastructure and business support. One of its success stories, Virtual Katy, a sound-editing software package was developed by the Lord of the Rings sound effects editor and recently secured $2 million in venture capital.

The Business Information Zone, www.biz.org.nz is a government initiative, which addresses the fundamentals of starting your own business as well as buying an established business. The Business Information Zone has links to business structures and the type of organisation you want to set up from being a sole trader to a limited liability company. Tax, ACC (Accident Compensation Commission), employing staff, health and safety and even grants and financial assistance are covered.

If this is the first time you have owned your own business then the section on putting together a business plan is going to be very important, especially if you need to raise capital. But before you start your new business venture, work through the useful checklist that aims to find out whether starting a business is right for you.

The link to buying an established business asks that you have carried out proper research (due diligence) on the company you intend to buy. Anyone interested in buying into the hospitality trade (running a restaurant or food business is a dream that many share) should read the case study on the couple that bought a coffee shop franchise.

While it could be useful to live in an urban cluster of others in the creative industries who might use your services, if your business is one that needs a strong local client base – for example a medical therapist or a masseuse, you will, of course need to do the research to find out if the population is big enough to sustain another local practitioner.

Whatever your business, trade or idea, bear in mind too that there are only just over four million people in the entire country and some businesses require a certain critical mass to be viable. Artists, writers, web designers, or IT professionals have the luxury of being based anywhere they choose and can take their pick from New Zealand's finest locations.

For business people who need to be close to clients or customers it doesn't mean that you have to be based in Auckland – after all, surely the whole point about making the move was to take advantage of the lifestyle and the slower pace of life. Think about the regional centres where the economy is doing well and somewhere that is close by to all the outdoor recreation you might be seeking. And if you really do need to be near a big city, in a recent poll of where Aucklanders would most like to move to, Christchurch came a close second to Nelson.

Doing Business with New Zealanders

The New Zealand business community has an air of informality about it that may delight, vex or just plain irritate you and it becomes more informal, the further away you go from the main centres. This doesn't necessarily mean that business people walk around in shorts and flip-flops but there is less standing on ceremony and certainly less of the deference than you would find in the UK or the USA. Introductions are carried out on first name terms.

Because the Christmas and the summer holiday are combined into one break, one irritating factor is that as a business owner you will have to get used to the entire nation shutting up shop from lunchtime on Christmas Eve and not re-opening again until the second or third week of January.

Trying to conduct any sort of business (unless you are in the retail trade) is a waste of time. It may take you a few years to adjust but many business people resign themselves to the shutdown and join the throng at the beach – where they are more likely to be able to network with fellow business people, all off on their summer holidays, as they are down at the local Chamber of Commerce.

Business owners should note that the standard office hours in New Zealand are 8.30am until 5.00pm Monday to Friday, although many owner operators and other business owners work longer.

Tax and Finance for Businesses

You should seek professional advice from an accountant who will advise you on all tax matters relating running your business – whether or not you should be registered for GST (Goods and Services Tax) or whether it is advantageous to set up a limited liability company if you are a sole trader. Registering for GST (like being VAT registered) requires regular administrational paperwork, which can be done via a software package.

Advantages and Disadvantages of Working from Home

It doesn't matter if your business is in Queenstown or Queensferry, working from home has its ups as well as downs.

Advantages:
- There are no extra costs to pay renting business premises.
- You do not have to find suitable office space or professional rooms.

- You do not have to waste time sitting in traffic commuting.
- You can work any hours you want.
- Freedom from office politics.

Disadvantages:
- Visitors and callers when they find you are 'at home' may not understand that you are in fact working.
- Working from home can be so convenient that you can never get away from it.
- Unless you employ the services of an office cleaner your office will remain messy unless you clean it.
- Sole traders may no longer have any administrative support staff.
- Social isolation and no one to bounce ideas off or consult when work isn't going so well.

RENTING OUT YOUR PROPERTY

With the cost of coastal retreats rocketing skywards and demand increasing, you might want to consider renting your holiday home or *bach*. You should get a good return in the peak season of January (if you are not using it yourself over the summer holiday).

Bach and holiday home owners still have to pay rates and maintenance on top of any mortgage payments. Any income you make could be spent on upgrading the property later, if it needs it. An occupied property will deter thieves.

If you are going to rent out though there are a number of ways that you can make your property more desirable.

Suggestions for Renting Out a Property

- Clean, tidy well-equipped kitchen
- Clean, tidy bathroom
- Allow pets – New Zealand is not as pet friendly as the UK or parts of Europe and many pet owners find going away difficult as they can't get anywhere to stay.
- Provide some recreational kit such as bikes, kayaks, golf clubs, and board games for wet weather.

Marketing Your Property

You can market a holiday property informally through friends, family and work contacts. But these networks only go so far and if you really want to reach out to a wider market you'll need to think about a marketing campaign. A good marketing campaign will cost you a few hundred dollars but these costs can be offset against tax.

If you are going to advertise in the print media it is important that your advertisement stands out from the rest. If you advertise that you take pets and the five other baches in the area make no mention of this, you may even get repeat business from pet owners, no longer forced to spend their Christmas break at home.

Create Your Own Website. Expensive websites have their place but not when you want to showcase your holiday house. Good photographs and a virtual tour – showing every room including kitchens, bathrooms and the outside area are a much better indication of what the house looks like than a lot of text that promises a lot. Holidaymakers want to see for themselves what the specification is, what the cooking facilities are like, whether cooking is done by electricity or gas, whether the appliances are new or old and whether the furniture is of a good standard. If a holidaymaker is booking your place because of its proximity to the beach the accuracy of the information relating to that is very important. Distances need to be exact, rather than approximations including how far it is to local shops, the petrol station, and the nearest supermarket. As most of your prospective tenants will be family groups, such factors as whether or not the local dairy is close enough for the kids to walk and buy an ice cream might seem trivial but could help 'sell' the property.

If you are not sure what to include on your website check out the competition on-line. Keep the prose to a minimum and let the images do the marketing for you. Holidaymakers are not coming to the area just to stay in your beach house.

Advertise on Other Websites. Websites advertising baches and holiday homes have multiplied in recent years. It can cost as little as $200 a year to advertise on an established site – good value when you consider that you could be getting $150- $200 a night for your property. Choosing a site is simply a matter of trying a few search engines to see which site comes up most frequently, whether it is straightforward to use and whether it offers homeowners any assistance such as an on-line calendar to help you manage bookings.

Exposure on a website allows you to see what others are charging and what facilities they have compared with yours. Make sure you set your rates competitively. Your place doesn't have to be an architectural statement with a lap pool – provided the price reflects that.

Websites merely bring your property to the attention of a wider market – they are not management agencies. Once a provisional booking has been made through a website the rest is up to the owner. A professional booking system with updated availability is very important. Provide a mobile phone number so that you can be reached in the daytime as well as the evening. Return e-mails and calls promptly. If you are targeting international visitors (and that is around one quarter of your potential market) you must be able to take credit card bookings.

Marketing to Satisfied Customers. Repeat business should be the aim of every holiday homeowner so don't forget to ask guests to sign the visitors book so that you can stay in touch. You could offer some kind of loyalty or discount scheme for regulars. An e-mail or two during the year with what's going on in the area will remind your former guests of their holiday and could be enough to persuade them to re-book.

Using a Property Manager. You could be paying up to 25% of the income from the property to a property manager in return for a total management service including finding tenants, organising key collection, supervising cleaning and linen change between tenancies, ensuring that the grounds are maintained, checking on wear and tear and finding tradesmen to carry out regular maintenance. Good service is vital in this business and when things do go wrong (as they invariably do with houses) there needs to be someone close by to sort out any problems. As property managers only get paid when the property is occupied that is their incentive to ensure that it is properly marketed. Property management charges can of course be offset against tax.

Before you buy a property in the area it would be worth talking to a property manager (from a different agency than the one you are buying from) to get a realistic picture of occupancy rates and how much you can charge. Sit down and do the sums first as if you are relying on the income to help pay the mortgage then a holiday home in a remote location may not be the wisest choice. Holiday home occupancy is seasonal and that season could be as short as twelve weeks, depending on the location.

SELLING ON

New Zealanders can, on average, expect to stay in one property for seven years. However long you thought you were going to stay, life may have got in the way and you could find that you need to sell up. As Helen Davies points out in the *Case History* section; marketing and real estate commission are very expensive in New Zealand. But although most New Zealanders grumble about the high costs of marketing and commission, the majority of houses are sold through an agent.

The average agent's commission is around 4% (expensive enough as it is) but this is only for the agent's services and excludes any marketing fee. The agent commission is paid solely by the seller and is not a split cost between buyer and seller – as it is in some countries. For a $600,000 house you will be paying an agent commission of around $24,000. On top of that you would be expected to pay around $3500 for 'marketing' a total spend of $27,500. For that you get a sign outside your house with colour photographs, colour advertising in the property press and on real estate websites such as Realenz and Opentoview.

Anyone that has ever tried to sell a house without an agent will know that this can be as time consuming as a full-time job but many sellers are aggrieved about the high costs. The agent may argue that they end up getting less than half the commission and that the real estate company will pocket the rest but that is no comfort to the hard-up seller.

Many of those who do end up trying to sell privately may be those who have bought recently and who may be too stretched to afford the commission. If an internet site like Trade Me becomes the dominant industry player, this could shift the power away from the agent back into the hands of the consumer. Currently Trade Me charges $50 and home sellers can display up to 20 photographs on the site. Although agents may be retained to run Open Homes and negotiate with buyers, a reduction in the hefty marketing fee would be a victory for consumers.

If you have enough time to wait until spring to sell your house that will be a bonus but if you need to sell it immediately then you should invite three local agents in the area to give you a market appraisal. You may not get an exact price but a guide price – 'in the region of.' Ask the three agents for the costs of marketing, their commission and the different prices for selling by negotiation, at auction or through a tender. Ask them to show you their figures of the current percentage of successful sales by auction. Ask every agent for a list of what needs doing to the property to prepare it for sale.

Grooming, Cleaning and Staging

While the terminology may be unfamiliar and more akin to presenting a show pony for the ring than a house to be sold – the principle is still the same. Your house and garden have to look their best before you put it on the market. The house should ideally be recently painted (outside as well as inside) as even a wide-angle lens cannot hide a grubby exterior. If you cannot afford to paint the exterior then the very least you will need to do is arrange for an external house cleaner to water blast with either a chemical wash or a high-pressure hose to clean the dirt off the outside.

Buyers prefer neutral décor as it makes it easier for them to imagine their furniture against a plain background. Not everyone likes colour. A green hallway, red dining room and an orange feature wall may reflect your bright personality but it might be advisable, if you can afford to redecorate, to paint these out to one neutral colour. If you cannot be bothered researching the latest looks and colours – or if your home is an older style property then resort to that good old standby – Spanish white (the New Zealand answer to Britain's Magnolia).

One homeowner in Hamilton was told to make some cosmetic changes to a recently renovated house. The house had been freshly painted and a brand new kitchen had been installed. The bathroom was the only room that had not been done up and was the least inviting room in the house. A café curtain and a plant gave this room the lift it needed.

The helpful agent pointed out that the house lacked 'street appeal.' With the assistance of a local gardener, a plan was drawn up to soften the view to the front of the house with appropriate planting. Two conifers in pots were placed in front of the front door to provide more of a welcome. Total spend including garden labour – less than $400. Although this was back in 2002 when the market had started to heat up in the regions, it took 24 hours to sell this house to a cash buyer who made an unconditional offer at the asking price.

As well as attending to all the tidying up, cleaning and painting needed, expensive houses are often 'staged'. To maximise the effect of the open-home marketing method, the owner's furniture is removed and replaced with one overall packaged look by a home staging company. This erases the owner's personality from the house on offer, especially if personal items are hidden away. Instead of being distracted by particular items in the house, potential buyers see the house looking like its been made over by a hotel chain, anonymous and devoid of someone else's personality.

Asking Price

Attend 'Open Homes' of similar houses in your local area to check out the competition for price, presentation and length of time needed to market a property. Assess the agents' valuations. Take the average of the three sales figures and use that as your asking price. The agent may of course decline to put an asking price on the property and let the market decide. But whichever strategy you choose – setting too high an asking price could hamper rather than help the marketing campaign.

As well as knowing the median house price in your area you should check how many days on average houses take to sell. Make sure that the agent gets feedback from potential buyers on what they thought of your property and if there is anything that might be putting them off. Cosmetic redecoration will not influence a sale if there is a more serious problem such as a boundary dispute with a neighbour or poor access.

Boundary disputes need to be clarified and addressed with a solicitor and poor access needs to be addressed. If you have fallen out with a neighbour then it is in your interests (and theirs) to have matters resolved either through an informal process, mediation or as a last resort via solicitors. If there is ongoing boundary dispute with neighbours and this is not disclosed to the buyer there could be legal repercussions.

CASE HISTORIES

SANDRO AND LAURA

Sandro and Laura run the organic Grey Heron bed and breakfast in Motueka, in the Nelson region. Originally from Liguria in Italy, they moved from a country that some would say has an enviable lifestyle – a rich cultural heritage, wonderful cuisine and climate to match, making it the ideal place to settle. But as Sandro and Laura point out, in order to earn a living in Italy these days, the majority of Italians have to base themselves in the bigger cities.

Many New Zealanders dream of buying a place in the Italian countryside – yet you've come to New Zealand. What was it that attracted you to the country and the Nelson region as a place to live?
We decided to migrate to New Zealand in order to have a better lifestyle. The Italian countryside is beautiful but very difficult for the average Italian to settle there – houses are very expensive and there are no jobs. The Italians have to stay in the big cities in order to have a job but the lifestyle in the bigger cities is terrible. We thought New Zealand was a quiet, friendly and safe place. We chose Nelson because of the nice climate, similar to the one we had in our region of origin, Liguria.

What was different about buying a house in New Zealand compared to Italy?
When we moved here the houses in NZ were far cheaper compared to the Italian ones. They are probably still cheaper but not that cheap!

How did you find adjusting to New Zealand life compared to where you lived before?
We took a while to adjust to the New Zealand lifestyle. In particular it was difficult for Laura – being a city girl. But the friendly environment made it easy to adapt.

What do you miss from home – regional cuisine, cultural life perhaps?
Of course we miss the Italian culture and the beautiful art-filled cities. We

don't miss the cooking much because we like cooking and we do a lot ourselves. We like to eat organic food, we try to make as much by hand as possible such as breads, cakes, panforte, jams as well as vegetarian and healthy
recipes. And the New Zealand lifestyle helps us a lot in achieving this.

How did you find getting residence in New Zealand?
Getting residence in New Zealand was quite difficult with the points system. There was a lot of bureaucracy and paperwork. But we were successful in the end.

Do you have any advice for others planning to do the same thing?
Always try to work out the good and bad expectations that you have. Try
to figure out how much you will miss family and friends before deciding to
move and don't think that here is paradise anyway! New Zealand appears
'green' on the surface but living here we are discovering that it is not that green
and we decided to go organic precisely because we found that there is genetic
modification and horticultural spraying. A lot of foreigners think that New
Zealand is the last resort in good living, and it could be in theory but stupid
governments don't only exist in Europe and North America, unfortunately!

HELEN DAVIES

Helen Davies moved with her family to a rural area just north of Auckland
in 2005 where the trees and greenery remind her of Wales.

What was it about New Zealand that first attracted you to live there?
We were attracted by the lifestyle but it turned out that where we wanted
to buy we weren't able to afford. We wanted to live in Coatesville in the
country. We didn't want to go coastal and we realised the price difference.
In the suburbs you can get a house for $400-$500,000 – around here it's
in the millions. We live in an area where you have to buy 5.5 acres. It's the
price of the land.

Cost of living.
I knew what food and electricity cost as we'd done our research. There are
hidden costs: things that are imported – which are cheaper in the UK. Al-
though meat is cheaper here and the fruit and veg quality is much better.
You change the way you eat. Petrol is cheaper. You still have to have your
WOF (MOT) done twice. If you worked it all out it would probably be

the same. I would say that because you're taxed higher in your wage any-way that it's the same. You're taxed on every dollar you earn.

On there being no NHS in New Zealand.
I used to work for the NHS so to me the NHS was a brilliant service. I find it an absolute pain to have to pay for the doctor. It's $28 for the children and $40 for me. People run the NHS down but it's a fantastic service.

How difficult was it to get in to the country?
Paul did his Certificate in Business Studies, which had to be verified from Swansea College, and then the qualifications had to be assessed by NZQA (New Zealand Qualifications Authority). We used the Emigration Group to help us. They were really good as we were both working full-time and didn't have time. They filled in the forms, although you pay for it (£3000). Paul got a job through a contact who was setting up a sales office in Auck-land making wood burning stoves.

Look see visit.
I thought I'd done my research. We came out in November 2004 and had a look around for a couple of weeks in the Auckland area as this is where Paul's job was going to be. Of course that was in the boom and houses were going like hot potatoes. We were looking to rent and rent out here (in the rural Coatesville/Riverhead area)was really expensive – $600 to $700 per week. We realised we'd really struggle to pay that level of rent for a long period of time on Paul's salary. We were in a Catch 22 situation as houses to buy were expensive as well. We were bringing the children – they didn't want to move to NZ and we wanted to make it as pleasurable for them as possible and we wanted them to be settled in the countryside. As well as rent being so expensive there were very few properties for rent to choose from. By then we'd sold our place in the UK.

On buying a house sight unseen over the internet.
When we went home (to Wales) we bought a house over the internet. We were faxed a contract which we didn't know, nor was it explained to us that what we were signing we couldn't back out of. We had basically signed an unconditional contract with no valuation, builder's report or any condi-tions in the contract. We had done our own research and had heard of Leaky Building Syndrome so there was a concern about that.

What happened when they arrived.
The house we bought had an electricity pylon right opposite it and this house that was supposed to be completely done up wasn't and we had to do it ourselves. (As well as that the Davies' found out that half of their front garden belonged to the local council.)

On buying a house in New Zealand.
You can buy a house in a day here. It's too easy to buy a house in New Zealand compared with the UK. In the UK the solicitor checks everything and asks for different reports. In New Zealand it's different. I would totally avoid buying a house at auction as you still have to pay for LIMS up front and then you could still lose out especially if the agent says the house is going to go for a certain amount and then it goes over that. Buying a house in New Zealand is a minefield.

On home maintenance and renovation.
Tradesmen cost a fortune and paint is much more expensive than in the UK.

On selling a house in New Zealand.
The cost of all the advertising and the commission is huge. It cost £250 to sell the old house – compared with $30,000 for the house here.

On living in New Zealand.
Auckland is not the rest of New Zealand. We came here as my husband's job was in Auckland. Property is more expensive in Auckland and we didn't realise how bad the traffic was. Paul spends three hours a day in traffic. But compared with Swansea, Auckland is a nice city. It's clean and close to the water. It has the lifestyle – the outdoor way of life, lots of people have boats and it's a nicer environment. The UK is overpopulated. There's more space and freedom to do things. They go out in all weather though. When my son was taking part in a school event we didn't think it was going to happen as it was raining so hard so when a friend rang and asked where we were and I said it would probably be cancelled she told us that, 'no, you're in New Zealand now.'

Advice for house buyers.
Always go and see a property for yourself rather than relying on what the agent tells you. Or if you know someone with a camcorder send them out. Talk to lots of agents as compared with the UK, agents are very pushy. One we dealt

with would ring us in the middle of the night when we were in the UK.

What are the main differences you've found about living in New Zealand compared with living in Wales?
People are more laid-back which is mostly a good thing but sometimes can be a bit frustrating. They don't have villages, which we found really strange. We wanted to be in a community but with space around us. That's why we came to the countryside. When you come down East Coast Bays road you see a sea of roofs. You think, you didn't come to New Zealand for that. You don't build behind each other in the UK and sell off your back garden.

What do you miss?
The only thing I really miss is the language because we speak Welsh. My children went to an all-Welsh school so English was a foreign language and now my son finds it difficult to speak Welsh and we haven't even been here a year. Welsh is my first language. We obviously miss our family and we feel guilty about taking our children away from the grandparents. Both sets have been out. You do miss family and friends. The culture as well. Both my husband and I have strong Welsh roots. Ffion my daughter sings.

MIKE COLE

Mike Cole and his family moved to New Zealand two and a half years ago. He set up his own business and now runs his own company BritsNZ which helps people with advice and guidance on moving to New Zealand.

You've started a brand new business in the past two years, which must be stressful enough – yet you've managed to have a house built as well. Why did you choose to build from scratch rather than buy a house?
Here in NZ buying a property is relatively straightforward (compared to the UK anyway) and although we went to many Open Homes we never quite found what we were truly looking for and nothing really grabbed us.. you know that sort of feeling you get when you walk in somewhere and it feels right. This could probably be put down to us just being somewhat fussy but also as there is quite a 'culture' difference between NZ and UK. Building looked a more attractive way of getting back into the property market as it allowed us to be creative. Coming from the south east of the UK it was something we could never have done there and so there was also an element of doing it because we could!

How long did it take to find the right section to build on?
We were guided by friends who had/were building also and so we opted to look in the same area and because at that time the section was well priced. Of course before we moved in the friends sold and moved elsewhere. From getting to NZ in October 2003 I think we eventually settled on the section April 2004.

What do people need to look out for when buying a section?
The list is long. It needs to be primarily north facing and needs to able to capture the sun most of the day, particularly in winter. Ideally it should be a flat section and have no fill in it, that is, the section is all original, natural ground…usually if there is fill on the section you will have to drive wooden piles which simply adds to the costs. It should be well draining and you need to be aware of the water table and of course what is around it…bush, houses, industry etc! You also need to feel comfortable in the neighbourhood and have an eye for what else is being built in the area. For instance, is the area going to suit your plans and give you a ready re-sale value?

What was it about Taranaki and New Plymouth that was so special that made you want live there?
Initially we had met the Mayor at an Emigrate show. He is a charismatic character and he and the video we saw of the area stuck in our minds. When we were job searching we remembered these things and therefore targeted the area and hey presto up popped the job we needed to get into NZ. But apart from that we are surrounded by stunning scenery, great rivers and surf beaches and a totally awesome mountain so what's not to like? We have a great climate which means warm but not oppressive summers and mild winters. Plus there are all the facilities we need locally.

The only downside to the area is that it is a little cut off…three hours north or south to the next largest town and this does give the people an introverted attitude…they are absolutely great and have helped us no end but they are slow to accept change!

How did you go about finding the right team to build the house – architects, builders and other trades people?
We took our time and asked as many local people as possible which of course threw up many different opinions but we gradually found the same names cropping up both positively and negatively and made decisions based on that.

One thing that does surprise (and worry us to a degree) is that too many people come over here and want everything in a hurry. They are supposedly coming for the rest of their lives so why do they need to make these key decisions so quickly? They certainly would not have made a house buying decision that quickly in the UK. As a consequence most people will move two or three times in the space of the first 12/18 months... something very few people do in the UK. People need to be encouraged to take their time and get into their new environment and find where is comfortable for them.

What kind of red tape did you encounter along the way?
To be honest not much red tape at all. The purchase of the section was slowed as we used a solicitor, as we had not seen a land purchase contract before and although we were assured it was a standard contract and could be dealt with via the selling agent we opted for caution. Plans went through the Council process with next to no problems and the council inspections of the build as it progressed threw up no oddities.

We did however discover that we had not understood just where our boundaries were and ended up having to build a retaining wall around two sides to provide us with the full size of what we had purchased so that caught us out somewhat!

What were some of the highs and the lows of the building process?
Highs – seeing our ideas appear as a plan, getting those plans through Council with next to no changes, then seeing the slab being created and poured and then seeing the house flat-packed waiting to be turned into our home and of course watching it being built!

Lows – in reality I think the only low was hassle with a flooring contractor who caused us no end of problems because of some pretty shoddy service and because even after ten months our slab was still too wet to apply some floor coverings!

Where did you live while the house was being built and how did the family cope?
We initially stayed in a motel for the first month (which was a godsend as our motel owner took us under her wing and helped us enormously). We then rented two different properties from the same landlord staying 18 months in one place and six months in another so making life pretty simple for us.

As we were in rented accommodation and had all our own stuff around us the family coped pretty well. The first rental was no more than twelve minutes from the city centre but was considered rural whilst the second was in town itself.

You were in the house in time for Christmas 2005 – how did that feel?

It was a great relief for my wife to at last have somewhere that was her own. We had rented in the UK before coming to NZ due to work problems and the potential need to be mobile (in reality it did help when we wanted to come to NZ as we only needed to give notice and leave whereas so many people are struggling to sell and that is affecting their migration plans!) and so she'd not had a home of here own for about five years…it was great to be in our home that we had created in time Christmas.

What advice would you give to anyone else who was contemplating having a house built in New Zealand?

Take your time and do not stop asking people who is good and as importantly who is not and go to those who on balance seem to be mentioned positively the most often. Never stop asking questions and remember your designer works for you so if you want something in the house make sure to demand it. Once you have your plans go and sit with them on the section and try and imagine what it will look like – even peg it out so you get a feel for size etc and go and see your friends and let them have a say. They may have some good ideas too! Once you have your builder on board make sure you have a fixed price contract and go and see progress regularly and befriend the guys working on the house (tea and cakes are always welcomed by builders – and do NOT forget the roof shout*!)(*Free drinks for the team when the roof goes on).

   If you have a budget make sure there is plenty of slack in it because you will definitely want things changed as it goes up and you see your plan taking actual shape.

It's such a big step moving half way across the world – and you and your family had your fair share of heartaches just to get accepted into New Zealand. What do you think the secret to a successful relocation is?

Knowing what you want to achieve and not being distracted from it no matter what. You have to have a complete focus on what you want to do and you must live the process 24/7. We were once asked what our contingency plan was if NZ did not happen – the answer was that there was no contingency plan we were going to get to NZ. You also have to change your attitude once in your new country. You are 'Johnny foreigner' and you have to make every effort to get out into the community and speak with people and find out things... never pass up any opportunity or invite and always be willing to listen and learn... and NEVER, NEVER, NEVER say 'we didn't do it like that at home'...that will not endear you to anyone. We have found that Kiwis respond very positively to people who make an effort whereas if you hold back they will not come forward.

Also dream the dream... individually think what you want your new life to be like before you leave the UK... write it down and share and compare it with your partner etc and periodically go back and revisit it and amend and refine, as you want. Take it with you on the flight and read it as you take-off and as you land in your new country and make it happen.

Be prepared for settling into NZ to be more expensive than you currently perceive it will be. Nearly everyone we have surveyed (for our trips back to the UK whether Poms or returning Kiwis) have commented that it cost more than they thought it would.

Finally, tell your family and friends your plans early... accept that there will be those who will be upset, but over time you will need their help and support so get the anguish out the way early and by the time you come to leave they should be there to support you. You know why you are doing this and if once explained people can't accept it that is their problem not yours.

Oh and one last thing... whatever else you do, do NOT let anyone, friend or family, come to the airport to see you off... it will be emotional enough but saying goodbye at the departure gate is just too distressing particularly when you have a 24+ hour flight ahead of you!

BIBLIOGRAPHY

Alpers, Antony – *Maori Myths and Tribal Legends*. (1964) Even though Alpers sources date back to Victorian England, he is a fine storyteller and researcher.

Automobile Association – *Regional Guides*.

Bed & Breakfast Book New Zealand (2005).

Bryant, G. and Scarrow E. – *The Complete New Zealand Gardener*.

Documentary series broadcast on TV One – *Frontier of Dreams*.

King, Michael – *The Penguin History of New Zealand*

Lonely Planet New Zealand (2005)

Magazines – *Cuisine, Listener, Metro, Property Press*

Newspapers – *New Zealand Herald, Weekly Telegraph*

Taylor, Paul – *Naked Eye Wonders – A Short Guide to the Stars as Seen from Aotearoa New Zealand*

The Rough Guide to New Zealand (2005).

Shaw, P. – *A History of New Zealand Architecture*.

Shaw, P. and Hallett, P. – *Spanish Mission Hastings – Styles of Five Decades*.

FURTHER READING

Barbara Anderson – *Long Hot Summer*. Defies the stereotype that New Zealand fiction is gloomy. Has a fine wit and gift for comic observation in this story of a holiday at the beach and a clash of cultures.

Fergus Barrowman (ed) – *The Picador Book of Contemporary New Zealand Fiction*

Janet Frame – *Faces in the Water, Owls Do Cry*.

Maurice Gee – *Plumb Trilogy*.

Keri Hulme – *The Bone People*.

Witi Ihimaera – *The Whale Rider*.

Lloyd Jones – *The Book of Fame*. The tale of the first All Black tour of England.

Elizabeth Knox – *The Vintner's Luck* – an imaginative and evocative book set amongst the vineyards in France written by a contemporary New Zealand writer.

Katherine Mansfield – *The Garden Party and Other Stories*.

Noel Virtue – *The Redemption of Elsdon Bird*

NEW ZEALAND ON FILM

An Angel at My Table, The Piano – Jane Campion. Janet Frame's autobiography and the tale of a Scottish mute mail order bride.

Heavenly Creatures, Lord of the Rings Trilogy – Peter Jackson. The New Zealand director who put Wellington on the map.

No 2 - Toa Fraser. A comedy set in Auckland's Polynesian community which won the Audience Award at the 2006 Sundance Film Festival.

Once Were Warriors – Lee Tamahori. As hard-hitting as Cathy Come Home comes this tragic tale set in modern South Auckland.

Scarfies – Robert Sarkies. Dunedin university students get up to no good.

The Navigator, Vigil – Vincent Ward. Two films from New Zealand's most significant art house director.

The World's Fastest Indian – Roger Donaldson. The tale of Southland motorcycling legend Burt Munro.

Utu – Geoff Murphy A tale of revenge set in the 1800s.

Whale Rider – Niki Caro. Set in rural Gisborne, the story of a girl destined for leadership.

INDEX

Complete guides to life abroad from Vacation Work

Live & Work Abroad

Live & Work in Australia & New Zealand £12.95
Live & Work in Belgium, The Netherlands & Luxembourg £10.99
Live & Work in China £11.95
Live & Work in France £11.95
Live & Work in Germany £10.99
Live & Work in Ireland £10.99
Live & Work in Italy £11.95
Live & Work in Japan £10.99
Live & Work in Portugal £11.95
Live & Work in Saudi & the Gulf £10.99
Live & Work in Scandinavia £10.99
Live & Work in Scotland £11.95
Live & Work in Spain £12.95
Live & Work in Spain & Portugal £10.99
Live & Work in the USA & Canada £12.95

Buying a House Abroad

Buying a House in France £11.95
Buying a House in Italy £11.95
Buying a House in Morocco £12.95
Buying a House in New Zealand £12.95
Buying a House in Portugal £11.95
Buying a House in Scotland £11.95
Buying a House in Spain £11.95
Buying a House on the Mediterranean £13.95

Property Investment

Where to Buy Property Abroad - An Investors Guide £12.95

Retiring Abroad

Retiring to Australia & New Zealand £10.99
Retiring to Cyprus £10.99
Retiring to France £10.99
Retiring to Italy £10.99
Retiring to Spain £10.99

Starting a Business Abroad

Starting a Business in Australia £12.95
Starting a Business in France £12.95
Starting a Business in Spain £12.95

**Available from good bookshops or direct from the publishers
Vacation Work, 9 Park End Street, Oxford OX1 1HJ
☎ 01865-241978 * Fax 01865-790885 * www.vacationwork.co.uk
In the US: available at bookstores everywhere
or from The Globe Pequot Press (www.GlobePequot.com)**